THE RAILWAY BEAT

A Century of
Canadian Pacific Police Service

Dedicated to Officers
J. Frith, J. Hallworth, R.G. MacIntosh,
W. Mackie, H. Talcott and A.J. Tierney,
all of whom gave their lives in the line of duty.

THE RAILWAY BEAT

A Century of
Canadian Pacific Police Service

David Laurence Jones

FIFTH
HOUSE

Published in Canada by Fifth House Ltd.,
195 Allstate Parkway, Markham, Ontario L3R 4T8

Published in the United States by Fifth House Ltd.,
311 Washington Street, Brighton, Massachusetts 02135

www.fifthhousepublishers.ca

10 9 8 7 6 5 4 3 2 1

Library and Archives Canada Cataloguing in Publication
ISBN 9781927083154
Cataloguing data available from Library and Archives Canada

Publisher Cataloging-in-Publication Data (U.S.)
ISBN 9781927083154
Data available on file

Fifth House Ltd. acknowledges with thanks the
Canada Council for the Arts, and the Ontario Arts Council
for their support of our publishing program. We acknowledge
the financial support of the Government of Canada through the
Canada Book Fund (CBF) for our publishing activities.

Design by Tanya Montini

Printed in Canada by Friesens

Table of Contents

Foreword   vi

Acknowledgements   vii

Frontier Justice: The Red-coated Police Force   1

Special Service: Railway Constables
and Labour Agents   31

Hands Up: The Gentleman Bandit   59

The Imperial Police: Enter the Professionals   81

Friends in High Places: Royalty and the
British Empire Exhibition   105

Competition and Chaos: Policing
the Front Lines   131

Home Guard: The Second World War
and its Aftermath   161

Specialty Squads: Bombs and the Cold War   197

Public Safety Officers: Educating the Public   229

The Beat Goes On: A Fresh Approach to Policing   269

Foreword

One hundred years ago, Canadian Pacific created a formal Department of Investigation to serve and protect its employees, customers, and physical assets. Significantly, our members also undertook to safeguard the public and its interests, whenever and wherever the company operated.

Over the years, as Canadian Pacific grew and diversified from a transcontinental railway into a multifaceted transportation conglomerate, so too did the responsibilities of the men and women in the police service dedicated to its wellbeing.

It is a testament to the professionalism of these officers that the fortunes of Canadian Pacific have grown in lockstep with those of the country as a whole and, indeed, have helped the company to expand its influence around the world and maintain a permanent economic presence in the United States. Few serious criminal incidents have occurred on their watch to mar the company's reputation at home or abroad.

David Jones has made good use of remaining departmental files, scarce public documentation and invaluable firsthand accounts to piece together a fine account of a century of Canadian Pacific Police Service, through its many successes and occasional failures, and for that I thank him.

Above all, however, I wish to thank every member of our dedicated police force, past and present, for serving Canadian Pacific's interests with honour and distinction, while maintaining strict neutrality of action and unwavering allegiance to the governing authorities in Canada and the United States.

I say with pride that the Canadian Pacific Police Service today stands shoulder to shoulder with the finest police forces in the world. To those who came before us and to those who shall follow, we offer this historical account of the trials and tribulations of the men and women on the railway beat.

Chief Ivan McClelland
Canadian Pacific Police Service
Calgary, Alberta

Acknowledgements

Before the advent of digital recording devices, any police department worth its salt could each year generate many cabinets full of files related to the cases in which it was involved, along with a considerable amount of administrative and training material essential to day-to-day operations.

Canadian Pacific Police Service has accumulated more than its fair share of such records over the last century, but the many relocations of the department's headquarters and the need to keep office and storage space to manageable levels inevitably led to the weeding and discarding of much of its closed, outdated and redundant files—a necessary measure for practical purposes, but a considerable impediment to historical research.

That said, however, while researching *The Railway Beat*, the department very generously allowed me to view whatever historical records were still extant in its files, including much of the material assembled by Inspector D.C. Duncan for the publication of a 75th anniversary commemorative book, in 1988.

In addition, I was very fortunate to have had access to the current chief of CPPS, Ivan McClellend, as well as to his two immediate predecessors Keith Leavitt and Gerry Moody, all of whom reviewed my drafts concerning the years of their tenures and offered helpful comments.

Other members of the department, past and present, to whom I am grateful for information, anecdotes, and advice are: Bruce Bennett, Dave Boggiss, Laurie Crittenden, Mike Curry, Gerry Fish, Doug Kinlock, Sue Layton and Rod Manson. I would also be remiss if I did not acknowledge the assistance of Darwin Pearson in providing contacts within CP Police and answering some of my interminable questions. Darwin worked as a house officer at Canadian Pacific's Chateau Lake Louise, under Inspector D.V. MacEachern, before going on to serve as Westin's chief security officer for many years.

As always, when researching matters related to Canadian Pacific, the CP Archives collection was invaluable, particularly the Van Horne and Shaughnessy executive correspondence, newspaper clippings, and extensive photographic files. For access to those materials I am indebted to Bob Kennell and Bob Parent (who also worked for a number of years with the CP Police call centre).

For details about the involvement of the North-West Mounted Police during the construction of the CPR, I relied on the candid reminiscences of former NWMP officer John Peter Turner in his two-volume set of books, entitled *The North-West Mounted Police 1873-1893*.

Goings-on within the Special Service Department that preceded CP's Department of Investigation were illuminated by Officer Robert G. Carpenter in his unpublished notes, which he called "Some investigations made in the service of the Canadian Pacific Railway Company—1900-1920." Some of the facts about Antonio Cordasco's reign as the primary labour agent for the CPR were gleaned from Gunther Peck's *Reinventing Free Labor: Padrones and Immigrant Workers in the North American West 1880-1930*.

Perhaps the most written about criminal activities in Canadian Pacific history are the two train robberies committed by Bill Miner and his cronies in 1904, and again in 1906. By far the best and most accurate account of these events is to be found in Peter Grauer's *Interred With Their Bones: Bill Miner in Canada 1903-1907*, which I used to supplement the many tidbits of information I found in CP's own files.

And for those intrigued by the ubiquity of graffiti on the sides of far too many pieces of railway equipment these days, you can find out more than you ever wanted—as well as view literally hundreds of colourful examples of this "art form"—by picking up a copy of *Freight Train Graffiti* by Roger Gastman, Darin Rowland and Ian Sattler.

Lastly I am thankful for the input of several people during the production stages of *The Railway Beat*: Larry Stillwell, Jim Dockrill, Nick Richbell and Rick Robinson for photo scans, my wife Erika Watters and colleague Michel Spenard for proofreading and, of course, all of the folks at Fifth House Publishers for taking on this project.

CHAPTER 1
Frontier Justice: The Red-coated Police Force

When a determined syndicate of nineteenth century venture capitalists built the Canadian Pacific Railway in the early 1880s, the CPR was the longest railway line in the world under one administration.

A vast continental wilderness separated the good citizens of the fledgling Canadian nation in the east from their would-be compatriots in the settlements on the Pacific coast. However, there was no single governing authority and no blanket system of law enforcement. The more than 2,000 miles of rugged, nearly uninhabited wilderness was, indeed, the "wild frontier."

The *British North America Act* of 1867 had established the Dominion of Canada as a semiautonomous and largely self-governing member of the British Empire, nestled in a small corner of the North American continent in close proximity to the more rebellious and expansion-minded United States of America.

Two years after Canadian Confederation, the Hudson Bay Company relinquished all claims to the lands west of the Great Lakes previously granted to that company under a charter from British King Charles I. When the federal government of Canada handed a cheque for $1.5 million to the owners of the former fur trading empire, the

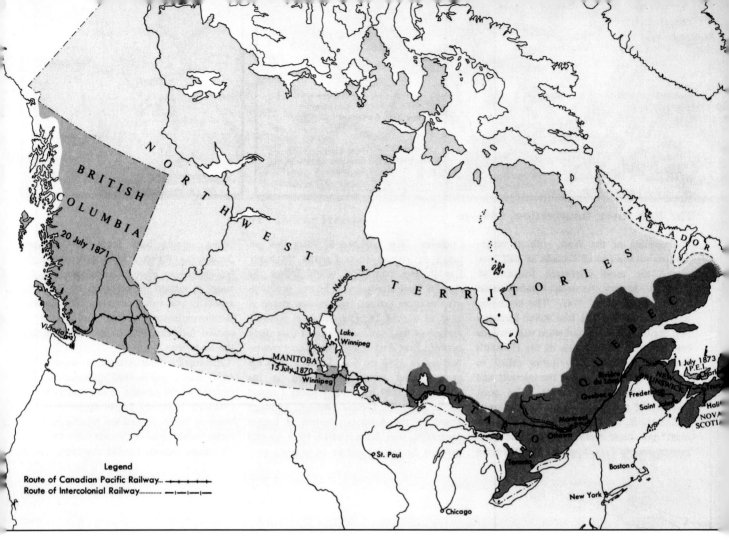

Before the Mounted Police came west, the proposed transcontinental railway ran through a sparsely populated, wild frontier.

lawmakers in Ottawa assumed all responsibility for the future security of these lands. The business of fully integrating the wild frontier with the Canadian nation had begun.

Across the border to the south, in the wake of the U.S. Civil War, restless and ambitious settlers were also looking toward the great western plains to achieve what they regarded as their 'manifest destiny' to create one nation from sea to sea. Men of influence such as Horace Greeley, then editor of the *New York Tribune*, encouraged his compatriots to follow the sun when he coined the phrase, "Go West, young man and grow up with the country."

For Canada's first prime minister, John A. Macdonald, the challenge was to establish a permanent political and economic link between the eastern provinces and the Pacific coast that would cement British Columbia's union with the Canadian federation and protect his own country's sovereignty from its southern neighbour's acquisitive instincts.

If successfully completed as proposed, the transcontinental rail link would forge the Canadian national dream into a steel banded reality.

To establish the rule of law and order across the country's vast new territories, Macdonald's government introduced a bill in 1873 to create the North-West Mounted Rifles. Not surprisingly, the news was greeted with considerable protest south of the border, where the Canadian initiative was regarded as overtly militaristic and overly aggressive. The matter was raised with some alarm in the U.S. Congress, and the Washington press hinted at possible reprisals. Macdonald, in a moment of inspiration, calmed the waters by substituting Police for Rifles in the name of the force, thereby making more explicit and less threatening the role the Mounties would play in ensuring domestic tranquility throughout the Canadian West.

Within a decade, with the country firmly committed to a national transcontinental railway link, the intrepid members of the North-West Mounted Police (NWMP) would become the first lawmen in the Canadian West and, by extension, the first Canadian Pacific Railway policemen. A decade earlier the Northern Pacific Railroad's directors had requested 5,000 soldiers to protect their line while it was constructed across the American plains. Canadian Pacific's general manager, William Van Horne, was content to rely on the more modest manpower provided by the newly established NWMP.

For the railway to be completed as planned, it would be essential to maintain law and order among the thousands of labourers living in rough and tumble construction camps along the line. Drinking, gambling and prostitution were rampant. The Mounties gave overall responsibility for this task to one of the first men to have signed up for the Force in 1873—Samuel Benfield Steele, a remarkable and formidable individual who would soon prove his worth both to the North-West Mounted Police and to the CPR.

Initially the strength of the North-West Mounted Police had been pegged by the federal government at 300 non-commissioned officers and men, but Section 5 of the *Mounted Police Act,* 42 Victoria, Chapter 36, provided that in case of extenuating circumstances the Force could be increased to a number not to exceed 500. An 1882 Order specified that "in consequence of the return to Canada, after an absence of three years, of about 4,000 of the most uncivilized Indians of the North-

Dashing and brave, Sam Steele set the tone for every movie and dime-store novel Mountie to come.

Steele of the Mounted

Samuel Benfield Steele was every inch the Hollywood Mountie: ruggedly handsome, fearless and impeccably turned out in his red serge uniform jacket.

Steele was born on January 5, 1849, on his family's homestead in Simcoe County, Canada West (now Ontario). His father, Elmes Steele, was a British veteran of the Napoleonic Wars who had come to Canada to seek more opportunities for his family.

Early on, Sam demonstrated his intellect, ability and thirst for adventure, finishing at the top of his class at a private school in Orillia, Ontario, and signing up with the local militia by convincing the recruiting officer that he was two years older than his actual age of fourteen. When his unit disbanded in 1871, Steele became the 23rd man to join the Canadian Permanent Force formed to take over the duties of British regular troops departing the Canadian frontier after the Red River Rebellion.

He was one of the original North-West Mounted Police following its creation in 1873. The next year he participated in the great march to the Canadian West where he maintained law and order, helped to eliminate the illegal whiskey trade, and kept the peace between warring bands of Indians.

During the construction of the CPR, Steele was in charge of policing the line across the Prairies and into the mountains of British Columbia, putting down a wildcat strike at Beavermouth in the Selkirk Mountains that threatened to mark the end of the railway, then on the verge of bankruptcy.

With the outbreak of the Riel Rebellion, Steele organized a force of more than 90 mounted policemen, ranchers and cowboys known as Steele's Scouts. Their pursuit of and battle with a band of Cree under Chief Big Bear shattered the rebellion's momentum at

Steele's Narrows, now a provincial park in central Saskatchewan. It was the last battle ever fought on Canadian soil.

During the 1890s, Steele was assigned to the Yukon, bringing law and order to the hordes of gold seekers rushing to the Klondike. Under his command, the NWMP set up police posts at the head of the mountain passes between Alaska and Canada. The Mounties made sure that each prospector had adequate supplies to survive the epic trek to the goldfields, while quietly relieving them of their firearms. For this Steele was credited with saving many lives. He went on to command the police and serve as a magistrate in Dawson City.

In 1900, Steele was handpicked by senior Canadian Pacific director, Lord Strathcona, to lead a Canadian regiment to the Boer War in South Africa. Having served with distinction, he stayed on after the war to serve as chief of the South African Police in the Transvaal. He returned to Canada in 1907 to resume command of the Canadian army in the west.

As a Major General in the First World War, Steele took the 25,000 men of the Second Canadian Division overseas. Too old to lead the force into action, he was placed in charge of training all Canadian troops then in Britain. In 1918, King George V made him a Knight Commander of the Bath.

Sir Sam Steele died in England, on January 30, 1919, at the age of 70, a victim of the great influenza epidemic.

West, the almost total disappearance from Canada of the buffalo, the rapid construction of the Canadian Pacific Railway, and the probable influx of white settlers and speculators during the present year, it would be prudent in the public interest to increase permanently the strength of the North-West Mounted Police to 500 non-commissioned officers and men."

Inspector Steele was placed in charge of the detachment that would police the construction of the railway and enforce the *Act for the Preservation of Peace in the Vicinity of Public Works*, a federal law that prohibited gambling and drinking within ten miles on either side of the railway line. With few lawmen in new towns along the

Shot during the mid-1920s near Amulet, Saskatchewan, the motion picture "Policing the Plains" romanticized the role of the Mounties in building the transcontinental railway.

route, Steele and his red coated adventurers would act as policemen, judges and jailers in the untamed west.

Suppression of the illegal whiskey trade had been a key factor in the establishment of the North-West Mounted Police, and alcohol was the biggest threat to the orderly progress of railway construction north of Lake Superior, across the Prairies and through the mountains. Drinking, gambling and prostitution were the main diversions for the armies of railway workers at the end of track and a large entourage of hangers-on took advantage of every opportunity to make a buck. With CPR wages burning a hole in their pockets, workers on the construction gangs were easy prey for unscrupulous card sharks, thieves, whores, confidence men and, especially, the ubiquitous bootleggers.

The purveyors of strong drink were nothing if not imaginative in their quest to deliver the goods to their captive and very thirsty clientele. Kegs of whiskey, rum and brandy were hidden inside barrels of kerosene, paint and other railway supplies. Cans of peas, corn and beans were deceptive covers for their more covert liquid contents. Countless eggs were blown out like so many Easter decorations to serve as miniature flasks for the illicit spirits, while hollowed out

The haphazard unloading of railway ties belies the speed with which the main line was spiked down across the prairies.

7

Bibles performed a new, unholy function for the faithful clients of the alcohol merchants. With few hiding places available across the vast sea of prairie grassland, the booze sellers took to stashing bottles awaiting distribution inside the carcasses of dead pack animals, or even burying large tanks of alcohol underground from where it could be pumped as required for resale.

The difficulties faced by the North-West Mounted Police in the suppression of this trade were compounded by a typically Canadian blurring of jurisdictions between federal, provincial, territorial and municipal authorities. Notwithstanding the provisions of the *Preservation of Peace Act*, the *Northwest Territories Act* spawned a system which allowed individuals to import alcohol under permit from the lieutenant governor, ostensibly for personal consumption. Importers purchased their liquid pleasures by the quart, half gallon or gallon from Winnipeg or Brandon, and were allowed to consume it in the privacy of their own homes or to deposit it at a local hotel saloon for the occasional social nip. Not surprisingly, the contents of bottles acquired in this way were quickly consumed and their containers immediately refilled with any manner of bootleg hooch, as often as not, a minimum amount of distilled alcohol mixed with a rather foul concoction that might include hot peppers, molasses, chewing tobacco or even red ink.

The Mounties, however, were able to keep fairly close tabs on the recurrent and insidious attempts of the whiskey traders to distribute their product among the construction gangs. The redcoats were kept very busy opening baggage, looking under wagon tarpaulins and staying one step ahead of their adversaries. Wherever and whenever they uncovered an illegal stash of alcohol, they opened it and poured it out on the ground in front of the offending parties. Frontier legend had it that the NWMP captured much of the illegal spirits for themselves by pouring it through buried blankets into hidden containers, but despite the slanderous and no doubt apocryphal accusations against the Mounties, they built a formidable reputation for honesty and evenhandedness in the administration of justice.

Asked at the time about the campaign to counter the whiskey traffic, North-West Mounted Police Commissioner Acheson Gosford Irvine was unequivocal: "Had this not been effectively stopped, I fear

I should have had to report a large number of depredations as having been committed," he said. "I venture to state that it is unparalleled in the history of railway building in a western country that not a single serious crime has been committed along the line of work."

That first season of policing the railway had also involved the pacification of certain Indian tribes in close proximity of the international boundary with the United States. A few years earlier, Sitting Bull's band of renegade Sioux had been repatriated peacefully to the U.S., and Mounted Police Superintendent James Morrow Walsh had made representations to both the Canadian and American governments on their behalf. Steele had taken command of Walsh's "B" Division of troopers and relocated them to a newly constructed full scale fort at Qu'Appelle, in what is now the province of Saskatchewan, in a good agricultural area through which the railway was expected to pass. The prevalent crime of horse stealing, engaged in by virtually all of the Plains Indians to prove their mettle and prowess, had been reduced considerably by increased vigilance, open dialogue with the natives and a good working relationship with officials of the U.S. Indian Department.

The CPR and its principals were extremely grateful for the protection furnished by the Mounted Police and made no bones about it. With the New Year, Commissioner Irvine received this tribute from railway construction boss, William Van Horne:

ABOVE: The 1920s motion picture, "Policing the Plains," building on the Mounties' already formidable mythology, put one of their red-coated constables literally at the end of track.

NEXT PAGE: The 'railway general' sends his thanks to the NWMP's commander in the West for maintaining "perfect order" along his rail line.

CANADIAN PACIFIC RAILWAY COMPANY.

OFFICE OF THE GENERAL MANAGER.

Winnipeg, Man. 1st Jany 1883.

Dear Sir,

Our work of construction for the year of 1882 has just closed, and I cannot permit the occasion to pass without acknowledging the obligations of the Company to the North Western Mounted Police, whose zeal and industry in preventing traffic in liquor, and preserving order along the line under construction, have contributed so much to the success-ful prosecution of the work. Indeed without the assistance of the officers and men of the splendid force under your command, it would have been impossible to have accom--plished as much as we did. On us great work within my

knowledge

knowledge, where so many men have been employed, has such perfect order prevailed.

On behalf of the Company and of all their officers, I wish to return thanks, and to acknowledge particularly our obligations to yourself and Major Walsh.

I am, Dear Sir,

Yours very truly.

W. C. VanHorne

General Manager.

Lt Col A.G. Irvine.
Commander
North Western Mounted Police.
Regina. N. W. T.

Piapot smiles for the studio
photographer in better days.

Showing no sign of fear, the feisty corporal pulled a watch from his pocket and barked at Piapot that he would give the chief exactly 15 minutes to comply with the order to pack up and leave.

The minutes slowly ticked by, no doubt inspiring some trepidation in the two Mounties. In wild displays of bravado, the armed Cree warriors raced around on their mounts, firing their weapons close to the faces of the stoic policemen, while the women and children in the camp pressed in close, adding their own taunts and invective to the volatile mix. Piapot himself stood defiantly with arms crossed.

"Time's up," stated Corporal Wilde succinctly, at the end of the designated period.

Climbing down from his mount and handing the reins to his companion, Wilde strode calmly toward Piapot's lodge and proceeded to kick out the centre pole. A howl of rage arose from the amassed mob of Indians and Piapot blanched visibly, aghast at the attack on his person and the blow to his dignity. However, the now alarmed chief was not so foolish as to strike back against the authority of the red coated lawmen, who were clearly ready to do whatever it took to win the day. Quickly sizing up the situation, Piapot instructed his followers to decamp immediately, and his entire entourage rode away, thoroughly chastened.

><+◊>•-O-•<◊+-<

Meanwhile, Inspector Steele also had his hands full, supervising the construction of the barracks and grounds for the North-West Mounted Police headquarters at Regina, supplies for which were arriving daily in overstuffed CPR boxcars. Along with overall responsibility for commanding the various detachments strung out along the line of railway construction, Steele was charged with many of the magisterial duties that arose along the line, often making legal pronouncements from his makeshift desk aboard a Red River cart. Later in his career, Steele claimed to have been able to assess the progress of railway construction merely by taking note of the number of supply trains that passed his impromptu office on a daily basis. Tellingly, he recalled one afternoon when a hard-driven locomotive had steamed past his magisterial perch with CPR General Manager Van Horne at the

Stylish Hudson Bay coats and red serge jackets add a splash of colour to dusty prairie station platforms.

Crowfoot himself. The appreciative chief had the pass framed and wore it proudly around his neck for the rest of his life.

Though open warfare between the various bands of Indians in Canada and the United States diminished greatly in the 1880s, it was still fairly common for small war parties to cross the "Medicine Line" between the two countries on horse stealing expeditions. Among the tempting targets north of the border were, of course, the large numbers of horses employed in the construction of the Canadian Pacific Railway. Apprehending the raiders was never an easy task. The thieves quickly escaped across vast distances, dividing the spoils and returning to camps many miles apart. While U.S. soldiers and sheriffs showed willingness to aid in the recovery of property stolen in Canada and did, in fact, repatriate many horses to the railway, the lawmen did not have the authority to arrest and punish the perpetrators.

On one occasion, several horses liberated from a CPR construction gang in the vicinity of Medicine Hat were recovered by the North-West Mounted Police with the help of a Montana trading company and the local sheriff.

"In connection with this matter," Police Commissioner Irvine informed Van Horne in a letter dated October 9, 1883, "I might mention that at the time these horses were run off, we did all in our power to recover them, owing however to the time which had been allowed to elapse prior to our receiving information as regards [to] the theft, the Indians who stole the horses were enabled to make good their escape and run the stolen property over the Boundary Line, we traced them to the vicinity of the South Piegan Agency in Montana, U.S. which led us to believe that the horses had been stolen by American Indians."

W. G. Conrad, acting on behalf of western railway supplier I. G. Baker and Co., soon had Sheriff James McDevitt of Fort Benton in the Montana Territory on the case. Ten of the twelve missing horses were recovered at a cost to the Railway of $25 each.

"I have every reason to believe," McDevitt said, "that taking these animals from the Piegans will have a visible effect in preventing them from making further war on the Northern Settlements." And it did.

In the same way, the Mounties reciprocated when Canadian Indians ran stolen U.S. horses north, but with harsher consequences calculated to stamp out the common practice among competing bands of warriors. Following the swift application of Canadian law, stolen property was returned to its owners and the horse thieves were sentenced to from two to five years of hard labour at the Manitoba Penitentiary.

But the duties of the Mounted Police assigned to the railway beat did not end with the suppression of the whiskey and stolen horse trades. Members of the Force were also recruited to represent the federal government as mail clerks and to prevent the destruction of CPR property during sporadic labour flare-ups.

In the absence of an organized mail service west of Moose Jaw, three constables from Regina were sworn in by the Canadian Postal Department to handle the job between Moose Jaw and Medicine Hat. Two more from Maple Creek between Medicine Hat and Calgary, and two from the Calgary detachment had responsibility as far as Laggan (now Lake Louise) in the mountains. All carried out the job with their usual efficiency.

In December 1883, when the railway reduced the amount of bonus money the workers could make, while refusing to give in to demands for compensatory increases in their rates of pay, a strike among CPR locomotive engineers and firemen tied up work all along the line. Once again, the NWMP, aided by provincial and city police officers, was called upon.

By an Act of the Dominion Parliament, "every person who, by any means or in any manner, or way, whatever, obstructs, interrupts or interferes," with the free use of the railway was guilty of a misdemeanor and, upon conviction, was made liable for a prison term from two to five years. There was also a clause dealing with postal service that provided sentences from two to ten years of hard labour for those convicted of disrupting "the passing or progress of any mail, or any car, or any conveyance, carrying the mail." Furthermore, there were provisions to deal with any person who might "willfully or maliciously displace or remove any railway switch or any rail of any railway, or

Standing at the east end of Calgary's first, temporary, railway station, from left, are land agents R.G. Marsh and W.T. Ramsay; *Calgary Herald* employee T.B. Braden; watchmaker G.E. Jacques; and Constable Fay.

injure, break down, rip up or destroy any railway track, or any railway bridge or fence of any railway bridge or any portion thereof or place any obstruction thereon whatsoever on any railway track or bridge with intent to injure any person, or interfere with any property passing over or along such railway, or to endanger human life." Not a terribly elegant listing of possible offenses against the CPR, but an exhaustive one nevertheless.

For the most part, the three or four thousand men involved in the strike action behaved in an orderly manner and formed a committee to negotiate with the railway. P. M. Arthur, Grand Master of the Brotherhood of Locomotive Engineers in the U.S., was said to have sent messages of support for a nascent northern chapter, while Northern Light Lodge No. 127 of the Brotherhood of Locomotive Firemen achieved full labour union status.

For several days, the one train operating in and out of Winnipeg was manned by CPR superintendents John Egan or John Niblock, and on more than one occasion accompanied by Winnipeg Police Chief Constantine and a pair of city officers. In Brandon, four special constables were sworn in to protect the company's property, two to guard the CPR shops and yard during the day and two at night. When one locomotive was taken to the tank for watering without a posse of policemen in attendance, a gang of strikers mounted the cab and attacked the driver and fireman, beating them badly.

In many cases, trains were placed at the disposal of striking engineers on the Port Arthur division so that they might get to Winnipeg to negotiate, but this privilege was halted when the striking men were found to have been stopping others from working on construction gangs. An engineer named Cuthbertson was charged with preventing the yardmaster at Rat Portage (later Kenora, Ontario) from rescuing one locomotive among several deserted by their crews on the main line. A railway handcar was stolen by a group of engineers east of Port Arthur.

The acts of petty vandalism and intimidation that occurred during the strike apparently had a negative effect on the support the locomotive engineers were getting from their brothers to the south. When a reporter from the Winnipeg Times contacted Grand Master Arthur about a supposed upcoming meeting with the CPR's Egan, the labour leader repudiated the actions of the Canadian strikers, claiming the strike was not a Brotherhood affair at all.

"I have not requested an audience with anyone," Arthur insisted. "and, so far as this office is concerned, no effort, whatever, has been made on behalf of the men, for the simple reason that the laws of the Brotherhood have not been complied with by them, ... If notice was given that a reduction in their wages would be made and they thought it unjust, after exhausting all means in their power to adjust the matter, they should have advised with me, as the laws of the Brotherhood require, and the strike might have been averted."

Most importantly, Arthur's comments were in line with the practical realities of the day.

"The men, of course," he concluded, "live in a comparatively small circle and do not know how slack the business of the country is just at present and how many Brothers are out of employment."

Throughout the dispute, the Mounties remained as neutral as possible, keeping watch mostly for random acts of vandalism against the railway and violence against its employees.

In a few cases, the railway was moved to prosecute the strikers in court. Three of the more rowdy men in Winnipeg—James Foster, John

Anderson and Pat Delaney—were charged with assaulting an engineer named Sawyer at a downtown saloon. During the proceedings, his Worship the Mayor gave the men quite a lecture about the error of their ways in assaulting people to sate their thirst for vengeance against the CPR.

Based on the evidence assembled and presented by CPR detective O'Keefe, the judge imposed a fine of ten dollars and costs on each man, or 21 days' hard labour.

The strike was over, but not so the troubles faced by the Mounted Police patrolling the westward advancement of the railway line, which had now reached the mountains where illicit liquor was reportedly being distilled in alarming quantities. To dry up the innumerable watering holes that were quickly established along the right-of-way, steps were taken immediately to widen the latitude of the *Canadian Act for the Preservation of Peace in the Vicinity of Public Works*, which imposed a dry belt for ten miles on either side of the railway line. In short order, the application of the law was extended to 20 miles on each side of the railway tracks, a distance that was deemed great enough to prevent idle construction workers from making the trek to one of the impromptu booze canteens custom made to empty pockets of their weekly wages.

Getting those earnings into the hands of the construction workers required six-man NWMP security teams to deliver the railway's payroll to end of track. To avoid ambushes from occurring at any of the hidden nooks and crannies along the mountain trails, two Mounties rode ahead of the cash, two accompanied the large and tempting consignments of cash, and two more followed to ensure that no nasty surprises came from behind. Despite the presence of any number of ne'er-do-wells seeking to prey upon the newcomers to the west, not one CPR payroll was lost under the watch of the North-West Mounted Police.

On Dominion Day (now Canada Day), July 1, 1884, five "soiled doves" were arrested by the Mounties in Laggan, not so much for plying their trade as for being too blatant about it. A couple of months later, Thomas Shaughnessy, assistant to CPR general manager William Van Horne, pointed out to general railway superintendent Egan just what a nuisance the ubiquitous sex trade had become, as witnessed by the Reverend Christopher Smith and his son while en route from Calgary to Winnipeg in a CPR sleeping car.

"They complain that a prostitute and a number of rough men who occupied the smoking room were very noisy and used bad language," Shaughnessy reported, "also that the prostitute was using the gentlemen's water closet, and being visited there by the men from the smoking room."

In a number of locations, "hostess houses", hastily constructed log cabins sprang up overnight. At Farwell (later Revelstoke), ladies of the night, such as black and buxom Madame Foster and come hither Irish Nell, did their best to relieve the loneliness of many a railway construction worker far from home, perhaps hosting a friendly game of cards while the men awaited more intimate pursuits. To discourage card sharks, in some settlements an unwritten rule was followed that required players to toss their packs of cards out the window after each game and open a new pack.

Though the railway workers were far from governmental machinations in the east, the corrosive effects of ultra-partisan politics could and did occasionally intrude. With many Americans on CPR construction gangs, the U.S. presidential election of 1884 drew more than its fair share of attention north of the border. In a tent at Kicking Horse Flats, a railway conductor who favoured New York Governor Grover Cleveland was viciously slashed with a razor by a booze fuelled barber. He preferred the Republican candidate and Speaker of the House James G. Blaine, despite rumours of the latter's influence peddling. The general mudslinging that ensued during the negative campaign did not deter "Grover the Good" from being ultimately propelled into the White House.

The misguided barber was promptly shot dead by a CPR brakeman awaiting his turn in the shop's revolving chair. Though immediately collared by the Mounted Police, the shooter was judged to be innocent by virtue of having acted in self defence on behalf of himself and his wounded conductor friend.

Out-of-control drinking continued apace.

In B.C., the provincial government took exception to restrictive Canadian liquor laws, being desirous of the great potential for tax revenues afforded by a soused citizenry. When a Mountie seized 16 bottles of beer within the railway dry belt, federal stipendiary magistrate George Hope Johnston fined the owner and confiscated the alcohol.

Sam Steele, seated, commanded the rugged NWMP detachment at Farwell (later Revelstoke), in British Columbia.

Crying foul for what he termed Johnston's theft of his property, the injured would be tippler was successful in convincing provincial Judge J. M. Sproat to have his own police force break into the federal lock-up, seize the bottles of beer and arrest the overzealous Mountie. In turn, Judge Johnston charged the provincial officers with assault.

In Manitoba, the lieutenant governor signed a proclamation extending the laws of his own small province far beyond his jurisdiction as far as Rat Portage setting off a firestorm of arrests and counter arrests in that area of the country.

Of course, such disputes did little to curb the abuse of alcohol among the railway workers, as evidenced by CPR superintendent Egan's missive to Van Horne on November 10, 1884.

"Saturday night," he wrote, "a couple of Sectionmen living at Rat Portage went over to Keewatin and got drunk, and coming home laid down between the rails with a bottle of whiskey, train came along round one of the curves and killed both of them."

The futility of trying to enforce rather wishy-washy regulations over such immense territories was not lost on North-West Mounted Police Inspecting Superintendent Lawrence William Herchmer. Apart from the general sentiment in the country that the somewhat arbitrary liquor statutes and the ludicrous permit system were virtually unenforceable, the Mounties themselves were known to enjoy a bracing tipple from time to time.

"The enforcement of the liquor laws is the most disagreeable and trying service," Herchmer wrote in an 1884 report to his superiors, "and in this particular, more than in any other, our weakness is apparent. Our men are generally young, and it is not possible to expect very young men to enforce these laws, unless they have a large portion of older and steadier men to set the example."

By 1885, the North-West Mounted Police had established a new western post at Beaver (later known as Beavermouth), in the Selkirk Mountains at the mouth of the Beaver River. The large number of unwanted attractions, both alcoholic and carnal, designed to waylay its workers in Donald, B.C., had prompted the railway to push the line through quickly to Beaver. But the construction delays caused by the need to erect three mammoth wooden trestles across Mountain Creek, Surprise Creek, and Stoney Creek to the west gave the purveyors of

illicit pleasures more than adequate time to set up shop across the river from the new police post.

Bigger troubles were also in the offing.

On March 26, a couple of hundred Plains Indians and Métis frontiersmen under the leadership of Louis Riel and Gabriel Dumont confronted and defeated a mixed force of Mounted Police and hastily recruited militiamen at Duck Lake in the District of Saskatchewan. The much anticipated second Northwest Rebellion had begun.

About the time Inspector Sam Steele had gotten the call to proceed east to help suppress the revolt, more than 1,200 CPR workers walked off the job in the vicinity of Beaver, and, in Steele's words, "a large number of loose characters were ready to urge them to any mischief." To add to his problems, the usually robust police officer was suffering from "mountain fever," a disease that had killed several men in the railway construction camps over the last few months. Accordingly, Steele's appropriately named second-in-command, Sergeant Billy Fury, was placed in charge when an armed mob threatened to shut down all work along the line.

Early NWMP frontier posts, like this one at Donald, British Columbia, were hastily erected, but functional 'wild west' structures.

Hotels, bars, and brothels were among the first buildings to rise from the woods in construction camps like this one at Beavermouth, in British Columbia.

Once again, the CPR was in financial difficulties and wages were late. Police Constable Kerr had been sent to end of track to arrest a contractor named Behan who was drunk, disorderly and causing no end of trouble. When Kerr was thrown to the ground by a group of strikers and forced to retreat, Steele insisted that, for the sake of the Force's reputation and effectiveness, the humiliation could not be set aside. "We must take the man at any cost," said the ailing inspector. "It will never do to let the remainder of the gang know they can play with us."

Accordingly, Sergeant Fury and three constables were dispatched to arrest the unrepentant desperado. They were quickly surrounded by an angry mob of armed men who badly beat the policemen and, once again, forced them to retreat to their post.

"Take your revolvers and shoot anyone who interferes with the arrest," shouted Steele, forcing himself out of bed to confront the situation. Standing beside federal civilian magistrate George Hope Johnston, he watched through a window as Fury and his constables walked between the saloons, dance halls and brothels across the bridge from Beaver, soon appearing with their prisoner "fighting like a fiend, while a woman in scarlet followed ... with wild shrieks and curses."

Calling for Johnston to come with him, Steele grabbed a rifle and headed outside to confront the strikers.

"Look at the bastard, his own death bed makes no difference to him," somebody in the crowd yelled. "You red-coated son of a bitch," echoed the charming woman in red.

"Listen to this and keep your hands off your guns, or I will shoot the first man who makes a hostile movement," Steele said, silencing the mob long enough for Johnston to read the Riot Act. "You have taken advantage of the fact that a rebellion has broken out in the North West and that I have only a handful of men," Steele admonished the men, "but as desperate diseases, and both disease and remedy are here, I warn you that if I find more than twelve of you standing together or any large crowd assembled, I will open fire upon you and mow you down! Now disperse and behave yourselves!"

The next day, Steele arrested several of the instigators and fined them each $100. The strikers stayed off the job until the railway made good on their back pay, but there was no more gunplay or intimidation.

Inspector Steele departed for the east to assemble "Steele's Scouts"—a group of 25 hard riding North-West Mounted Policemen and assorted ranchers and cowboys that would soon see action against the rebellious Indians and Métis. Meanwhile, Johnston swore in a force of special civilian constables to police CPR construction in his absence. James Walker, a former NWMP superintendent who was now ranching near Calgary, was given command of the home guard while another rancher, Major John Stewart of Pincher Creek, established a corps known as the Rocky Mountain Rangers to patrol north of the international border.

The insurrection in the northwest proved to be a boon to the CPR, potentially saving the entire transcontinental railway project from collapse. In the preceding months Prime Minister John A. Macdonald had been loath to ask the Canadian Parliament for further financial aide for the railway, having gone once too often to the well for help. Van Horne's offer to transport troops from the east to the battlefront freed the government to extend additional funds, while the British could see for themselves the strategic and military value of getting the line up and running. Riel and Dumont had saved the day!

When the last rails were laid at Craigellachie, B.C., on November 7,

A double-barreled shotgun and a dog with a good nose were the tools of the trade for this 'watchman' in the railyard.

lions of dollars per year. Those concerns would soon be official railway police business too.

In 1865, Pennsylvania was the first state to grant state-wide police powers to railway agents to counter the rising post-war depredations against the ubiquitous rail lines that were beginning to blanket the eastern regions of the continent. While the new police forces were still expected to engage directly in strikebreaking activities, ostensibly they were focused on "preventing vandalism and theft, maintaining security at scenes of derailments and accidents, and patrolling in search of trespassers and track obstructions."

Some of the early railroad companies in the United States seeking to avoid the expense of hiring police constables for protection appointed "watchmen," who supplied their services to the railways in exchange for nothing more than the privilege of collecting and selling grain sweepings from the freight cars in the yards. Basically, the scheme was a disaster as the watchmen were too intent upon their grain business and they did not always limit themselves to sweepings. The thefts only got worse.

Another ploy initiated by the railways was to pay watchmen regular wages and keep them under the charge of a chief watchman in each large yard who would report to the local yardmaster and his assistants. Unfortunately, the men hired for this task were often elderly and unable to perform other duties in addition to keeping watch, so they were paid a correspondingly low rate of pay and had limited success in preventing crime. In addition, it was not uncommon for the yard officers themselves to be involved in the systematic pillaging of rail freight, to which the watchmen usually turned a blind eye for fear of being fired.

There was no coordination of effort and little contact whatsoever between these yard watchmen and the special railway constables who also reported to local railway operating officers. The incidents of theft, both in rail yards and while cars were in transit, continued to increase.

In the first years of CPR operations the railway paid detectives $50 a month in major centres, while constables made $1.25 a day to patrol on the more populated divisions and as much as $2.50 to work the demanding Lake Superior section. Policemen were also assigned to individual stations at Quebec Gate Station (later known as Place Viger Station and Hotel), in Montreal and in Ottawa. Men were also hired for special duties such as guarding the railway's pay car, protecting valuable freight consignments and accompanying very important persons in transit with the CPR.

Along with its rapidly expanding railway network, Canadian Pacific was busy building what would become known as the "World's Most Complete Transportation System."

From the beginning, Van Horne envisioned a single management structure to handle all of the Company's many and varied involvements. Even as the rails were being laid across the country, telegraph wires were being strung along the CPR right of way providing unprecedented communications possibilities—not just for the purpose of conducting the railway's core business more efficiently, but also to establish a commercial telegraph service for the general public. At the same time, the wires connected law enforcement agencies more closely from coast to coast. The Company's hotel, shipping and trucking interests entered into in the 1880s, and expanded throughout the ensuing century, added to the many assets and properties in need of police protection. Its eventual acquisition of ten small Canadian regional airlines and "bush" operations and their service expansion across the country and around the world required even more security.

In the early years of operation, overlapping federal and provincial jurisdictions made for some grey areas when it came to law enforcement. In particular, the enactment of the *Dominion Railway Act* in 1888 led that year to an almost comic encounter between the CPR and the Province of Manitoba.

The CPR's original charter included a monopoly clause that would allow its founders to recover their initial investment and place the national enterprise on a sound financial footing. It read as follows:

> For 20 years from the date hereof, no line of railway shall be authorized by the Dominion Parliament to be constructed south of the Canadian Pacific Railway, except such lines as shall run south-west or to the westward of south-west; nor to within 15 miles of latitude 49. And in the establishment of any new provinces in the Northwest Territories, provision shall be made for continuing such prohibition after such establishment until the expiration of the same period.

Though there was initially little opposition in Manitoba to the monopoly clause, it was not long before provincial legislators demanded the right to approve other railway charters within their own borders, some of which were sure to conflict with the CPR agreement. Early attempts by the provincial government to do just that were thwarted by the federal Department of Justice. When Manitoba's economic boom collapsed in 1882, much of the blame for the province's ills was laid at the CPR's doorstep.

Five years later, John Norquay, the Conservative premier of Manitoba, decided to push back with a new railway bill that the provincial legislature adopted unanimously. The proposal called for a line to be built from Winnipeg to the U.S. border at West Lynne, and on to Pembina in Minnesota, where it would connect with the Northern Pacific and provide a link with American railroads in competition with the CPR-controlled Pembina line and the St. Paul, Minneapolis & Manitoba Railway.

In due course, the federal government disallowed the bill, but, despite the ruling, local businessmen were determined to press ahead with the proposed Red River Valley Railway. Though the CPR made several attempts to stop the project with injunctions, whenever federal authorities tried to serve papers on various senior officers of the provincial railway, they were conveniently unavailable.

Construction of the new line proceeded south from Winnipeg and north from the United States border, but at some point the track would have to cross the CPR just west of the Manitoba capital, and a major

conflict was inevitable. By October 1888, Red River Valley Railway construction had reached the CPR on both sides of its main line.

The matter came to a head on the twentieth of October, when Chief Clark of the Manitoba Provincial Police swore in 53 constables drawn from Winnipeg's Board of Trade members and other prominent citizens, to protect the workers who were to install a "diamond" crossing on the CPR to allow the provincial line to cross over.

When they arrived at the proposed intersection, they discovered three CPR locomotives and five railway cars blocking the point of crossing. Four of the cars were filled with workmen from the local Canadian Pacific shops armed with pickaxes and other potential weapons. At the rear was the private car of William Whyte, general superintendent of the CPR's western division. Whyte was authorized by Van Horne himself to do everything possible to prevent any tampering with the CPR. He was accompanied by two justices of the peace who had previously sworn in all of the CPR workmen as provincial constables to protect the railway's property, as allowed under the *Dominion Railway Act* passed by Parliament that same year.

With little training and virtually no centralized control, most of the men reported to whoever the highest ranking railway official was in the area where they were hired.

Chief Clark, accompanied by all of the provincial cabinet ministers in the province at the time, as well as Chief McRae and five other members of the Winnipeg Police Force, immediately served notice on all of the Canadian Pacific men that their appointments as provincial police had been cancelled. The justices of the peace then promptly swore them in again as "special constables." Threats were made, the local militia was called out, and by early evening the provincial forces returned to Winnipeg, while about 300 CPR men were left to guard the site.

Again, the CPR called for an injunction, but its arguments were rejected by the courts.

In short order, 300 Winnipeg citizens, sworn in as special constables, proceeded to a nearby location on the CPR right of way, lifted some of the track, and installed a diamond with 120 feet of track on either side. Twenty of the constables were left to protect their work.

Whyte and the CPR reacted immediately. Reassembling his forces, the railway officer counterattacked the next day. The *Winnipeg Free Press* reported that "to put it mildly, the specials did not distinguish themselves by bravery or devotion to duty," so it was not surprising that the diamond was soon ripped out and brought back to the CPR yard where it was displayed triumphantly. When the general superintendent had his men put up a barricade on both sides of the CPR line, it was immediately dubbed Fort Whyte by the locals.

A few weeks passed with a number of minor incidents keeping everybody on edge. Sporadic fisticuffs broke out; each side appealed to Ottawa to intervene on its behalf. By the end of October the matter had been elevated to the Supreme Court of Canada where it was eventually settled in favour of Manitoba. The provincial line was allowed to cross over the CPR. The so-called Battle of Fort Whyte was over.

Not long afterwards, the CPR built a station near the point of confrontation and called it Fort Whyte, apparently with tongue firmly in cheek.

The expansion of the various business interests of the CPR brought more opportunities for criminal activity. The railway's long, thin artery of commerce was far more vulnerable to criminal acts than most other enterprises. The practice of hiring watchmen, constables and investigators haphazardly, with no overall strategy for

coordinating their efforts, had done little to reduce the losses suffered by the Company.

"A gang of safe blowers is working extensively along the lines of railway in the eastern part of the Province of Ontario," said W. S. Stout, general manager of the Dominion Express Company, a CPR subsidiary, in a warning to the Company's agents. "It is necessary that you should take extra precautions in the care of any money or valuables which you may have in your charge and make an effort to effect prompt delivery of such."

To combat the upsurge of theft, as well as to put much more vigour into its policing practices in and around its many properties and to protect its corporate assets during a new century of expansion and development, the CPR created a "Special Service Department".

ABOVE: With Canadian Pacific's purchase of the well-established Dominion Express Company, the railway added another link to its rapidly expanding intermodal chain.

NEXT PAGE: Following the lead of the pioneer Pinkerton's Detective Agency, CPR's Special Service Department kept detailed files on criminals.

CANADIAN PACIFIC RAILWAY COMPANY
SPECIAL SERVICE DEPARTMENT

Handwriting of accused—

by return mail
Yours truly
D R Donaldson
Care Prospect Hotel
Bristol
Ct

Name	- -	Gordon C. Metcalfe.
Aliases	- -	F. S. Ballard, J. Cochrane, D. R. Donaldson, G. H. French, T. L. Potter, George E. Metcalfe, Clark Karnochan, J. Wright, J. A. Duncan, Neal A. Florence, E. A. Hobart, James A. Ramsey.
Born	- -	Claims to have been born in Inverness, Scotland, having come to America early in life. From conversation, however, his accent would indicate that he came from the Western States.
Age	- -	About 38 years.
Height	- -	6 feet.
Weight	- -	175 pounds.
Build	- -	Very erect, carries shoulders well back and head up.
Hair	- -	Brownish.
Eyes	- -	Blue.
Complexion	-	Fair but "muddy." Was generally flushed with liquor.
Moustache	-	Brown.
Occupation	-	Telegraph Operator and Train Dispatcher. Writes and operates with both hands.
Teeth	- -	Discolored with tobacco (he is an incessant smoker of cigarettes and also chews) and protrude a little while speaking, over the nether lip. Lower back teeth gone.
Habits	- -	He drinks heavily at times and is fond of women.
Other characteristics.		He has a very peculiar voice, speaking from the throat rather than from the chest, and has a quick, nervous way of delivery.
		He is a thorough railroader, and can speak intelligently on all branches.

The above is an accurate likeness and description of "Gordon C. Metcalfe," who was arrested, on the instigation of this Department, at Bristol, Connecticut, on the 25th day of June, 1902, charged with having stolen $350 from the Station Agent of the Canadian Pacific Railway at Sault Ste. Marie, Ontario, in December, 1901. He was committed for extradition by the United States Commissioner at Hartford, Connecticut, on the 26th day of June, and afterwards consented to return with the officers to Canada on another charge of having, in October, 1900, stolen from the Dominion Express Company, a money package containing $520.85, from Neepawa Station, Manitoba, on the Canadian Pacific Railway, under the name of F. S. Ballard. He was duly brought back to Canada, and on being arraigned at Sault Ste. Marie, Ontario, he pleaded guilty to the Soo charge, and on July 17th following, he was sentenced to five years penal servitude in Kingston Penitentiary. He is now serving his time. On the expiration of this sentence, it is the intention of the Dominion Express Company to take up the Neepawa charge.

This Department has been endeavoring for some months to get an accurate history of Metcalfe. The result of enquiries is set out below, but owing to Metcalfe's many aliases and the many roads he has operated on, if the information is not as complete and accurate as desirable, it is to be hoped that the deficiencies or discrepancies will be excused.

Metcalfe's method was to secure a position as telegraph operator or relieving agent under an assumed name on forged or stolen recommendations, generally applying to some railway when operators or agents were scarce. He never, apparently, stayed in any place very long, but cleared out within a few days with all funds in sight, before his character and antecedents could be enquired into. It is suspected that he took the names and records of other operators with whom, at various times, he came in contact. As nearly as can be ascertained, his right name is George Edward Metcalfe, and he was raised at Somonauk, Illinois.

The first record I have of him is in 1890, when, for about two weeks, he was employed on the L. E. & St. L. C. R. R., at Booneville, Indiana, leaving with a shortage. In June, 1892, he was employed on the C. B. & Q., at Thayer, Iowa, under the name of Neal A. Florence, when he stole $300 belonging to the American Express Company. He was located in Milwaukee in 1896, and taken to Creston, Iowa, for trial on this charge. He claimed it was a case of mistaken identity and gave his name as George E. Metcalfe, and residence as Palatka, Florida. About this time the L. & N. Railroad also arrested him for impersonating a travelling auditor at Paris, Kentucky, and getting $300 from an Agent, and again at Pleasureville, Kentucky, when he got $53 from the Agent. He was admitted to bail but jumped. In February, 1895, he was ticket clerk on the Illinois Central at LaSalle, Illinois. In 1898, as Gordon C. Metcalfe, he worked at St. John, New Brunswick, on the Atlantic Division of the Canadian Pacific Railway, absconding with the General Superintendent's annual passes. In the same year, under the name of E. A. Hobart, he swindled the American Express Company and the Boston and Maine Railroad at Byfield, Massachusetts, out of a considerable sum ; also, under another alias, at Groton, Vermont. In February, 1902, he was bill clerk on the Grand Trunk Railway at Fenton, Mich., leaving with a shortage, and in March of the same year he was checked in as James A. Ramsey, at Dunlow, West Virginia, on the N. and W. Railway and Southern Express Company, and on the 2nd of April he disappeared with $300. At other times, under the other aliases mentioned above, he has worked for the N. Y. C. & H. R. R. R., Maine Central, Central Vermont, Plant System, Peoria and Eastern, Northern Pacific, N. Y., N. H. & H., and possibly many other roads. Whether there are any other charges against him, I am at present unable to state.

At Palatka, Florida, while working on the Florida Southern Railway, he married, but left his wife six or seven years ago, and also, in 1898, while in St. John, New Brunswick, he married again. He has children by both these wives.

The object of this circular is to advise all roads interested and to request that any information regarding this criminal be forwarded to the undersigned at an early date.

A. C. LANCEY,
Chief Inspector, C.P.R.,

MONTREAL, December 1st, 1902.

George Edson Burns, a native of London, Ontario, who had studied law before entering CPR service in the auditor's office, was chosen to head up the new department. Chief Burns reported directly to David McNicoll, the railway's vice-president and general manager in Montreal.

In early 1900, the Special Service Department was organized in two divisions—a headquarters in Montreal and a branch office in Winnipeg. In Montreal, five inspectors—Joseph Guertin, Isaac MacKay, Ludger Crevier, William Crowe and Robert Carpenter—were responsible for everything from that city east to Saint John, New Brunswick. They reported directly to Chief Burns. Inspector Charles Baillie joined them a year later. In Winnipeg, assistant departmental chief, A. C. Lancey and inspectors Levi Hussey and William MacLeod covered all of the territory between the Lakehead and the Pacific Coast. A uniformed branch, supervised by Sergeant James McGovern out of Montreal, also reported to Burns. McGovern had considerable knowledge of the CPR's business, having for many years been a member of the railway police at Hochelaga in Montreal where all of the Company's shops were then located. All watchmen, constables, detectives and investigators previously reporting to local railway officials across the CPR network were incorporated into the new department.

Though most of the men hired for Special Service had no formal background in law enforcement, generally speaking they were chosen for their proven ability, honesty and conscientiousness.

One such recruit was Robert Carpenter, who worked for the CPR as a weighmaster at Outremont Yard and later as a car checker before joining the new police department. Carpenter first became acquainted with Special Service in 1900 when he reported the ongoing theft of coal at Hochelaga by men, women and children from the houses just east of the yard. During the ensuing interviews with the department, Chief Burns learned that he was a personal friend of the car checker's father, Silas H. Carpenter, a former chief of detectives with the Montreal Police Force and a founding member of the Canadian Secret Service Agency. The Agency was the first of its kind in Canada, handling all criminal investigative work in the Province of Quebec for the federal government and all of the Pinkerton Detective Agency work in eastern Canada.

The Special Service Department's offices were set up in CPR's first

ABOVE: Half of Montreal's police force was needed to supplement the railway's own ad-hoc security arrangements when the first transcontinental train steamed West from Dalhousie Square Station.

LEFT: Windsor Station is festooned with decorations for the visit of the Duke and Duchess of Cornwall and York, in 1901, the first of many royal tours for which the railway police would provide security.

Pinkerton's unsleeping eye oversaw a spying and security apparatus with a greater reach than the US federal government.

Pinkerton's Private Eyes

The Pinkerton National Detective Agency was the first large scale, full security service in North America, and not only did it lead the way for all of the private law enforcement agencies that would follow in the latter half of the nineteenth century, it also pioneered many of the tactics and techniques adopted in the ensuing years by the U.S. Federal Bureau of Investigation (FBI) and the Central Intelligence Agency (CIA) that are still in use today.

Established in 1850 by Scottish immigrant Allan Pinkerton, the famous agency developed a specialty for capturing train robbers. One of Pinkerton's first great patrons was George McClellan, vice-president of the Illinois Central Railroad and later commander of the U.S. Federal Army of the Potomac during the American Civil War.

Pinkerton's historic leap from small time detective to the nation's top intelligence operative came when he was recruited by McClellan to take charge of Abraham Lincoln's personal security during the American Civil War and to gather military intelligence behind Confederate lines—in effect to establish the first U.S. secret service. His role in foiling an attempt on Lincoln's life as the newly elected president's train made a pre-inaugural stop in Baltimore, cemented his standing as the nation's foremost 'spook.'

After the war, Pinkerton's agency built its reputation pursuing such famed American frontier characters as Jesse James, the Younger Brothers, the Dalton Gang and Butch Cassidy's Wild Bunch. Valuable items moving by rail overtook and quickly surpassed stagecoach shipments as the prime target of Pinkerton's adversaries. Pinkerton's men went from working side by side with the Postal Service and Wells Fargo officials to becoming the number one provider of security and investigative services to nearly every railway company on the continent.

Pinkerton's company logo featured a disembodied eye and the motto "We Never Sleep". It watched over the agency's three storey headquarters in Chicago and it stared from the company's letterhead and most of its advertisements, giving birth to the public image of the 'private eye,' as well as the lurid dime store novels that featured detectives for hire.

By the 1870s, Pinkerton's had developed the world's largest criminal database and library of mug shots.

Before the turn of the century, much of the agency's business came from mining companies and factory owners who hired the private security company to keep suspected unionists out of the work force and to infiltrate their ranks. The heavy-handed tactics used to break up strikes, and the adverse publicity from a number of deaths that occurred in violent confrontations during labour disputes, occasionally plunged the private eye business into public disrepute.

Despite some setbacks, however, Pinkerton's agency did manage to maintain its supremacy in the field of private security services throughout much of the 20th century. Over the years, many Pinkerton agents worked closely with Canadian Pacific police officers, notably on the famous Bill Miner train robberies in British Columbia.

In 1999, Pinkerton's was acquired by Securitas Services USA Inc. The storied detective agency that once boasted more men in its ranks than the U.S. Army was merged under the Securitas brand with its biggest rival, the William Burns Detective Agency. The new company is an industry leader in the provision of security services to companies around the world.

Montreal terminal, variously known as Dalhousie Square Station or Quebec Gate Barracks Station, where its officers could easily keep an ear to the rail. The following year, the department's police were moved to the west wing of the railway's headquarters building and new Montreal terminal, Windsor Station, where they occupied two rooms on the first floor.

Among their regular duties, members of Special Service were responsible for the many Chinese workers travelling back and forth across Canada on the way to labour-intensive jobs in Europe, Cuba, Mexico and the U.S. Because the railway was subject to stiff fines from the federal government if any of the workers went missing while in

the obstructions on the track. However, the suspect must have gotten word of the charges, because he fled town for his grandmother's home on the Quebec side of the border before the railway police could arrive at his door.

When they discovered where he had gone, CPR Investigators Carpenter and Crevier hired a team of horses and drove to the grandmother's house where they arrested the wanted man and brought him about 14 miles to Sweetsburg, Quebec, the nearest point where there was a magistrate and a jail. It was late at night when they arrived, so the two policemen kept their prisoner in a nearby hotel, where they took turns guarding him through the night.

In the morning, they were surprised to be confronted by a lawyer sent by the suspect's family in Richford to represent him. Accepting the advice of the attorney to save some time and effort, the investigators allowed their prisoner to board the morning train for Richford where they arranged for him to be arrested immediately upon arrival by a local constable.

In due course, the man was convicted and received a nominal sentence, but the case was far from closed. Shortly after the conviction, the railway received a claim for damages on the grounds that the young man had been kidnapped from his grandmother's home, hauled off to Sweetsburg, and whisked across the border without a hearing from a magistrate. Though the investigators had acted in good faith and the man had ultimately been found guilty of the charges against him, the Company had to pay $400 to settle the claim. It was a lesson in jurisprudence that Carpenter and Crevier would not soon forget.

Of course, the railway was also vulnerable to internal fraud, and Special Service was expected to handle these cases as well.

In 1900, an astute Company auditor exposed a conspiracy that was tapping into the CPR's passenger revenues. Periodically, auditors were sent out by the railway to intercept trains and take over all tickets and cash fares from the conductors, after which the trains would be checked in the presence of the conductors to see that all passengers were accounted for. One of the more than 25 conductors allegedly involved in the suspected conspiracy had approached the auditor with a proposition to warn the conductors in advance of such a spot check. The auditor, in turn, had conferred with his own boss, who had counseled him to go along with the plot until a sufficient amount of evidence could be obtained to warrant a formal charge against the scheming conductors.

In the end, only five CPR conductors were convicted and sentenced, but the depth and extent of the investigation gave notice to the broader contingent of Company employees that the days of turning a blind eye to internal theft and fraud were over.

A new era of checks and balances had dawned and a new level of transparency was expected in all of the railway's business activities. More confrontations were bound to occur.

While the railway police were still getting acclimatized to the new department's overall mandate, a fresh wrinkle was introduced; a strike among railway track workers was called on June 1, 1901.

While both British Columbia and Manitoba had police forces that could be relied upon to assist the railway police with any disturbances, the vast areas in the Northwest Territories which still included what are now the provinces of Alberta and Saskatchewan were a different story. To ensure relative peace in those locations, the Special Service called upon the assistance of the railway's old friends in the North-West Mounted Police.

In the early days of the strike, trouble broke out at Gull Lake where at the time there was only a lone CPR operator, a water tank and a section house for railway crews—no community existed. When a railway extra gang threatened to trash the place, a CPR investigator and two Mounted Police constables from Maple Creek were sent out to bring the boys the 40 miles back to town, where they could blow off steam at the local watering holes.

In Tilley, some 125 miles east of Calgary, a railway gang led by a tough foreman, formerly of the Royal Irish Constabulary, sent a wire to Calgary threatening to wreck a train if the railway didn't settle with the maintenance-of-way workers. Before the matter could be settled, CPR Investigator Carpenter and Special Constable Bob Barker who were dispatched to deal with the situation were forced to pull their guns and drag the protesting Irishman up in front of NWMP Superintendent Lieutenant-Colonel G. E. Sanders. Prosecuting the case was Company solicitor Richard Bedford Bennett, then a partner of Senator James Lougheed who later became prime minister of Canada. The defense was conducted by Paddy Nolan, a colourful figure in Calgary legal circles at the time.

Before the trial, Nolan suggested to Bennett that if the charges against his client were withdrawn, he would not lay charges against the railway police for drawing their weapons at Tilley. Bennett, however, did not waver in his quest to prosecute the recalcitrant foreman successfully. No counter charges were laid.

Some additional excitement was caused at Calgary, when 33 Italian workers who had previously been taken to Revelstoke, B.C. as strikebreakers, stampeded aboard an eastbound CPR train demanding to be taken to Calgary where they would have access to the extracurricular activities to be found in the saloons and brothels there. Arrangements were made by the Special Service Department to run the train right through the Calgary town site and straight out to the nearby Mounted Police barracks where Superintendent Sanders gave the men the choice between serving time or returning peacefully to Revelstoke, which they did with no further trouble.

The railway police expressed their gratitude to their red-coated associates by donating a keg of beer to be consumed at a concert the Mounties were staging that night.

Once the initial threat to the railway's day-to-day operations had been addressed, the Special Service Department settled down to attend to its new role as overseer of the CPR's labour bureau. Along with its responsibility for discouraging vandalism and protecting CPR employees from intimidation, Burns's department took on the task of finding reliable, docile seasonal workers.

Even before the recent unrest, the railway had shown itself to be a very labour intensive industry, particularly during the warmer months when most of the trackwork and roadbed maintenance was scheduled. It required workers willing to work in the wild, men who would tolerate exploitation for the chance to make ready cash, men untainted by unionism. When the Canadian government tightened up its immigration policies with anti-Chinese legislation in the first decade of the 20th century, it was mostly Italian labourers who filled the gap for seasonal workers.

"Italians are the only class of labour we can employ who can live for a year on the wages they earn in six months," Burns said of the

Even as Antonio Cordasco was being crowned 'King of the Workers,' the labour boss was losing his grip on his cushy monopoly.

CPR's hiring strategy at the time. "If we have the Italians, there is no danger of their jumping their jobs and leaving us in the lurch."

For a number of years, the railway had been using the services of Montreal labour agent Antonio Cordasco to obtain a sufficient number of track workers each summer to carry out its regular maintenance and expansion plans. With the onset of winter, the seasonal workers would return to their homes in Italy and the eastern United States, or they looked for a place where they could find cheap room and board until they were rehired the following spring. As a reward for helping to break up the track workers' strike, the CPR made Cordasco sole Italian labour agent in the fall of 1901.

Cordasco had an office on Craig Street, not far from the CPR headquarters, where he also carried on an importing business dealing with olive oil, Italian wines and other provisions. As labour agent for the CPR, he was paid a dollar for every worker he recruited, and with that incentive Cordasco was able to sign up more than 12,000 men for the railway between the years 1901 and 1904. Along with the CPR, his other major clients included the Dominion Coal Company, the Canadian Northern Railway and a particular Canadian labour contractor, H. J. Beemer, who supplied men to the City of Montreal to work on sewer lines and other municipal projects.

The new labour boss was part of the *padrone* system endemic to North American heavy industry at the time. Typically, the *padrone* was an ethnic entrepreneur who not only provided foreign workers to industry, but who often took on the job of supplying those workers with food while employed, transportation to the job site, and room and board during down times. He usually found a way to collect a fee from both worker and employer.

Cordasco knew how to tap into the labour markets in the "Little Italys" of the eastern United States. During the winter months, he would register workers for a dollar apiece and foremen for three, promising each man gainful employment with the railway in the spring, on the basis of the job-seeker's place on the contractor's list. The CPR also extended his sphere of influence by setting Cordasco up as an agent for its subsidiary steamship line and helped him become an agent for the Compagnie Générale Transatlantique and several others.

Most of the Italian workers who were recruited and worked under

Seasonal railway workers, most of whom are Italian, hunker down in a Rocky Mountains cabin before shipping home.

the *padrone* system were paid directly by the CPR, but there was no hope of even being hired if your name did not appear on Cordasco's registration list. At times, though, the labour boss collected the wages himself and then paid the workers their cut after deducting the cost of putting them up. In one instance, a couple of Cordasco's workers provided a letter to the railway which read: "We the undersigned, signed with a cross mark because we can neither write or read, both of us, we authorize Mr. A. Cordasco to draw our wages for work done in the month of October last."

The railway settled with the striking maintenance-of-way workers by September 1, 1901, just in time for the royal tour later that month of the Duke and Duchess of Cornwall. While in Canada, Their Royal Highnesses would be protected by the Dominion Police, commanded

Luxury and security went hand-in-hand in what were said to be the finest set of railway cars ever constructed.

by Commissioner Lieutenant-Colonel Percy Sherwood. (The Dominion Police had been created by the Government of Canada in 1869.) With Sherwood were a couple of detectives from his own force, as well as members from the CPR's Special Service Department and the Toronto and Montreal city police forces.

Four special trains were provided for the royal party. The first and fourth, by order of departure, conveyed the grooms, horses and carriages. The CPR's Chief Burns and Sergeant McGovern rode aboard the lead train to check on all security and logistics issues. Accompanying them was Dominion Police Inspector Rufus G. Chamberlin. In 1913 he would serve as the first chief of CPR's new Department of Investigation.

The second train carried the Canadian Governor-General and his wife, Their Excellencies the Earl and Countess of Minto and their entourage, along with the prime minister, The Right Honourable Sir Wilfrid Laurier and a party of his colleagues and friends.

The third, or royal train proper, was devoted to Their Royal Highnesses and was said to be among the finest set of railway cars ever constructed. The ten-car train was 730 feet long and weighed nearly 600 tons. All of the cars had enclosed vestibules and each was connected to an end-to-end telephone line; the first time this service had been installed by the railway. The entire train was lit by electricity and equipped with electric bells. The exterior of all the cars was mahogany.

The day coach, *Cornwall*, at the rear end of the train included an observation platform from which the royal couple could view the passing scenery. Coupled to it was the night coach, *York*, housing the bed chambers, bathrooms and accommodations for Their Royal Highnesses and their attendants.

"The train was designed and constructed for the purpose for which it is to be used," stated a CPR royal tour guide book. "Having in view the long run it is intended to make, the essentials for comfort and safety have been kept in mind in its construction, and it is believed that the train presents all that is best in Canadian railway equipment."

Perhaps not surprisingly, given the amount of advanced planning conducted and the strength of the various police forces assigned to this prestigious duty, the trip went very smoothly, according to schedule, and without any untoward incidents.

The most important investigation carried out by the railway police that winter involved the mysterious origins of a serious fire at a coal mine in Michel, B.C., in which both the CPR and the Crow's Nest Pass Coal Company suffered heavy damages. Members of the Special Service Department interviewed dozens of men engaged in mining and logging activities from as far away as Bull River and Fort Steele. They were able to gather enough evidence to prove that the fire had been started by a contractor employed by the mining company to clear a strip of land east of the town. While burning some debris, the fire had gotten away from the contractor's men and into the town.

The new century, increasingly, was one of labour unrest in North America. Various loosely organized "brotherhoods" acted as bargaining units and mutual aid societies for their members. The American Federation of Labor (AFL) was the largest and most conservative union. It encouraged workers to organize according to their trade rather than along industrial lines. However, there were more radical elements in the labour movement who rebelled against the AFL's leadership and continued to seek industry specific bargaining units to fight for workers' rights. One of these groups, the United Brotherhood of Railway Employees (UBRE) sought to unify all railway workers.

In Canada, the CPR's railway workers attempted to establish a chapter of the UBRE in Vancouver in the early months of 1903. By February, the Railway had decided to put the brakes on the union movement at all costs. Several of the key Brotherhood of Railway Employees instigators were indentified and dismissed by the Special Service Department, one of whose members had gone undercover as secretary to the union. The firings brought on a confrontation the railway hoped would break the union, while the CPR could still claim in public that recent labour unrest was merely the result of rapacious workers demanding unrealistic wage increases.

Generally speaking, the fledgling union had broad support from railway employees in the Vancouver terminals, in the offices, on the docks, and in the freight sheds. Clerks, baggage handlers and train crews stood shoulder to shoulder with their brothers and sisters in the British Columbia Coast Steamships (BCCS) organization, one of the Canadian Pacific's marine divisions. Many other local union members, including a number of longshoremen and stevedores, picketed in sympathy and even walked off the job.

In the preceding months, the Special Service Department had signed on additional constables in anticipation of the need for more security in the west. The Department, of course, was also called upon to fulfill its other role as a strikebreaking force and labour agency.

Two railcars full of men, under the command of CPR Inspector Isaac McKay, left Montreal on the morning of January 24 to join Inspector William MacLeod and Constable Robert Bullock at the Pacific terminus of the transcontinental railway. The Canadian Pacific's docks and freight sheds in Vancouver were built on piles, just offshore from the railway yard and approachable only by way of a bridge at either end. This made the job of policing the dock area rather easy.

Each night at least one CPR constable was quartered in the Department's offices in the Vancouver Station to be available at all times. Rank and file strikebreakers were housed on the Yosemite, a wooden side- wheel steamship tied up at the east end of the dock, where they were less likely to have any unpleasant encounters with angry workers on the picket line. A dining car was quietly parked in a corner of the yard near the station to serve meals to the replacement workers.

When extra seamen recruited from the Atlantic Coast kept disappearing upon arrival in town before they could show up for work,

a CPR inspector discovered a striking BCCS fireman named Williams passing out threatening notes to the men as they disembarked from their trains. The enterprising Williams was arrested on a charge of intimidation, convicted and sentenced to pay a fine of $50 or spend three months in jail. The fine was paid, in all probability by the UBRE.

The strike continued for three months. Several minor altercations between the strikers and the strikebreakers were stifled by the strong force of railway constables, which grew to some 65 men before the matter was settled. But worse was yet to come.

On April 13, 1903, an enthusiastic fistfight broke out when a mob of strikers and longshoremen assaulted the east end of the CPR docks and declared their intention to wreck the Yosemite. Though the railway police were successful in containing the violence and dispersing most of the participants, small bands of hotheads from both sides lingered in the railyard throughout the day.

Later that evening Frank Rogers, a prominent socialist and local union organizer, approached the waterfront picket line in the company of two other sympathetic longshoremen. It was less than an hour since the general mêlée at the docks. At the same time, two of the hired strikebreakers were being escorted to the scene of the dust-up by special police officers, as they searched for a lost hat and umbrella.

Tied up at the CPR docks, the paddle-wheeler *Yosemite* served as a floating hotel for the railway's strikebreaking forces during a labour dust-up in Vancouver.

Shouts and then shots were exchanged. Nobody was sure who fired first, but both the picketers and the Vancouver media blamed the gunfire on "thugs" hired by the railway to guard the company's property.

By the time the smoke had cleared, Rogers was on his knees with a bullet in his stomach. His companions quickly spirited him off to the Great Western Hotel on nearby Water Street, where his condition was stabilized before he was taken by ambulance to the old city hospital on Cambie. Though he was a strong young man still in his thirties, two days later Rogers died from his wounds.

A $500 reward was posted for the arrest of Rogers' murderers and, almost immediately, two railway constables were charged. In short order, one of the two was released, but a judge determined there was enough evidence to send the other, one James MacGregor, to trial. The CPR hired a top lawyer for the defense of the man, who had been brought in from Montreal to work during the strike as a "clerk."

During the preliminary hearing, a key witness had been William F. Armstrong, a companion of Rogers on that fateful might. Armstrong testified that shortly after the incident MacGregor had admitted to firing the fatal shot from the office shed in the CPR railyard. However, at trial Armstrong changed part of his testimony, casting doubt on his entire previous statement. The coroner's report concluded that Rogers had been "murdered by person or persons unknown," and the crime went unsolved.

After the strike, the United Brotherhood of Railway Employees withered away. Several other unions that had struck in sympathy, including the longshoremen organization, were also dismantled in the wake of the labour strife. The railway had won the battle, but its all-out war on the union movement had propelled its Special Service Department into disrepute in much the same way as similar strikebreaking activities had turned public opinion south of the border against private police forces and detective agencies. And in the east, more trouble was brewing.

On January 23, 1904, a "Great Parade" of more than 2,000 Italian labourers wended its way through the streets of Montreal in honour of Antonio Cordasco, steamship agent and CPR labour bureau chief, proclaimed that day to be "King of the Workers." The following month, a huge banquet celebrated the King's newly recognized status, but even as an ersatz crown was being placed upon his head by two Italian foremen, Cordasco was under public fire for questionable business practices.

In true Canadian form, a Royal Commission was appointed to inquire into the immigration of Italian labourers to Montreal and the alleged fraudulent practices of employment agencies in general. On the stand, CPR Police Chief Burns admitted that he had given Cordasco a monopoly as the company's sole agent for Italian labourers, but he also began to distance himself and the CPR from the "King."

"I have never regarded Cordasco as an employee of the company," Burns insisted. "We simply engaged him as an employment agent, and it was his own business; he could collect whatever fees he liked from the men."

And collect he apparently did, from employee and employer alike. While Burns paid the labour boss $5 a head to recruit seasonal workers, the workers also were each expected personally to cough up a commission of $3 before they were hired by Cordasco's agency. In serving both groups, Cordasco may have been deserving of the fees he extracted, but the amounts were deemed outrageous by most standards of decency.

That Cordasco's sway over the Italian migrant work force had the tacit approval of the Company was made apparent to most of the foremen and others at the banquet in his honour by the presence of the chief superintendent of the CPR's Vancouver Division: Richard Marpole. In each of the preceding three years, the Company had secured Cordasco's position by hiring several thousand workers from him, as well as allowing him to supply the workers with the food and supplies they would need while on the job.

However, under oath, it became abundantly clear that Cordasco was buying supplies inexpensively in Montreal and charging an exorbitant markup to workers at various remote CPR sites in Northern Ontario. It also surfaced that the CPR had resisted calls from the local Italian Immigration Aid Society to redress the situation and allow competition from other brokers.

"I have taken up the question of the employment of labour with the proper authorities and have to advise you that it is not the intention of this company to change the arrangements of the employment of Italian immigrant labour which has been in effect the last few years," Burns gestured with his pistol for the railway men to jump down from the locomotive. One of the other masked men covered them with a rifle.

The bandit leader and his companions then walked the hapless locomotive crew down the track toward the express and baggage cars and spread out to secure the area. While mail clerks William Thorburn and W. F. Lough and Dominion Express messenger Herbert Mitchell crouched in the dark suspecting the worst, brakeman William Abbott at the tail end of the train also sensed that something was amiss.

"As I poked my head out of the car, I came face to face with a masked fellow holding a gun that looked as big as a sewer pipe," Abbott later recalled. "He told me to get inside unless I wanted my head blown off, so I climbed back inside... quickly."

Pandemonium reigned in the passenger cars.

As soon as conductor John Ward realized that a robbery was in progress, he rushed through the train to warn those on board. A CPR engineer H. B. Walkem and the railway's superintendent of buildings Alex Wilson were also on the train returning home from a work assignment. They took it upon themselves to explain what was happening and calm everyone down. But it was Judge W. Norman Bole of New Westminster, B.C., a colourful and well regarded character, who took full control of the situation.

The judge was travelling in the company of William Harold Malkin, a grocery distributor known as the "Jam King," who would later go on to serve as mayor of Vancouver. Bole recapped his strategy to the *New Westminster Columbian* a few days later.

"Is there any gentleman present who has a weapon about him?" the judge had asked the assembled passengers when he had become aware of the situation. Getting no response, he continued, "Then I find I am the only person here who is in a state to defend this car from those wretches. How many of you gentlemen are willing to stand by me and fight this gang, prevent them from entering this car?" Every man was said to have stepped to the judge's side.

Robert Wilson, a CPR clerk who was also on board the train that night, described to the *Victoria Colonist* the mad panic that ensued among the passengers to hide anything of value.

"Talk about queer hiding places, I saw more off hiding places for valuables discovered in a few minutes than I ever thought was

In the mail Car

possible," Wilson said. "As soon as the news of the holdup was communicated to the passengers, there was the greatest scramble I ever saw to hide money, watches and other valuables. The majority of the women passengers resorted to the usual hosiery receptacle for their jewelry and other valuables, while the men stowed rolls of bills away in their shoes, hatbands and other unlikely places."

Judge Bole apparently handled his men like a general.

"Everything movable was piled against the doors at each end of the car so that it would be impossible to open them," Wilson said. "All the valuables having been stowed away in all sorts of odd corners, the lights were put out in the centre of the car, leaving it black as the night outside. The Pullman sleeper with its darkened interior and brilliantly illuminated corridors presented an eerie appearance, and the uncanny look of the car was enhanced by the knowledge of the fact that a determined man crouched in the darkness was ready to seed deadly missiles into the first bandit that set foot within those fatal paths of light."

But the bandits were focused on other prizes.

Even the most mild-mannered railway clerk kept at least one firearm close at hand while sorting Her Majesty's mail en route.

Uncoupling the coaches, they returned to the front of the train, where they once again boarded the locomotive and had Scott pull the baggage, mail and express cars forward. A mile or so up the track, the gang leader ordered the train to a halt. When the bandits had Engineer Scott tap on the door of the express car, it was flung open by messenger Mitchell.

"Hold up your hands or I'll blow your head off," commanded one of the robbers, holding up a sack of dynamite in front of the Dominion Express man's face. Mitchell, fearing that the bandits would blow up the entire car, quickly handed over his standard issue .38 calibre Smith & Wesson revolver. With a rifle in his ribs, he was frog marched over to the car's strongbox from which was extracted $914.37 in currency and about $6,000 worth of gold dust from the Cariboo Gold Mines at Ashcroft, B.C.

Some said the robbers had also made off with somewhere between $60,000 and $80,000 in bearer bonds from a registered mail sack. Although a subject of conjecture for decades to come, the rumour was never confirmed by the CPR or the authorities.

That night, with cash and gold in hand, the train robbers ordered the locomotive engineer to drive his engine further west to the Whonnock milepost and "stop there, just in front of the church." As they made toward their designated drop off point, the leader of the gang engaged in small talk with Engineer Scott, and even returned to the railway man a gold watch and a bit of cash that had previously been taken from him.

"That's all right, my boy," the masked man intoned in the friendly manner that would help to make him a folk hero in the eyes of many. "Put that back in your pocket. I don't want any man's money that works for wages," said the gentleman bandit.

As the engine pulled up in Whonnock, the train robbers jumped from the cab and leaped down the embankment to a rowboat awaiting them in the Fraser River. "Go back and get your train," the gang leader shouted to the crew members.

"Good night, boys. Sorry to have troubled you," he added, before disappearing into the night.

It didn't take long to get things hopping when news of the CPR's first train robbery began to circulate. The station operator fired off his official report in a telegraph message to H. E. Beasley, the CPR superintendent in Vancouver. By chance, Beasley was meeting with CPR Inspector William MacLeod and Police Chief Burns on Burns's last official visit to the west coast before the Special Service Department was disbanded. Joining the emergency session in short order were Vancouver chief of police Samuel North, and B.C. Provincial Police constable Colin Campbell, along with assistant federal postmaster F. E. Harrison and representatives of the

Dominion Express Company. By 2:00 a.m., a special CPR train was on its way to the scene of the crime with Beasley, MacLeod, North, Campbell and a reporter from the *Vancouver Province* all on board.

At the site of the confrontation, CPR fireman Creelman walked the police officers and railway officials through the hold up. Though several sets of footprints backed up the train crew's version of events, no new evidence was discovered.

Within days, detectives from Pinkerton's famous agency were side by side with the provincial police hot on the trail of the perpetrators. Descriptions of the robbers' appearance and mannerisms provided by Scott, Creelman and others had convinced the investigators that they were looking for none other than the famous "gentleman bandit" Bill Miner and his accomplices. Pinkerton superintendent James E. Dye and five investigators were soon joined in the hunt by several members of the Thiel Detective Agency's office in Seattle.

"I got a break," Dye told the *Vancouver Sun* many years later, "when I found a half-finished meal by the side of the railroad tracks near Hammond. It was an old frying pan, chopped up vegetables with milk poured over it. It was a messy looking affair."

The Pinkerton man deduced that the meal had been prepared by somebody suffering from stomach ulcers, a condition he recalled Miner having. He sent to Seattle for pictures of the notorious train robber who had "served his apprenticeship knocking off stage coaches in California gold country." When the mug shots were circulated, sure enough, the CPR train crew members fingered Bill as the leader of the bandits.

'The Gentleman Bandit' became a local folk hero.

Old Bill Miner

Despite having been the subject of countless poems, songs, stage productions, books and movies, Bill Miner is still the most mysterious bandit in the pantheon of Old West bad guys.

More popular in his day, though less remembered, than equally infamous contemporaries such as Jesse James and Billy the Kid, Miner has been mythologized over the years as the Gentleman Bandit, the Robin Hood of North America, and the Grey Fox. His tombstone reads: "Last of the Famous Western Bandits." Pinkerton called him the "Master Criminal of the American West."

Few things about his life seem certain. When imprisoned in California at San Quentin, he said he was born in 1847, but he gave 1842 as his birth date when sent to a penitentiary in New Westminster, British Columbia. Not even his name seems to have been pinned down for certain, alternately cited by various researchers as William A. McDonald or Ezra Allen Miner. Some say he was a homosexual, but offer no conclusive evidence.

Whatever the facts, the man known to posterity as "Old Bill Miner" began his criminal career as a young petty thief before building a reputation as a stagecoach bandit, train robber and escape artist, and in Canada, he earned his notoriety by robbing Canadian Pacific Railway trains on two separate occasions in 1904 and 1906.

The attacks on the CPR were neither the first nor the last robberies to occur in Canada, although both claims have been made repeatedly.

Miner is now a full-fledged folk hero. His name and face grace the signboards of numerous restaurants, saloons, pubs and roadhouses, mostly in B.C. One popular steakhouse even offers

"Billy Miner Pie" on its menu. Bald Mountain, near Princeton, B.C., in the same vicinity where George Edwards (one of Miner's many aliases), took up residence while in Canada, was renamed Mount Miner. There's even a small theatre group in Armstrong, B.C. which calls itself the Bill Miner Society for Cultural Advancement.

Not bad for the man who may or may not have coined the phrase: "Hands up!"

The train robbery provided the *Vancouver Province* with a great opportunity to engage its readership. "Professional robbers of the cleverest type and equipped with plenty of boldness and nerve are credited with having committed the robbery," the newspaper stated.

Richard Marpole, general superintendent for the CPR's Pacific Division, was hard pressed to juggle his regular duties with his newfound celebrity as official railway spokesman during the manhunt that ensued. In interviews with the *Province*, he assured an excited citizenry that the railway and the government were sparing no effort to bring the culprits to justice, estimating that there were upwards of 40 law enforcement officers combing the countryside for clues to their whereabouts.

The CPR and the Dominion Express Company jointly offered a $5,000 reward for the "capture and conviction" of the men who robbed the express and mail car, and another $1,000 for "reliable information leading to the arrest and conviction of these individuals." On top of that, the B.C. provincial government put up an additional $1,500.

The Pinkerton agency had all but concluded that it was, indeed, Bill Miner they sought. Most of the local newspapers had joined in the speculation. But the bandits somehow managed to evade capture. Generally it was supposed that the trio had vanished across the border where they were said to be, no doubt, holed up in one of the small towns in the western United States.

In later years it emerged that Miner had simply returned to his previous haunts in the neighbourhood of Princeton, B.C., where he went by the name of George Edwards, a very respectable and well liked member of the community.

$500 Reward

The above reward will be paid for the arrest and detention of **WILLIAM** (Bill) **MINER**, alias **Edwards**, who escaped from the New Westminster Penitentiary, at New Westminster, British Columbia, on the 8th August, 1907, where he was serving a life sentence for train robbery.

DESCRIPTION:

Age 65 years; 138 pounds; 5 feet 8½ inches; dark complexion; brown eyes; grey hair; slight build; face spotted; tattoo base of left thumb, star and ballet girl right forearm; wrist joint-bones large; moles centre of breast, 1 under left breast, 1 on right shoulder, 1 on left shoulder-blade; discoloration left buttock; scars on left shin, right leg, inside, at knee, 2 on neck.

Communicate with

LT.-COL. A. P. SHERWOOD,

Commissioner Dominion Police,
Ottawa, Canada.

The 'Grey Fox' used all his wiles to escape a life sentence in the New Westminster Penitentiary.

The theft, paltry though it was, triggered a manhunt in which CPR agents were joined by provincial officers, North-West Mounted Police, and of course, agents from both the Pinkerton and Thiel agencies.

The day after the robbery, senior CPR detectives William McLaws and R. E. Bullick arrived in Kamloops to coordinate the CPR's response. Agent McLaws, from the CPR police office in Winnipeg, was appointed officer in charge. He and Superintendent Brown of Seattle's Thiel agency interviewed as many witnesses as they could find and began to put together profiles of the train robbers.

At first there was conflicting information and much confusion about the identity of the outlaws.

"McLaws wires difficult [to] get information from railway employees, who seem to have more information than they care to divulge," the CPR's David McNicholl was informed by Vice President William Whyte. "Everything points to it being done by local men, or at least some local men being with them at time of hold-up. Robbers left horses hobbled at least five miles from railway line. ... They made no attempt to get express. These facts might point to attempt to cause company trouble by dishonest employees," he surmised. "Outlaws now supposed to be in heavy timbered, hilly country south of Campbell's Meadows, which is difficult section to travel. No word from posse since Friday, nor from constable sent in with first lot of bloodhounds."

CPR Superintendent Kilpatrick and Trainmaster Elson, both working out of Revelstoke, actively aided provincial police with the pursuit, arranging for transportation, messaging, and the provision of supplies for the manhunt. Kilpatrick even had his private car moved to Kamloops, where he personally joined in the search. General Superintendent Marpole's car No. 10 joined the group shortly thereafter.

By Saturday, four days after the robbery, a posse of Mounted Police

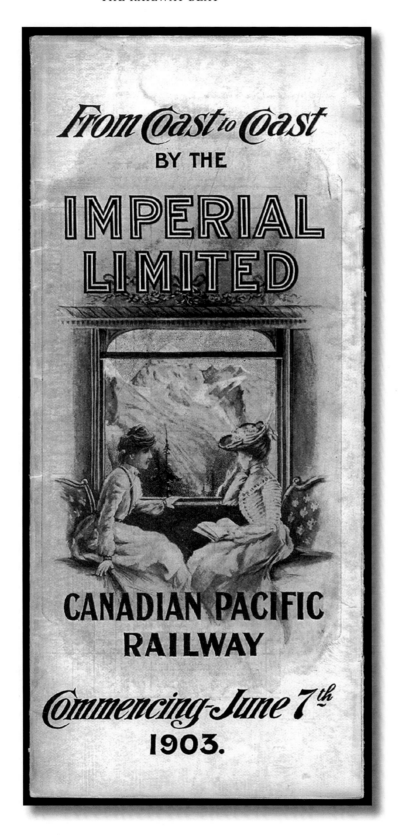

From Coast to Coast
BY THE
IMPERIAL
LIMITED
CANADIAN PACIFIC
RAILWAY
Commencing June 7th
1903.

In the early years of the 20th century, the transcontinental *Imperial Limited* was CPR's most luxurious public offering.

arrived on the scene from Calgary, Banff and elsewhere in the west, under the command of Commissioner A. Bowen Perry. Among them were sergeants T. M. Shoebotham, John J. Wilson and Percy Thomas, along with corporals James Stewart, C. R. Peters, James Tabuteau and John T. Browning. The Mounties worked closely with provincial police officers and their hired Indian trackers to divide the search area and put as many boots on the ground as possible.

On horses freshly broken and supplied by a local man named John Roper Hull, the Mounted Police spent two days scouring the bush. In the daytime they were pounded by rain, but at night they were comfortably ensconced with local ranchers.

On Monday, May 14, the Mounties grabbed their rifles, revolvers and trail supplies at first light to resume their search. Sergeants Shoebotham and Wilson, and Constables Stewart, Browning and Peters had paused at midday for a quick meal when B.C. Constable William Fernie rode up out of breath.

"We were about to saddle up after lunch when Provincial Constable Fernie rode in and told us he had seen and talked to three men, two or three miles back, and he thought they were the wanted men," Browning recalled many years later. "We left with him at once at a gallop to the place at which he had seen them; he did not know in what direction they were headed."

The Mounties spread out looking for tracks, and before long Corporal Stewart saw smoke from a campfire and waved the other policemen over to where three men could be clearly seen. Wilson was first to address the men, stating they were looking for three men who had recently held up a CPR train. The tall one replied they had not seen anyone.

"Well, boys," Wilson said, "you answer the description of the men we are looking for. Throw 'em up!"

At this, one of the men around the campfire drew his gun and fired, ran toward the bush and hollered "Look out boys, the game is up." But one of the lawmen managed to wing the fleeing gunman in the leg and the three suspects were soon disarmed and held under cover.

As the Mounties were searching the men, one of them revealed a distinctive tattoo on his right forearm—a ballet dancer.

"We have something more than the Kamloops train robbers here," said Sergeant Shoebotham. "We have captured Bill Miner, the notorious American bandit with a $20,000 reward on his head."

The outlaws were bound hand and foot, loaded onto a wagon and driven to a nearby ranch. There the manager, a Mr. Graves, told the Mounties they had made a big mistake. "Why, this old man is George Edwards, a local rancher and highly respected neighbour," he said.

It was the same story when the prisoners were transferred to Kamloops, where everybody refused to believe that the apparent leader of the three suspects was the legendary U.S. train robber. Eventually, however, though he stuck with the name Edwards, Miner confessed that he had robbed the train at Ducks, thinking it carried more than $100,000 in relief funds for victims of the recent earthquake in San Francisco. Alas, the cash shipment had moved by train a day before the robbery.

The men were brought to trial and found guilty.

"At the trial," Corporal Browning said, "it came out in the evidence of the Express messenger of the car that was held up, that the tallest of the bandits was wearing black goggles and he had broken open a carton of liver pills and put one in his pocket. The .38 revolver we took off Miner was identified as the one belonging to the Express messenger held up at Mission Junction the previous year."

One of Miner's accomplices was identified as Lewis Colquhoun, an Ontario man Miner had met in Phoenix, Arizona, several years before. Before turning to train robbery, Colquhoun had been employed by the Great Northern Railroad, as well as by the CPR, putting in telegraph lines. He also did a brief stint working for Pat Burns, the famous Canadian cattle and meat packing baron.

The smallest train robber, the one who caught a bullet in his knee, was charged as Thomas "Shorty" Dunn, but was more commonly known among his associates as "Little Billy," a horse wrangler, trapper and packer from Wisconsin.

Miner and Dunn were sentenced to life imprisonment, Colquhoun to 25 years. Colquhoun died of tuberculosis in 1911 while still in New Westminster Penitentiary. His body was shipped to his former home in Collingwood, Ontario, for burial. Dunn was paroled in 1918, but drowned nine years later when his boat capsized in an isolated estuary of Ootsa Lake, not far from Kamloops where Little Billy was trapping and prospecting.

LEFT: Lewis "Scotty" Colquhoun died of tuberculosis while in prison.

RIGHT: Shorty Dunn was also known as "Little Billy."

Miner escaped the B.C. pen with three other inmates on August 9, 1907, under strange circumstances. The prisoners somehow managed to dig their way under a couple of fences at the rear of the New Westminster Penitentiary brickmaking yard, an escape that remains controversial to this day. The man who had famously told a judge that "no prison walls can hold me" was once again on the loose.

For some, the evidence didn't add up. It was said the holes under the fences were too small for men to crawl through; others claimed that the guard on duty that day had allowed the men to escape through an unlocked gate. Speculation was high that Miner's escape had been "arranged" or at least aided by the CPR, said to be desperate to recover bonds stolen, but unreported, during the Mission Junction robbery in 1904. The rumours were never confirmed.

For nine days, 35 armed men, including penitentiary guards, provincial police and special constables beat the bush looking for the escaped convicts. Mounted Police Sergeant John Wilson complained to a reporter from the *Vancouver News Advertiser* about the lack of enthusiasm for the chase and, particularly, about the meager $500 bounty belatedly posted by the Dominion Police for Miner's capture.

"The reward offered is not large enough to get him, as he has too many friends in B.C.," the Mounties put forth. "Bill is one of the smoothest fellows you ever saw, when he's not robbing trains, always willing to spend his money, and making friends with women and children. He makes a point of never taking anything from a man who works for wages, but believes that corporations are not to be pitied, and has no compunction about taking a toll on them."

Though Miner was able to avoid capture and escape to the U.S., predictably, he was unable to stay on the straight and narrow. On February 18, 1911, he was caught after holding up a train in Georgia and handed a 20 year sentence in that state's Milledgeville prison. True to form, Old Bill escaped twice more, but each time was recaptured and returned to prison. He died there on September 2, 1913, at the age of 64.

With Bill out of the picture, things might have returned to normal for CPR operating crews in the rugged mountains of B.C., but they didn't.

Locomotive engineer Matt Crawford was at the throttle on the fateful night of June 21, 1909, when a dramatic train robbery once again unfolded on the CPR.

"I picked up train No. 97 at Revelstoke," Crawford told the *Vancouver Province* many years later. "She was the through passenger to the Coast, and was running four hours late, but my orders did not call for me to make up time. We took on water at Sicamous and again at Notch Hill. This must have been where the gunman boarded us. We slowed down going through Shuswap and were just picking up speed again, when I heard a gruff voice."

At first Crawford thought it was his fireman Harry Carpenter but when he turned to look, a masked man with an oversized frock coat was pointing two revolvers at his head.

"Here, you," said the bandit, motioning with one gun for the fireman to approach. He was half-hidden in the shadow of the locomotive tender. To engineer Crawford he shouted, "You keep going,"

The railway men struggled to calm themselves.

"He moved closer, and I told him that it was not necessary to keep us covered," Crawford said, "that we could not do him any harm. He lowered his guns, but kept his fingers on the triggers. He was swearing terrifically and kept saying: "I'm going to have this train."

When the train was about five miles west of Shuswap, a red light glowed beside the track and Crawford began to slow his engine. Under a fresh torrent of profanity, the engineer told the bandit that despite the situation, he could not ignore a signal light.

"Well, if it's your duty, do it, but keep your damn mouth shut," was the reply, as once again a menacing gun barrel loomed large.

Conductor Sam Elliot and brakeman Ashton jumped from the train and started forward to see what was happening, but had to quickly clamber back aboard as the train lurched ahead. Just east of the station at Ducks, the locomotive rounded a curve and the crew could see a bonfire burning alongside the tracks.

"Stop!" yelled the bandit, waving his guns in agitation and throwing a coal pick from the tender to the road bed below.

Forced to climb down from the locomotive cab, Crawford and Carpenter were confronted by two more masked men, one of whom appeared out of the gloom with three sticks of dynamite in his hands. The men were hustled down to the first express car behind the engine.

Armed with the commandeered pick, the bandits banged on the door and, hearing nothing from inside, opened a hole with the tool large enough to see that the car was empty. The same scenario unfolded beside the second car.

"Now the cursing was terrible," recalled Crawford.

The bandits proceeded to the third car; it was a combination mail coach and express car. The leader shouted to open the door, threatening to blow the car up.

"Go ahead and do your blowing," was the cool reply of the mail clerk, busy inside hiding the registered mail. "What you are looking for went on ahead by train No. 5."

It was later reported that a shipment of silver from Trail, B.C., to a Vancouver bank had been slated to move by Train No. 97, but had been rerouted. Had the bandits been more successful in pinpointing the bullion, they may have been dismayed to find that the loot they coveted consisted of 6,000 pounds of silver lead ingots, weighing about 90 pounds apiece. They were also unaware apparently that the Dominion Express Company had assigned heavily armed guards to accompany every valuable shipment since the Bill Miner train holdups of 1904 and 1906.

Confident the robbers would find nothing of value, the clerk eventually flung open the side door of the mail and express car and the masked bandits climbed in, but none of the expected padlocked boxes was to be found. No attempt was made to touch the mail or rob the passengers. Empty handed, the man in the frock coat and his accomplices vanished into the night.

At daybreak, a heavily armed posse left Kamloops for the holdup scene on a special CPR train. Aboard was B.C. Provincial Constable Bill Fernie, one of the heroes of the Miner capture, as well as some Indian trackers and Mounted Police officers. Within 24 hours, agents from the CPR, Pinkerton's and Thiel had also joined the hunt.

At first, the investigators assumed Old Bill was back at it. Despite being jailed for life, Miner was still at large after his escape from New Westminster Penitentiary. But the train crew looked over the mug shots of the "Gentleman Bandit" and shook their heads emphatically.

Days passed before any details began to emerge. After a series of interviews with the locals, the police officers determined the bandits had taken a boat across Shuswap Lake. Next, four stolen saddle horses from the Pioneer Poultry Ranch, near Kamloops, were found wandering aimlessly on the range.

The rumours persisted about Bill Miner's involvement, but CPR conductor Sam Elliot, who had been on the train held up by Miner three years earlier and had had a good up-close look at the famous train robber during his trial, swore up and down that this was not the case.

Nearly a week passed before government agent W. J. Christie stationed at Ashcroft, B.C., got an urgent telegram to be on the lookout for three men floating down the North Thompson River on a skiff. Isaac Decker, a former CPR employee who often acted as a special constable for the province was called upon by the B.C. Provincial Police to watch the river.

Decker didn't have long to wait. He hardly had time to scramble down the embankment to the water's edge before, sure enough; a rowboat with two men aboard came around the bend and into view. It was later learned that a third man had been landed shortly before.

Armed with an old Winchester rifle, Decker motioned the men

toward the shore. As soon as the boat ground up onto the beach, one of the men jumped out with a coat folded over his arm. Before words could be exchanged, he aimed a revolver at the constable from under the garment and fired. At the same time, Decker shot from the hip, putting a bullet through the would-be assassin's brain.

The second man in the boat grabbed a shotgun, sprang ashore and shot the wounded Decker where he lay. He then proceeded to very coolly bend over his dead companion and remove all his identification papers and, tucking the man's revolver into his belt, climbed the bank to the railway track and disappeared. Decker lingered between life and death for several hours before expiring.

A short time later, engineer Crawford was able to identify the dead bandit as the man with the frock coat who had held up Train No. 97.

News of the violent encounter and the two deaths electrified the countryside. Railroad police and hired detectives swarmed the scene with bloodhounds and a small arsenal of hastily assembled weapons. The investigators were still trying to determine the identity of the man with the frock coat who now lay in the morgue. The break came when more police arrived from Seattle, Tacoma and Portland to join in the hunt. Looking over the photos of the dead bandit, a veteran of the Southern Pacific Police solved the mystery.

"That's Dave Haney," he stated unequivocally.

"You sure?" queried Chief Constable Joe Burr, an ex-stage coach driver and longtime provincial police officer.

"Absolutely," retorted the American officer. "I recognize him well. And his brother must have been with him; they were never far apart."

"The man with him," said Burr, "is the one we want for murder. He's about 40 years old, stout, broad-shouldered and clean-shaven."

A consensus was building.

"That sure sounds like it could be Bill Haney," the American officer said.

The notorious Haneys! In and out of U.S. federal prisons for the last 20 years, they were wanted for more than one railroad job, and now it looked like the cold and cunning brothers had upped the ante with their first foray into Canada when they stuck up the CPR's *Imperial Limited*.

William Haney was wanted by the American authorities. He was sought by both the Pinkerton and Thiel agencies. The B.C. Provincial Police offered $2,500 for his arrest and conviction; the CPR put up an additional $1,500. The heat was on, but Haney was nowhere to be found.

Hardly a week went by without a new telegram arriving at police headquarters in Victoria to say that Bill Haney had been seen somewhere. Reports came from as far away as Sydney, Australia. But it was always the same story: the tips proved to be false alarms prompted largely by the substantial reward on offer.

Every state, provincial and federal penitentiary now had Haney's description and mug shots. Every police department and law enforcement agency on both sides of the border had Haney "wanted" notices papering the walls. As well as the B.C. government and CPR rewards totaling $4,000 for William Haney's capture, the CPR was said to have set aside a couple of thousand dollars to help educate Isaac Decker's son, Archie, a young boy of twelve when his father died in the line of duty. The railway also intended to offer Archie a job when he graduated from school, but the orphaned boy was killed during the First World War while fighting in France with the Canadian Forces.

Ten years after the killing of Special Constable Isaac Decker, stray reports and sightings of Haney were still being investigated by B.C. Provincial Police. Bill Haney was never seen or heard from again, at least not by any law enforcement officers.

Meanwhile, trouble was brewing among the more than 1,000 men working in the CPR's Fort William freight sheds. Looking for a wage increase the men (collectively cited at the time as perhaps the most militant railway work force in the country), suddenly walked off the job on the morning of August 9, 1909.

The wildcat strike was described as the most violent labour dispute to date. Within days, the railway had brought in up to 30 special constables to assist the local police force in keeping a lid on the protest, but a gun battle was unavoidable. During it, Inspector Ball of the CPR Special Police was shot in the abdomen and in one eye, which later had to be removed. Railway Constable J. Carpenter received several shots to the legs, one bullet shattering his knee. Another constable, J. Hallworth, was critically wounded and later died of his injuries. Sergeant Taylor of the Fort William City Police was shot in the rear end.

On August 13, a contingent of Royal Canadian Mounted Rifles

Following a short stint as a railway constable, Victor McLaglen went on to stardom in Hollywood.

The Magnificent Brute

Though his trackside stint was a short one, Victor McLaglen (1886-1959) was without a doubt the most dashing figure to sign up with the railway police since Sam Steele patrolled the construction camps of the CPR.

McLaglen joined Canadian Pacific as a constable in 1906 just after the disbanding of the railway's Special Service Department and the return of control for policing and security to senior railway operating people at the local level. A boy soldier who later earned a living as a wrestler and heavyweight boxer, McLaglen was deployed by the CPR to duties in and around the Company boat docks at Owen Sound, Ontario.

For whatever reason, on April 18, 1907 he went AWOL, never to return to policing.

Twenty-eight years later, in 1935, Victor McLaglen won the Academy Award as Best Motion Picture Actor for his leading role in *The Informer.* The road from reluctant CPR policeman to successful, highly respected thespian had been a long and circuitous one.

McLaglen was born in Tunbridge Wells, Kent. His father, an Anglican clergyman, moved the family from Britain to take up the position of Bishop of Claremont in South Africa while Victor was still a child.

During the war in South Africa, an underaged McLaglen served as a Life Guard at Windsor Castle before his early release was secured by his father. The young adventurer then came to Canada where he indulged his pugnacious nature in the boxing ring. He toured with a number of circuses, Wild West shows and vaudeville acts, sometimes offering $25 to anybody who could go three rounds with him.

When the First World War broke out, McLaglen signed up with the Irish Fusiliers. Most of his soldiering took place in the Middle East, and he eventually earned the rank of provost marshal, or head of the British military police for the city of Baghdad.

In the early 1920s he broke into British films, and soon moved to Hollywood, where he won several roles as a somewhat thuggish, but kindhearted man of action. He made more than 120 movies between 1920 and 1958, among them *The Magnificent Brute*, in which McLaglen's physical prowess was showcased front and centre.

He was married three times and died at the age of 72 on November 7, 1959.

Canadians in the small towns of Ontario remembered McLaglen best for his robust physique. "That man had the most perfect control of his muscles I have ever seen," recalled Chief Carson, head of the police force in Owen Sound, the very place where Victor McLaglen had pinned on his railway police badge at the age of 20.

(a Canadian militia, not to be confused with John A. MacDonald's Mounted Police) arrived in town by train to restore order. The strike ended the next day. Sixteen of the ringleaders were convicted of various gun-related offences and sentenced to terms between 30 days and nine months.

Late in 1912 in Cochrane, Alberta, a CPR trainman named Roy Blair discovered a couple of transients riding in an empty refrigerator car on his westbound passenger train. When he ordered them down from the car, one of the men drew a pistol and shot Blair dead on the spot. The killer's accomplice, a man named Crawford, was caught shortly afterward, but the gunman had made his escape.

It wasn't until three years later that Alfred Cuddy, chief of Calgary City Police, received a wire from the warden at Walla Walla, Washington state penitentiary that a prisoner held there, one "Shorty" Lyons, had confessed to the murder at Cochrane.

CPR Investigator Carpenter and Royal Northwest Mounted Police (the name having been officially changed in 1904) Inspector of Detectives Richardson obtained a warrant, travelled to the U.S. and were successful in bringing him back to Canada to face justice.

At his trial in Calgary, Carpenter was able to produce the man's accomplice as a witness along with the conductor and the second brakeman who had been on the train the night Blair was slain. Lyons

McADAM JCT

A railway police officer takes place of pride, front and centre with railway officers and other workers at McAdam Junction, New Brunswick.

was sentenced to be hanged, but the decision was later commuted to life imprisonment, which the convicted killer served in Prince Albert Penitentiary.

One more relatively minor occurrence, on December 2, 1912, marked the end of an era which would not be missed by the CPR. A masked man boarded the observation car of the *Imperial Limited* just as the train was departing Vancouver for its transcontinental run. This time passengers were targeted and those enjoying the view from the rear observation deck as the train rolled out of the station were collectively relieved of $309, two watches and a ring. CPR posted a reward of $500, but nobody ever stepped forward to collect.

CHAPTER 4
The Imperial Police:
Enter the Professionals

By 1912, theft of freight from both yards and trains, combined with the tendency of company assets to walk off the property when not locked down was costing the CPR well over a million dollars annually. The volume of complaints was enormous, as was the disruption in the smooth flow of business, consuming valuable administrative hours and complicating the day to day lives of local railway superintendents and other officials who, as often as not, lived in close proximity to the railway's customers. Though the CPR undertook to reimburse its customers for the full value of their stolen goods, the efforts of the harried railway clerks in the freight claims department could not fully compensate the victims for their inconvenience and lost business.

Organized gangs operated in railway yards and on moving trains all too frequently with the connivance of the company's own employees. Nineteenth-century hiring practices were loose and there was no reliable means for the railway to weed out undesirables from the pool of available labourers, particularly when seeking men for seasonal and piecemeal work. Disenfranchised and transient workers struggling to eke out a living in isolated communities across the country could easily give in to their own temptation or become marks for the many fraudsters, con men and small time crooks operating up and down

To ensure the new force would live up to its billing, a potential recruit was required to meet three specific criteria before being considered:

First, he had to have served a term of enlistment with the Imperial army or Mounted Police.

Second, he would have to display a service medal to establish his credentials because as the CPR emphasized, "that ribbon means that the wearer has been trained in a school that means rigid discipline, lessons that teach him how to hold his temper and to recognize that the public is a hard master." For a number of years railway management required members to wear their military ribbons whenever they were in police uniform. Psychologically, the railway looked to a smart, martial uniform to provide both a deterrent to crime and a security blanket for a jittery public in the years leading up to the First World War.

Last, a successful candidate had to be formally discharged from his former position with the army or police force "without a shadow of a blemish."

Along with news of the new force's formation came the announcement that the chief of the department would be headquartered in Winnipeg and would report directly to CPR Vice President Bury. While the police would undeniably be involved in the detection and discouragement of crime, as well as in a general watchfulness that would protect the company's property from the depredations to which it was currently vulnerable, other, softer, public duties were held up as equally important. Along with being on hand in major centres to ensure travelers were informed about the arrival and departure times of the CPR's passenger trains, the new kinder and gentler professional railway police officer would be able to "answer the thousands of questions that only the public can ask."

Key to changing the public's perception of any railway cop's undeniably thuggish image would be the smart, military style outift that would serve as his mark of distinction. Chosen personally by Bury for the railway's police force, the new look was an instant hit with the travelling public and drew several enquiries from other railway companies in Canada and the United States. Canada's Governor-General, the Duke of Connaught, had made the point of complimenting Bury on the excellence of the CPR police while on an official tour of

western Canada, during the course of which he had recognized several of the men from the British army.

The January 1913 edition of *Canadian Railway and Marine World*, the most prominent and respected industry journal of the day, noted that 80 members had already been acquired of the 150 men needed for the new police force. The article went on to enthuse that the new force could no doubt "be solidified almost instantly into a unit of Imperial defense."

It was a positive note upon which to launch a significant evolution in railway police work. The strong links to Empire that were alluded to, as well as the obvious military efficiency with which the new force intended to operate, can only have lent credibility to the initiative in both Canada and Britain. In any case, whether initial public reaction was a factor or not, the CPR was prepared to go one step further. Before the news about a new police force in the Canadian West had made the rounds of railway and law enforcement circles, the initiative had been expanded to blanket the railway's entire system.

At about the same time, *Canadian Railway and Marine World* was advising its readers of the somewhat romantic Imperial police force then being created by George Bury. CPR President Thomas

A CP constable stands guard over the mail and express car, while the train boards passengers at Smiths Falls, Ontario.

Rufus Chamberlin was the only man considered for the top job.

Rufus Gardner Chamberlin

THE FIRST CHIEF
OF A NEW POLICE DEPARTMENT

When the CPR created the Department of Investigation in 1913, President Thomas Shaughnessy had just one man in mind to fill the position of railway police chief: Rufus Gardner Chamberlin.

Chamberlin was then Chief of the Vancouver City Police Department and well known to Shaughnessy through the railway's many and deep connections with that city.

The CPR's first chief was born in Chelsea, Quebec, on August 4, 1863. By age 21 he had joined the illustrious ranks of the Dominion Police in Ottawa.

The Dominion Police Force was created in 1869 to provide basic security services on Parliament Hill. Along with operating rudimentary detective and secret services branches, the fledgling force provided fire protection on the Hill and even ran the mail service between various government buildings in the nation's capital.

As a constable in this highly visible, full service constabulary, Chamberlin was an impressive figure from the heels of his spit polished boots to the tip of his spiked steel helmet.

By 1903, he had been promoted to inspector with the Dominion Police Force's secret service, playing a major role in all of the Force's important cases. Four years later, his quiet competence, sterling service record and many professional connections in the law enforcement and business communities had earned him the high profile position of police chief in Vancouver where he was instrumental in quelling the unfortunate rash of anti-Asian riots that erupted in the city soon after his appointment.

The Dominion Police were superseded in 1920 when the Royal Canadian Mounted Police were given full authority throughout Canada.

Rufus Chamberlin was a crack shot with both rifle and revolver. The championship trophy he won on behalf of the Dominion Police in competition with other forces across the country was a shiny testament to his superb marksmanship.

The chief also approved of and gave his patronage to any number of physical activities. In Vancouver, he encouraged his men to compete in athletic competitions whenever possible. When two members of his department won the Police Amateur Athletic Association championship against competitors from Montreal, Ottawa, Toronto, Hamilton and Winnipeg, they were flag bearers for the culture of fitness nurtured by Chamberlin.

Aside from his work, the Ottawa Silver Seven hockey team (later the Ottawa Senators) never had a more ardent supporter.

As head of the CPR's new, system wide, integrated police service, Chamberlin encouraged every member to stay fit and maintain their firearms expertise. Over the course of his ten year career with the railway, he developed a modus operandi that would guide the Department of Investigation for decades to come.

One of the highlights of his career came in 1919, when Chamberlin was appointed by the federal government as a Commissioner of Police for the Dominion. That same year, and again in 1923, he accompanied His Royal Highness, Edward, the Prince of Wales, on extended royal tours across Canada. He had become one of the most capable and respected law enforcement officers on the continent.

Chamberlin passed away suddenly on December 23, 1923, at Montreal's Royal Victoria Hospital. He had appeared to be on the road to recovery after undergoing minor surgery when he contracted pneumonia and died.

The Prince of Wales, with whom the chief had formed a lasting friendship, sent Mrs. Chamberlin a cablegram expressing his deepest sympathy for her loss.

Major William McLeod was appointed to be his deputy in Winnipeg, while A. Hector Cadieux was assistant chief in Montreal.

The mandate for the new, expanded police force called for about 400 men, give or take. Four hundred men to cover more than 12,000 track miles and nearly as many railway stations, yards and other assets across Canada and into the United States. Company steamship activities and docking facilities, in particular, required constant attention, and then there were the numerous company hotels across the Dominion.

There was much for the Department of Investigation to do.

Its members wasted no time before plunging into the complex, globe spanning activities of the "World's Greatest Transportation System." The CPR ran a vast commercial empire that never slept. To survive, the Department had to combine tact, diplomacy and providence with solid, measureable results and use its limited resources wisely, targeting specific areas of concern as needed while maintaining flexibility always. Its members had to learn not just how the CPR operated, but how the company's many thousands of customers ran their businesses as well. They had to use a firm hand without alienating the public, projecting an aura of reassurance rather than menace.

In very short order, travelers regarded the presence of a uniformed railway police constable, particularly in large centres, as normal. The public cleansing of the railway policeman's image was accompanied by an about face in the way individual members began to interact with other CPR employees. The former antagonistic relationship slowly gave way to one of cooperation and, in many cases, genuine understanding and friendship.

Railway constables and sergeants were expected to be turned out in full uniform at all times on the job except, of course, when the men were involved in special investigations or assigned to undercover duty.

The 1851 *Railway Act* had outlined the regulations by which railways would be governed in Canada. An amendment in 1861 allowed for the appointment of railway constables and gave them the authority to make arrests on trains and on company property. Further iterations of the *Act,* modified in the 1880s and several times during the early decades of the 20th century, expanded the jurisdiction of railway police officers. It included all territory within a quarter mile on either side of the CPR right of way and within the same distance from all of the company's wharves, quays, landing places, warehouses, lands and premises.

In jurisdictions where several constables were required on a single shift, sergeants were assigned to supervise the work and report on the Department's activities to the district inspector. On the wharves in Montreal and Vancouver where police officers worked eight hour shifts around the clock, there was always a sergeant on duty.

In each of the CPR districts where railway operations were overseen by a general superintendent, roughly coinciding with each province from New Brunswick west, an inspector from the Department of Investigation was also stationed. While the inspectors reported directly to the chief of police and his assistant, they also worked closely with the local superintendents and other senior railway officers in the field. The district inspectors supervised the work of however many constables and sergeants might be assigned to them, and could recommend men for promotion or suspend them for insubordination or breaches of proper conduct, if necessary.

One regional inspector in the east and another in the west were assigned full time to the timely and orderly distribution of uniforms, revolvers and other necessary equipment. These regional administrators also handled all the paperwork associated with the job applications, references and medical examinations required by the Department.

Plainclothes investigators were assigned to general detective work, watching not only for signs of professional criminal activity, but also setting up safeguards to stamp out the rampant theft, fraud and payroll padding of the past.

Initially, 12 investigators were assigned to Montreal and its environs, six or seven to the Winnipeg area and two, three or as many as five in the various districts as needed. Those numbers, of course, varied with the years, and would ebb and flow along with the economic health of the railway and the political wellbeing of the country as a whole.

One important duty was the protection of valuable silk shipments from the Orient to markets on the east coast of North America. In 1913, the CPR had astounded the world by moving raw silk from Yokohama to New York City via its steamship *Empress of Asia* and

The *Empress of Asia* was luxuriously appointed throughout, with plenty of imaginative places to stash illicit things.

transcontinental railway lines in a previously unheard of 17 days. Armed guards accompanied the shipments at all times and the Department of Investigation provided security at all points where transfers were made, crews were changed out, and fuel and water were taken on.

Often the railway police were the closest to the action when a business along the railway line was struck by bandits.

On the morning of May 22, 1914, three men killed the paymaster of the Canada Cement Company at Exshaw, Alberta, in the course of a robbery. Paymaster John Wilson, accompanied by company clerk James Gordon, had been carrying more than $2,300 to the nearby CPR train station in a canvas bag when he was set upon by the trio. Reaching for an automatic pistol hidden in his pocket, Wilson was shot once in the chest and again through the mouth and brain. Gordon got lucky and walked away from the hold-up with a bullet hole in his trousers.

CPR Inspector R. G. Carpenter and his sergeant, George Smith, along with some officers from the Royal Northwest Mounted Police were soon on their way to the scene on a track car made from a converted 1912 Ford. By the time they arrived, an impromptu posse consisting of a handful of Canada Cement Company employees and the proprietor of a local hotel had already crossed the Kananaskis River by canoe and wounded one of the bandits in a shootout. The man was later identified as a Russian named Max Manelik. The other two thieves got away.

In Exshaw, the officers on the scene joined forces with Mounted Police Sergeant Paddy Ryan and three provincial policemen from Canmore. Inspector Carpenter's father, Silas Carpenter, then Commissioner of the Dominion Police at Banff, was also there. Guards were quickly posted at all the nearby bridges. Sergeant James Murray from the Calgary office of the Department of Investigation was asked to search all eastbound trains as they passed through Cochrane, a move that soon paid off when a second man, Sergey Konick, was captured by Murray the next night with all of the stolen money.

A Mounted Police constable had begun to search an eastbound freight from the front end while the CPR sergeant did the same from the rear. It wasn't long before Sergeant Murray saw Konick jump down and walk toward the end of the train. Lying prone until the suspect was nearly on top of him, Murray leapt on Konick and wrestled him to the ground.

It was more than a week later before the third hold-up man was cornered in a Calgary basement. The fugitive had somehow made his way undetected to Calgary, where he contacted an acquaintance looking for food and money. Unfortunately for him, his so-called friend immediately contacted Chief of Police Cuddy. As quickly as Cuddy could meet up with CPR Inspector Carpenter, the two men were staking out the abandoned store in which the desperate criminal, now known also to be a Russian by the name of Sokoloff, was said to be holed up.

The basement was basically a large hole under part of the building. There was no drain. The chief sent for a fire hose and filled the hole with water until it rose as high as the floor joists.

"When the water began to raise, Sokoloff climbed up on the ground under the store floor between the joists, and when the water reached that level, he decided it was time to quit," Carpenter later recalled.

"He called out to us that he would surrender and a hole was chopped in the floor over the spot from which we heard him call. His arms were wedged alongside his body between the joists and his .45 Luger and a belt of ammunition was lying on his stomach, his face was white and shining with perspiration and there was no fight left in him."

That same year, the Department of Investigation responded to two large scale catastrophes.

On the fateful night of May 29, 1914, more than 1,000 people died when the CPR's luxury liner *Empress of Ireland* sank in the frigid waters of St. Lawrence River. Rammed by the Norwegian collier *Storstad*, just off the south shore town of Rimouski, Quebec, the pride of the railway's ocean going fleet vanished beneath the waves in a brief 14 minutes. In the aftermath of the disaster, CPR constables were assigned to the dock areas and relief vessels where the bodies of passengers and their valuables were being recovered. The Department coordinated the efforts of city and provincial police involved in the recovery efforts.

Less than a month later on June 19th, a severe explosion rocked the Alberta town of Hillcrest Mines. Four CPR constables with first aid expertise were dispatched immediately from Calgary to provide relief, however, when they arrived at Hillcrest there were no survivors. One hundred and eighty-nine men, about half of the mine's total work force, were killed in a blast caused by a lethal mix of methane gas and coal dust.

Bigger challenges yet loomed on the horizon. Even as the Department of Investigation was stretching its organizational wings across the CPR system, storm clouds foreshadowed the coming Great War.

When Britain declared war on Germany on August 4, 1914, the Canadian Pacific played its part in supporting the British cause. One hundred thousand miles of company telegraph wires hummed night and day with messages mobilizing the rolling stock that would be required to move troops and supplies overseas.

At the outbreak of the hostilities, the Department of Investigation asked all of its members to be on the lookout for subversive activities and to keep their ears open for any information related to the enemy. By virtue of Canada's close relationship with Britain, the mother country's declaration of war automatically included the overseas Dominion in the epic struggle. When the news broke, an entire colony of ex-

TOP: In just fourteen minutes, the pride of the CPR's steamship fleet vanished beneath the waves.

LEFT: A CP constable sits with divers among the gear to be used in a salvage attempt on the sunken *Empress of Ireland*.

The railways and the railway
police were intimately involved with
the movement of troops
to the European theatre.

German army officers who had settled at Hussar, Alberta bolted for the United States via the CPR and the border crossing at North Portal, Saskatchewan. They got as far as Gibraltar en route to Italy before they were taken off the liner on which they were sailing by officers from a British war ship. They were interned for the duration of the war.

More than 11,000 CPR employees enlisted from virtually every service arm the transportation giant. Among them were 76 constables from the Department of Investigation, most of whom were veterans of the South African or Boer War.

The British Admiralty requisitioned most of the company's fleet on both the Atlantic and Pacific to serve as armed cruisers and troop transports. Fifty-two Canadian Pacific steamships moved almost one million soldiers to the various theatres of war in Europe, the Mediterranean, India, China, Egypt, Gallipoli and Mesopotamia. More than four million tons of cargo, munitions and supplies were also ferried into position. Twenty-seven of the vessels survived the conflict and returned to CPR service. Twelve sank, mostly targets of the ravenous U-boats that patrolled the major shipping lanes. One of the company's oldest liners, the elegant *Empress of India*, was converted to a hospital ship by, appropriately enough, India's Maharajah of Gwalior.

Within the first few months of the war, it became evident that Great Britain and her allies were unable to manufacture a sufficient number of shells to keep pace with the enormous demands for ammunition. At the time, Canada had virtually no munitions industry, but the CPR took up the challenge presented by Canadian war minister Sam Hughes and the federal government to turn out shells from its Angus Shops, a vast industrial complex located in Montreal.

As Canada's leading railway and industrial juggernaut, the CPR also took a leading role in the formation of the Canadian Overseas Railway Construction Corps, a group of skilled railway engineers and administrators who helped rebuild Europe's war torn rail infrastructure, even as the combatants were raining death down upon one another.

On the home front, the CPR gave absolute priority to troops and supply trains. Because there was every reason to expect sabotage attempts, 2,000 special sentries were enlisted to stand guard over strategic stretches of the right of way. Bridges were especially vulnerable. All of these recruits reported to the Department of Investigation.

One incident, in particular, led to this blanket precaution.

Early in the war one of Kaiser Wilhelm's agents, the master spy Franz von Papen, targeted the Vanceboro Bridge which crossed the St. Croix River between Maine and New Brunswick. Assuming correctly that large quantities of supplies as well as fully loaded troop trains had to funnel across this short span, von Papen laid out a plan to destroy it.

To this end, he enlisted the aid of an underling, Oberleutnant Werner Horn, to carry out the task.

On December 30, 1914, Horn arrived in the quaint little town of Vanceboro, Maine with sabotage on his mind. In his suitcase were 27 kilograms of explosives. Twice while trying to place the charge, he was forced to hang over the edge of the bridge to avoid troop trains. Although Horn did finally manage to achieve a loud bang for his efforts, there was very little accompanying damage to the bridge. In the brutal, sub-zero weather Horn's nitroglycerin had become almost inert. Struck by a fit of remorse, the hapless saboteur confessed to his crime and spent the remainder of the war incarcerated.

The following summer, Pinkerton agents uncovered a plot to sabotage CPR infrastructure in British Columbia. The prime suspect, a Dutchman by the name of J. H. van Koolbergen, was followed from San Francisco to Victoria, B.C., where he was watched closely by the authorities.

Pinkerton's notified the CPR's Department of Investigation about their suspicions and company investigators uncovered some interesting facts about van Koolbergen: the suspected German agent had once lived in Montreal where he married a French Canadian. Moving to Calgary in the boom years that preceded the war, van Koolbergen was involved in a series of fraudulent real estate deals before leaving town for points unknown.

When the CPR and the Calgary City Police discussed their options, they decided to issue a warrant for van Koolbergen's arrest on the outstanding charges of fraud as it would also have the useful effect of taking him out of the sabotage business. While in Calgary awaiting trial, van Koolbergen made numerous, detailed statements to the police about his connections with an extensive German spy ring working out of San Francisco and, in particular, outlined what had transpired when he was called to meet with a Leutnant von Brincken in that city's German consulate.

"Not knowing what he wanted, I went to see him," van Koolbergen said of his meeting with von Brincken. "He was very pleasant and told me that he was an officer in the German army and, at present, working in the secret service of the German Empire under Franz Bopp, the Imperial German consul.

"I went to the consulate and met Franz Bopp and then saw von Brincken in another room," he further confessed. "He asked me if I would do something for him in Canada and I answered him, 'Sure, I will do something, even blow up bridges if there's money in it.' And he said, 'you are the man; if that is so, you can make good money.'"

The Germans had apparently wanted van Koolbergen to dynamite one of the CPR's spectacular bridges or, even better, to blow up the eight kilometre long Connaught Tunnel that took the railway's transcontinental main line more than 1,000 metres beneath the summit of the mighty Selkirk Mountains.

His confessions spelled the end to van Koolbergen's spying activities and enabled the Canadian government to press the U.S. authorities for the incarceration of Bopp and von Brincken as well.

As a further disincentive to sabotage, CPR police acquired a small motorboat with which to patrol the company's Vancouver docks. Some of the Canadian federal customs officers at the docks also took advantage of the cabin cruiser to carry out their duties.

The 1917 Bolshevik revolution added a new dimension to the ongoing world conflict. A great many Russians living in Canada and the United States wished to return to the mother country, some to enlist with the counter revolutionary White Army, and others to swell the ranks of the ultimately victorious Reds.

The CPR's Department of Investigation issued orders to its constables on steamship duty to search all baggage leaving the country for arms of all description. In the process, investigators uncovered five large cases of printed material and a disassembled printing press on one of the company's Pacific *Empresses* bound for Vladivostok. But when they reported the extensive stash of Communist propaganda to the Canadian authorities, they were instructed to let it be loaded aboard the ship to avoid potential trouble. During the voyage across the Pacific the whole works disappeared over the side.

In support of the Whites, large quantities of war materiel had previously been shipped to Russia from the United States and Canada.

Patrolling the Vancouver yards, a CPR inspector does a quick check around the engine before a silk train and its high-value cargo depart for markets on the East Coast.

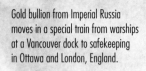

In payment for these supplies, the besieged Russian government sent several shipments of gold by warship to Vancouver. The gold, packed in 200 pound cases, was unloaded at night on the CPR docks and loaded directly onto steel baggage cars.

As soon as the transfers were made, the clandestine "silk trains" would leave for an undisclosed destination accompanied by Dominion Express officials and guards from the railway's Department of Investigation. No mention of gold was ever made. All of the shipments were made without incident.

During the course of the war, the CPR was occasionally called

upon to transport Chinese labourers to Europe to work on damaged infrastructure. On one such move a riot broke out aboard the company's *Empress of Asia* which the ship's officers were unable to control. A number of Mongolians en route to France and awaiting immigration clearance from Canadian officials had been gambling with members of the ship's crew. When an argument turned into a full blown riot, a CPR investigator and four constables with rifles and fixed bayonets were hard-pressed to restore order.

At the end of hostilities in 1918, the door was thrown wide open for those who had left the CPR to return to their jobs. More than 7,000 former employees were reinstated, while an additional 11,000 ex-servicemen were also offered employment.

Large numbers of passengers and a great deal of freight had been protected while in transit. Members of the Department of Investigation now went back to riding trains and patrolling yards. Uniformed constables were once again posted at company stations, restaurants and hotels where they provided security and assisted travelers in a variety of ways.

CHAPTER 5
Friends in High Places:
Royalty and the
British Empire Exhibition

As life returned to normal after the war, Canadians looked upon their shattered economy with considerable anxiety. The cost of living had shot up by more than 75% during the conflict years. Workers' wages, however, had not kept pace. Servicemen returned from overseas to find war industries closing down at home and economic deflation worldwide. Unemployment grew.

Edward Wentworth Beatty had inherited the mantle of CPR president from Sir Thomas Shaughnessy one month before the end of the hostilities. The company benefitted from a spike in business as trainloads of goods and materials were sent overseas to rebuild the European economy. However, wages, prices and freight rates all took a while to stabilize.

The first three presidents of the CPR—George Stephen, William Van Horne and Thomas Shaughnessy—had all been founding fathers and creators of the company. Through some very trying times, the young and dashing Beatty would have to conserve what they had built.

Many labour leaders in the post war years believed capitalism was doomed. The more radical among them looked at the birth of proletarian power in the Russian Empire as a model for the future. They resented the Canadian government for sending troops to counter what they viewed to be a just revolution.

Soldiers returning from the battlefields of Europe, who had risked everything for their country and were now trying to provide a decent life for their families back home, expected their demands for better working conditions and more job security to be taken seriously. So, too, did all the men and women who had heeded the call of the assembly lines and supply chains of the wartime economy. From great sacrifice a strong desire for social change had been born.

Strike threats proliferated across the country and nowhere more so than in Winnipeg where the Winnipeg Trades and Labour Council pushed for a coordinated strike among the nation's workers to improve their bargaining position. "If necessary, a general strike of the whole Dominion would be called," threatened the council's *Winnipeg Labour News*, as it rode the wave of discontent.

The workers movement took a dramatic leap when 239 delegates representing big labour met at a convention in Calgary in the spring of 1919. The delegates voted overwhelmingly to create a gigantic economic alliance of all tradesmen in Canada that they named One Big Union (OBU).

The Calgary Convention set a deadline of June 1 for a general strike if demands for a six hour work day and other concessions were not met by employers, but workers in the country's third largest city jumped the gun. On May 15, electricians, carpenters, plumbers, clerks, cooks, caretakers and hundreds of others walked off the job in Winnipeg. In less than two hours, most of the workers in the city were on strike.

"Strike committee governs city," the *Winnipeg Tribune* declared, a day before the paper and its two competitors, the *Free Press* and the *Telegram*, ceased publication. Their typesetters and pressmen joined the workers on the street contributing to the general sense of chaos and confusion.

Not everybody agreed with the workers' tactics, however, and an organized opposition rallied in the Board of Trade building on Main Street. A "Citizens' Committee of One Thousand" took shape and attempted to maintain essential services throughout the city. Volunteer businessmen and professionals from the middle class, and returning "loyalist" soldiers rode fire trucks, staffed the waterworks department and delivered mail. City police stayed on the job—reluctantly.

In Ottawa, Prime Minister Robert Borden pledged to maintain law and order. A detachment of Royal Northwest Mounted Police returning home from overseas was diverted to Winnipeg, and the city called out four units of local militiamen. Ominously, 20 Lewis machine guns were loaded aboard CPR troop trains bound for the troubles.

When many of the city police refused to sign a no strike pledge, city council dismissed all but 15 of the 140 men on the force. Fresh from the battlefields of Europe, 700 soldiers were signed up as special police. The Canadian Pacific's Department of Investigation bolstered its handful of local constables with members from its detachments in Brandon, Medicine Hat and Kenora to protect the company's properties as best they could from any possible depredations.

A detachment of special mounted police clashed with the mobs that congregated downtown, cracking heads with their clubs and, in turn, falling victim to a fusillade of flying stones. Some were dragged from their horses and beaten by the mobs. A week later, 50 mounted police and about 500 special officers descended upon the homes of known strike leaders in the early morning hours, rousing them from their beds and hustling them off to the city's Rupert Street jail.

Despite the attempt by the authorities to decapitate the movement, by June 21 the situation was at its bleakest, culminating that day in a violent riot centred on Winnipeg's Market Square, a day that came to be known as "Bloody Saturday."

Around noon, thousands of agitated, chanting decommissioned soldiers and a sea of striking workers marched on the CPR's Royal Alexandra Hotel where Labour Minister Robertson and other anti-strike leaders were engaged in contingency planning. CPR police escorted a workers' delegation inside for talks.

Law enforcement officers and citizens clashed at Portage and Main, as tin cans, stones and chunks of concrete flew. One bleeding Mountie and then another went down to the pavement, leaving riderless and panicked horses to add to the general pandemonium. A streetcar was swarmed by the mob, windows broken, cushions torn out.

As the besieged streetcar was torched, the Mounted Police drew their revolvers and fired a volley into the air in an attempt to rein in the worst of the agitators. "My God, they're shooting to kill," somebody yelled. Scores of injured and wounded were lying in the streets. A man later identified

as Mike Sokolowiski dropped dead with a bullet in his heart. The special police attacked with guns and nightsticks, while the crowd struck back with anything that could be hurled in anger. Military ambulances and Red Cross workers waded into the fray to tend to the casualties.

At the peak of the frenzy, Mayor Gray emerged under guard to read the Riot Act from the steps of City Hall.

With the arrival of several vehicles full of soldiers, machine guns and fixed bayonets in hand, the crowd quickly dispersed and order was restored. Ninety-one persons landed in jail; 30 or more were in the hospital, including six Mounties and two other police officers who had been thrown from a roof. Bloody Saturday claimed its second victim when rioter Steve Schezerbanowes died from gangrene as a result of gunshot wounds to both legs.

The courtroom trials that followed were political sideshows. The authorities tried to paint the strikers as hell bent on undermining the Canadian way of life and setting up a Soviet form of government. Ultimately, however, it was determined that the strike leaders' overriding

The Royal Alexandra Hotel,
a prominent Winnipeg social centre,
became a convenient meeting point
for impromptu labour negotiations.

motivation had been to secure the principle of collective bargaining for working people and that no seditious conspiracy had taken place.

One of the most prominent among the strike leaders, alderman and social activist John Queen, went on to serve seven terms as mayor of Winnipeg and was also elected to the Manitoba legislature. The One Big Union faded away and morphed into several smaller labour organizations, largely based on specific trades.

Within months, labour struggles were bumped from newspaper headlines in favor of banner announcements of what would be the social event of the year 1919: a royal visit from H.R.H. the Prince of Wales. Prince Charming, the most eligible bachelor in the Empire, was sailing for Canada.

The Canadian Pacific organized most of the tour logistics and hosted the royal entourage across its own transportation network for a large portion of the round trip. Their conveyance, meticulously prepared by the CPR to make the proper impression for the occasion, was described by W. Douglas Newton, official tour correspondent and chronicler:

As his car neared the top of the hill, two Montreal flappers, whose extreme youth was only exceeded by their extreme daring, sprang onto the footboard and held him up with autograph books. He immediately produced a fountain pen, and sitting once more on the back of the car, wrote his name as the car went along, and the young ladies from Montreal clung on to it.

This delightful act was too much for one of the maidens, for, on getting her book back, she kissed the Prince impulsively, and then in a sudden attack of deferred modesty, sprang from the car and ran for her blushes' sake.

A CP constable at the entrance to Vancouver Station keeps onlookers at a respectful distance, while the Prince chats with members of his ceremonial guard.

During breaks in the formal ceremonies at several of the train's scheduled stops, the Prince of Wales engaged in lengthy conversations with former soldiers of the Canadian Corps, some of whom he had met on his visits to the front lines during the First World War. As a representative of the Crown, he was also pleased to meet and shake hands with loyal Canadians who had served the Empire in the Boer War, put down the Rebellion in the North-West, or ridden in the great western march of the Mounted Police.

The royal tour had been carefully planned to include plenty of time for the type of activities which appealed to Prince Edward, whether they be dancing the night away with the charming female socialites of cosmopolitan Toronto and Vancouver or saddling up for a manly cattle drive with the rugged ranchers of southern Alberta. During his visit to Canada, the prince gained such an affinity for the people and, in particular, the western lifestyle that he returned four years later on a shorter, unofficial trip, during which he purchased a hobby ranch south of Calgary.

During his initial three month tour and on his several subsequent visits, the Prince of Wales came to know many CPR constables by name and voiced his admiration for the men's professional look and military bearing on more than one occasion. The 1919 royal procession paraded through virtually all the main cities west of Quebec and a good number of smaller locations, particularly in Ontario and British Columbia. But despite the broad scope of the tour and the ambitious itinerary of public events, the prince preferred to socialize less formally and he hosted impromptu receptions almost daily. During the long stretches between stops he could shed the burden of public service and get to know his fellow travelers on a more personal level. Whenever the Prince was in the care of the CPR, Chief Chamberlin was close at hand, standing with the guest of honour on any number of reviewing platforms or relaxing over a pot of tea. They became fast friends and confidants.

The Department of Investigation was making friends in high places, both inside and outside of the company.

In the end, the royal tour was a pleasant but fleeting distraction for Canadians. With the prince back aboard HMS *Renown*, the focus of the man in the street returned to the day to day pursuit of making ends meet. In the east, few new factories had come on line to replace the

The Prince insisted on meeting each of the men assigned to the security detail for his first royal tour of Canada.

closed munitions plants and war industries; in the west below average crop yields left many workers idle. By the early 1920s, unemployment had reached 17%.

Times were tough. The Department of Investigation laid numerous charges against confidence men and gamblers who preyed upon the company's clientele on its trains and in its stations and hotels. While most of the constables were building good working relationships on the ground with company employees, others were combating the still too prevalent frauds and small time criminal conspiracies perpetrated by an inside few. In many of these cases the money trail, or discrepancies between ridership numbers and those accounted for with ticket sales, pointed to the culprits. At other times, employees or agents of the company were caught turning a blind eye to theft on the company wharves, in its freight sheds and yards, or in other locations where merchandise was handled.

And there were still those who thought passenger trains were easy pickings.

On the evening of August 2, 1920, westbound CPR Train No. 63 steamed out of Lethbridge, Alberta, bound for Crowsnest, B.C. George Akoff, Ausby Auloff and Tom Basoff attracted little attention among the other passengers in the first and second class coaches.

The trip was uneventful until the train pulled away from the platform at Coleman, one stop east of Crowsnest. Conductor Sam Jones had just collected the fares from the passengers who had boarded at Coleman and was heading for the baggage car when Akoff came out of the lavatory waving an automatic pistol in the air. Thinking the man drunk, Jones told him to put the gun away and take his seat, but soon discovered the seriousness of the situation when an armed Bassoff took up a position at the opposite end of the car. Auloff then entered the car and ordered the passengers to throw up their hands.

Conductor Jones was pulling the signal cord to alert the locomotive engineer that something was amiss, when a bullet from Auloff's gun whistled past his head and embedded itself in the car's woodwork. Jones, brakeman J. Hickey and baggageman J. H. Staples were then hustled by Basoff out onto the rear platform, while Auloff relieved the passengers of their money and other valuables. The greedy Auloff even helped himself to the conductor's gold pocket watch, an act that would ultimately lead to his arrest more than five years later. The total take from the hold-up amounted to slightly less than $600.

The engineer, not knowing why the signal cord had been pulled, made an unscheduled stop in Sentinel. The three Russians took the opportunity to jump down from the train. They headed back down the track at a run, carrying two bundles and a suitcase full of loot.

Though the men were well-known in the area, not a trace of them was discovered for three days. CPR investigators had joined members of the Mounted Police and Alberta Provincial Police to form a posse, and were scouring the bush and conducting a systematic search of nearby lumber camps.

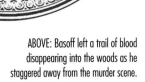

ABOVE: Basoff left a trail of blood disappearing into the woods as he staggered away from the murder scene.

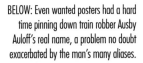

BELOW: Even wanted posters had a hard time pinning down train robber Ausby Auloff's real name, a problem no doubt exacerbated by the man's many aliases.

x Illustrating how Bassof appeared when shooting Bailey dead. Bailey was unharmed in the building.

BELLEVUE CAFE & ROOMS

The murder at the Bellevue Cafe was reenacted in great detail by police investigators.

A grain dealer spotted the fugitives going into a café next door to where he lived in Bellevue, Alberta, a small town seven miles east of Coleman. Corporal Ussher of the newly named Royal Canadian Mounted Police and Alberta Provincial Constable Baillie were the first to respond. Ussher entered the café by the back door, Baillie through the front. A wild firefight ensued.

Akoff was shot seven times, through the neck, in the shoulder and in the chest. Both of the policemen were wounded and fell to the floor. Basoff, a huge lumberjack of a man, wrestled Ussher's gun from him and used it to kill both men where they lay. Akoff staggered to the door and fell dead on the sidewalk.

Basoff then limped from the restaurant, a gun in either hand, dripping a trail of blood down the road. He disappeared into the woods, leaving Ussher's empty pistol lying on the street. As much as the arriving posse members tried, they were unable to discover where

Basoff had hidden himself, though some suspected he had made his way to the endless piles of rubble not too far away, the permanent legacy of an enormous slide that had occurred 16 years earlier, burying the town of Frank and a long stretch of railway track.

A search through the slide path, which included chunks of rock the size of buildings, was all but impossible so pickets were placed all along the railway line.

The next day Basoff appeared from among the debris to beg at a farmhouse for food. The farmer's wife had no idea who he was and, taking pity on him, gave Basoff something to eat, after which he staggered off, hatless, coatless and limping badly.

Again, law enforcement officers combed the area for two days straight, finding no trace of the injured fugitive.

Nine days after the train robbery, CPR locomotive engineer Tom Hammond was operating a pusher engine between Burmis and Pincher, when he saw a man lying still near the tracks. In the days that followed, CPR constable J. S. Glover described the ensuing search of the railyard at Pincher:

> I heard someone moving in a vacant lot south of the hotel and bending down made out the form of a man in the darkness. I went over to see who he was and, flashing my torch in his face, I recognized him from the police description as Tom Basoff. I then covered him with my revolver and ordered him to put his hands up. Upon his refusal to do so, I kicked him on the right elbow. At that, he put his hands high above his head.

A Colt .45 was found in Basoff's shirt, and after his capture he spoke freely, telling a CPR investigator that Auloff had split from the other two men shortly after the robbery, taking the money and heading west. He denied any part in the murder at Bellevue, but his protestations were in vain. Basoff was tried, convicted of murder and hanged at McLeod, Alberta.

The dragnet for Auloff was gradually withdrawn and, with time, he was all but forgotten. Five years later, however, his luck ran out when

RCMP Constable Ernest Ussher, shot down in cold blood, was laid to rest with full honours on August 11, 1920.

he tried to sell the watch—serial No. 22554511—he had stolen from Sam Jones, to a dealer in Great Falls, Montana, who checked the timepiece's provenance. Auloff was convicted and served a seven year sentence.

Bad economic times bred bad behaviour. On occasion, the stress of trying to make ends meet could push people over the edge.

Many small towns along the railway line had their own resident gangs of boxcar thieves whose members were more than willing to take on what was often a lone law enforcement officer in an isolated location, far from the public eye and potential backup.

In the wee hours of April 8, 1922, a CPR constable was on the losing end of a gun battle in the railway yard at Moose Jaw, Saskatchewan. "One of three men caught pilfering a CPR freight car shot and instantly killed Canadian Pacific Railway Special Constable A. J. Tierney, at 12:25 a.m. today," said the *Moose Jaw Evening Times*. While stalking the thieves, the constable approached the freight car in question passing through a circle of light from a nearby streetlamp. At that moment, two shots rang out from the dark and Tierney dropped dead with a bullet through his heart. Investigations by the railway police uncovered only raisins and canned fruit dropped by the thieves in their haste to escape. Two suspects were held briefly for questioning, but there was insufficient evidence to support a conviction; nobody was ever officially charged with the killing.

The next month, after a number of boxcar thefts, CPR Constable P. Evans was on a stakeout in the railyards at Smiths Falls, Ontario. Just after eight o'clock on the evening of May 28, Evans had concealed himself underneath one of the boxcars on which a broken seal had been discovered. Before long, a man climbed over the fence at the edge of the property, crouched down and made his way toward the car.

As Evans manoeuvred to get a clear view from his hiding spot, the man broke the seal on one of the side doors, opened the car and groped around for the first case of merchandise he could reach. As he bent over to place his booty on the ground, the would-be boxcar thief came face to face with a wide eyed, startled railway constable.

Quick to react, the thief fired five or six shots from an automatic pistol that appeared in his hand before either man had time to think straight. One round went clean through the constable's pant leg; a second caught him square in the left thigh and he cried out in pain. With the thief in full flight across the yard, Evans managed to squeeze off a few shots of his own, but none found its target. And though an investigation was launched immediately, no one was ever charged. Evans made a full recovery.

⊱┄⟡┄○┄⟡┄⊰

The period between the two world wars was a time of feverish competition for the Canadian Pacific and its new Crown owned competitor, Canadian National Railways, cobbled together in 1918 from several bankrupt Canadian railways and those previously owned and operated by the government. Both of the Canadian transcontinental railways built branch lines across the Prairies at a near ruinous pace while competing fiercely for business.

The Canadian Pacific's activities literally spanned the world with the help of its extensive network of agents in both Europe and Asia, as well as through its global steamship cruise business. Its clientele included commercial travelers, government officials, missionaries, students and tourists. An important link in the transportation network of the British Empire, the company promoted itself as "The Imperial Highway." It offered the only "All-Red Route" between the

Mother Country and its possessions in the South China Sea, referring of course to the fact that by crossing Canada to get to the Far East, travelers need never leave the Empire, coloured red on all world maps.

As a prominent participant at the 1924 British Empire Exhibition in the London suburb of Wembley, the company heralded its many services. A forerunner of modern world's fairs, the ambitious trade show showcased the Empire's great Dominions overseas, as well as Britain's lesser colonies and dependencies.

This greatest trade show the world had ever seen was the brainchild of Lord Strathcona, a founding director of the CPR, the man who drove the Last Spike in the railway's transcontinental main line and a noted British imperialist.

The exhibition covered 89 hectares and included 24 kilometres of streets named in grand fashion for the event by Rudyard Kipling. The CPR pavilion stood proudly, side by side with the main Canadian government building at the very crossroads of the grounds, and in front of an artificial lake on Empire Way.

The Canadian Pacific pavilion stood proudly, side-by-side with the Canadian government building on 'Empire Way.'

Twenty-seven million people visited the greatest trade show the world had ever seen.

The four railway constables sent to Wembley were chosen for their spotless records, as well as their bachelor status.

GEORGE STEPHEN
LORD MOUNT STEPHEN
FIRST PRESIDENT
OF THE
CANADIAN PACIFIC
RAILWAY COMPANY
1881–1888

The CPR's two story pavilion was constructed and supervised by the company's director of exhibits, E. R. Bruce. The impressive structure featured full sized bronze sculptures of buffalo on either side of the main entrance and presented 560 square metres of display space on the main floor alone, all of which was employed to sing loudly the praises of the company's rail, steamship, hotel, colonization, and telegraph, express and other services.

In a bid to match the fine impression made at the Canadian pavilion by the uniformed Mounted Police officers who stood ceremonial guard over the property, Canadian Pacific decided to bring over four of its own immaculately turned out policemen from Canada to provide security for its building and surrounding environs. Sergeant C. Rippington and Constables A. Darie, C. Lappes and S. Corbett were chosen for their spotless service records, as well as for their status as bachelors, an important consideration given the long period of time they would be away from home. Upon arrival in the U.K., they were sworn in as peace officers at Scotland Yard.

Over the course of the fair's 150 days, 27 million people (more than half the population of Great Britain), explored the grounds and visited the pavilions. They could not help but notice the spit polished and camera ready security force quietly maintaining order and providing excellent public relations for the CPR.

In the early 1920s, the CPR was operating on nearly 15,000 miles of track in Canada and another 5,000 or so in the U.S. Many of the cities and towns through which the railway ran owed their very existence to the railway, and, in large measure their growth depended on an ongoing relationship with the company that now formally styled itself as "The World's Greatest Transportation System." Employees, suppliers and customers lived in close proximity to CPR tracks, shops and yards. Workers looked to the railway for good, steady employment and community issues were often intertwined with those of the company. The railway, of course, preferred to keep those relationships on a solid business footing—cordial, efficient and profitable. However, there were times when economic, political and even religious issues could interfere with this harmonious coexistence, sometimes with disastrous results.

Seldom was this more apparent than in the early hours of October

The Doukhobors had long since expanded their holdings in the west, including the more than 21,000 acres of land in the B.C. interior on which they farmed, maintained orchards, made and sold jam and operated brick plants. The majority still lived on communes and supported The Lordly's leadership, but about 40 per cent of the once monolithic Doukhobor community had become independent.

On that momentous night in October 1924, when the 64-year-old Verigin boarded CPR Train No. 11, he was very much the central figure in a nasty, ongoing religious civil war. He had many enemies inside and outside the faith, and one way or another; the Doukhobor community had alienated most of Canadian society. Trouble bubbled ominously just below the surface, and the controversial leader was marked for a violent end. Just past one in the morning, a terrific explosion detonated right under the railway car seat on which The Lordly and his 20-year-old female companion were dozing.

The blast blew the end door off the train's baggage car, lifting conductor Joseph Turner clean off his feet. Flames licked around a gaping hole in the floor where Verigin and several other passengers had been seated in the first class coach. The fire began to consume the car's exquisite inlaid panels. The roof was gone. A great amount of glass and debris rained down on and around the tracks.

"The smoke and fire at this time was very bad," Conductor Turner said in his official statement, two days after the explosion. "There certainly was no sign of life in the car. I told the brakeman and baggageman that we would set a brake on the sleeper, block it and, if possible, pull the burning car away, which we did—about a coach length—cut off from the head end and pulled the baggage car away. What was left of the day coach at this time was a mass of flames, but I observed very distinctly that the gas tanks were practically intact, showing no sign of having been disturbed in any way by the explosion."

Turner's final statement was significant, as the initial news reports in the local papers had pointed to the railway car's Pintsch gas lighting system. "Gas tank explodes under day coach," proclaimed the misleading headlines in the October 29 edition of the *Nelson Daily News*. "Explodes west of Farron, spreading death and injury."

The Royal Canadian Mounted Police became a national police force in February 1920 when the RNWMP merged with the Dominion

Police Force. It had about a 1,000 members spread across the country by 1924. They soon had men at the scene of the blast. In British Columbia, criminal investigations were normally carried out by the provincial police, formed in 1858 and now having a complement of about 200 officers. The first among them to respond were from nearby Grand Forks—Constable G. F. Killam and coroner Charles Kingston.

Peter Verigin was found dead, face down on the ground more than 40 feet from the train. One of his legs had been blown off in the explosion. Some 15 to 20 feet from Verigin's corpse was the body of John McKie, member of the B.C. legislature for the local Grand Forks–Greenwood riding. Seven other passengers, including the unfortunate Mary Streleoff, who was found still breathing but dying, were either killed outright or succumbed to their injuries in the coming days.

Three other Doukhobors going home on the coach after working a shift as CPR sectionmen escaped the death and destruction unscathed.

Coroner Kingston took charge of all the bodies and had them brought aboard the intact sleeping car. The CPR rushed another locomotive to the scene and arranged for the removal of the dead to Grand Forks where an inquest was to occur. The injured were taken to the hospital in Nelson. Within eight hours of the explosion, a special CPR train was en route to the little town of Farron, B.C., with a hastily assembled passenger list of several Doukhobors including the leader's nephew, Larion Verigin, and Mary's uncle, Anton Streleoff.

B.C. Police Staff Sergeant Ernest Gammon and CPR Constable E. J. House were also on board to take charge of the crime scene investigation and to comb through the wreckage.

Constable House was lauded by the Department of Investigation for his quick work in discovering the source of the explosion. Going over the surrounding area inch by inch, he located and recovered several parts from a clock mechanism more than 200 feet

There were many suspects, but no one was ever charged with murdering the Doukhobor leader.

$1,000 REWARD

The Canadian Pacific Railway Company offers a reward of One Thousand Dollars ($1,000) for information leading to the arrest and conviction of the person or persons responsible for the explosion which occurred in Passenger Coach No. 1586, Train No. 11, of the Canadian Pacific Railway Company, and which caused the death of a number of persons on the said train one mile west of Farron, British Columbia, on the 29th day of October, 1924.

F. W. PETERS,
General Superintendent,
British Columbia District,
Canadian Pacific Railway.

Vancouver, B. C.,
December 4th, 1924.

away from ground zero. In the ensuing days his work would enable the Department to piece together a horrifying story of murder and mayhem. The source of the explosion on Train No. 11 was ultimately shown to be a time bomb in a suitcase stashed directly under the seat of Peter Verigin.

But who was responsible?

The suspects were many.

The Sons of Freedom were prime candidates. They had not followed the path of the Doukhobor majority for many years. Several of the dissident group of Doukhobors had already torched the spiritual leader's impressive summer home in Brilliant, B.C., just months before.

Another possible conspirator was the leader's long-time companion, Anastasia Holubova, the young woman whose position at Verigin's side had been usurped by an even younger Mary Streleoff in the months leading up to the explosion.

Holubova's exalted status within the Doukhobor community was such that she was able to form her own "Lordly Commune" of about 200 members in subsequent years, so her public snubbing at the hands of Verigin might have been cause for revenge.

The CPR's Department of Investigation agreed that it was almost certainly the religious leader's fellow Doukhobors who had done him in, but there were so many factions and investigative turkey trails that few could keep track of all the players.

Even Verigin's son, who was still living in Russia at the time, fell under a cloud of suspicion. The offspring of "The Lordly" and his long estranged ex-wife, Peter Petrovich Verigin had not even met his father until 1902 when the Doukhobor leader had visited him and his mother while en route from Siberia to Canada. In 1905, when the younger Peter traveled to Canada, he showed nothing but contempt for his father's lifestyle. Significantly though, after his father's death, Peter P. Verigin was chosen to lead the Canadian Doukhobors.

Adding to these known facts in the case was the testimony of conductor Turner that one of the two Doukhobors who had climbed aboard CPR Train No. 11 at Castlegar, B.C., and had been seen depositing two cases under Verigin's seat, bore an uncanny resemblance to Joseph P. Shukin, chief aide to the dead leader's son. The two suspect men had disembarked at Farron while a café car was being added to the tail end of the ill-fated train.

The magnificent new hotel was the full-time stomping ground for a small squad of house detectives.

A series of devastating hotel fires struck Lake Louise, above, Banff Springs, and Quebec's Chateau Frontenac.

and railway revitalization. The wooden wing of the company's Chateau Lake Louise burned down in 1924 and was almost immediately replaced by a much more substantial concrete structure. Fires at Quebec's Château Frontenac and the Banff Springs Hotel necessitated equally prompt rebuilds, and new members of the hotel chain were added in Regina and Toronto with the Hotel Saskatchewan and the Royal York Hotel.

The Royal York, in particular, would add a whole new dimension to Panet's responsibilities and those of the Department. The magnificent edifice on Front Street, right across from the equally stunning and modern Union Station, was so successful in its first season of operation that a new addition was added, making it the largest hotel in the British Commonwealth with 1,600 rooms. A small squad of up to 20 railway policemen under the direction of a CPR investigator and later an assistant inspector handled the job of full-time "house detectives." From time to time, many of the Company's other hotels were also assigned full time police officers, particularly during special events or while celebrity guests were staying in them.

Among the more tedious, but prestigious jobs to which a railway constable could be assigned was station duty, where the long hours

Chief Edouard de Bellefeuille Panet

TOP MILITARY ADMINISTRATOR
TAKES THE REINS

Chamberlin was succeeded as Chief of the Department of Investigation by Brigadier-General (later Major-General) Edouard de Bellefeuille Panet, C.M.G., D.S.O., Legion of Honour.

Panet was born in Ottawa, August 24, 1881, and was educated at Ashbury College, Ottawa University and the Royal Military College at Kingston, Ontario.

An excellent administrator with a fine military record, General Panet was well qualified to deal with his new duties.

Commissioned as a lieutenant in the Royal Canadian Artillery in 1902, he gained his captaincy two years later. In 1911 he became a major in the Royal Canadian Horse Artillery. At the outbreak of the First World War, Panet went overseas with the First Canadian Division. In two years he rose from deputy assistant adjutant general to assistant quartermaster general for the entire Canadian Corps with the rank of lieutenant-colonel. He was mentioned in dispatches six times and was made a brigadier-general and quartermaster general for the Canadian Corps in 1919.

General Panet received the Distinguished Service Order in 1917 and was named Commander of the Order of St. Michael and St. George in 1918. He was awarded the Legion of Honor the same year, before resigning his commission in the permanent army in November 1919. He was later decorated with the Belgian Military Cross.

In 1921, Panet was chosen to be the first head of the Quebec Liquor Commission (now the Société des alcools du Quebec) Police.

After the First World War, the United States had opted to keep prohibition in effect, while the Canadian federal government transferred full powers over the production and distribution of alcohol to the provinces. Quebec and British Columbia were the first

Panet served as aide-de-camp for two Canadian governors-general.

to turn the taps back on, setting up government controlled liquor stores. The Prairie Provinces followed shortly after with Ontario not far behind. By the end of the 1920s, the only dry province was Prince Edward Island where prohibition remained in effect until 1948. Canadian distilleries and breweries flourished, as did bootleggers on either side of the Canada–U.S. border.

In November 1924, Panet received a tip that a Belgian schooner at the docks in Montreal had just transferred a large load of alcohol onto a barge owned and operated by a Captain Tremblay who, in turn, intended to smuggle the booze to a marketplace of willing consumers south of the border. Sure enough, when the Quebec Liquor Commission Police swooped down they found Tremblay in the company of two of New York's most prominent bootleggers. Unfortunately, they also found that the suspect shipment was under the protection of one J. A. E. Bisaillon, a shameless smuggler himself who just happened to hold the position of "chief preventive officer" for Montreal, reporting directly to the federal Minister of Customs. Tremblay was eventually arrested and charged with smuggling. Bisaillon was charged with conspiracy, but later acquitted of all charges. As for Panet, he soon resigned his post to become chief of the Canadian Pacific Department of Investigation on July 15, 1925. As chief, Panet built on Chamberlin's successes, emphasizing training, professionalism and military efficiency. His own considerable experience was acknowledged and rewarded when he served as aide-de-camp for two Canadian governors-general, The Marquess of Willingdon and the Earl of Bessborough, from 1926 until 1934.

With the Second World War, General Panet was named the country's first Director of Internment Operations. From 1940 to 1943, he headed Montreal's military district, becoming a major-general in 1940. From February until July of 1946, he served as a member of a Royal Commission on civil service salaries, classifications and conditions of employment for senior administrative officers. He was a member of the University Club, Montreal Club and Quebec Garrison Club.

Panet retired from the Canadian Pacific at age 65 on September 1, 1946.

CPR founding president, George Stephen, stands guard on his pedestal in Montreal's Windsor Station, while a couple of railway police officers watch over things at ground level.

of inactivity could be as hazardous to one's career as chasing down boxcar thieves in the dead of night. The job called for considerable tact, judgement and discretion. The CPR's headquarters building and Montreal terminal at Windsor Station, in particular, required constant patrols to clear the smoking and waiting rooms of idlers, who were just as often likely to be railway retirees and pensioners, gathered to discuss old times as if they were street people or the unemployed. In all cases, the officers were expected never to lose their tempers or treat the public curtly or with contempt, no matter how sticky the situation they were confronted with or how foolish a question they were asked.

Despite their training, however, on more than one occasion Chief Panet received complaints about constables being inattentive and idling their time away.

Boxing matches were hugely popular in the 1920s and one of the biggest and best remembered is the heavyweight title fight between the defending champion Jack Dempsey and challenger Gene Tunney on September 23, 1926.

More than 120,000 enthusiastic spectators jammed into Philadelphia's Municipal Stadium to witness the bout that day, while fight fans around the world crowded about their radios to follow the feints and jabs of the legendary bout. After ten punishing rounds in the pouring rain, Tunney was declared the victor, a feat he would repeat a year later in a rematch with Dempsey.

The constable on duty at the main entrance to Montreal's Windsor Station the morning after the fight was still caught up in the excitement, judging from the tone of a subsequent memo from Panet to his men.

Panet's terse note that day reminded all members of the Department that "no constable can do his duty properly unless his mind is on his work from the time he goes on duty until the time he goes off duty." Specifically, he had been informed that the constable at Montreal's main passenger terminus and headquarters building had been "more interested in discussing the fight with the taxi agent and others than he was in attending to passengers who were looking for taxis." Worst of all, "this was quite noticeable and the discussion was overheard by parties not connected with the Company."

Incidents of rebuke, however, were more than overshadowed by the kudos earned by the railway's boys in blue for their many displays of extreme valour.

In 1927, Acting Sergeant Edward O'Brien was awarded a bronze medal for saving an elderly lady from certain death beneath a train at the railway station in Sudbury, Ontario. The woman had apparently misjudged the speed of an approaching train and ran from the waiting room directly in front of the locomotive. In the blink of an eye, Sergeant O'Brien had assessed the situation and reacted without hesitation, jumping onto the track and heaving the petrified woman bodily to safety by a margin of only inches.

The following year, in the same neck of the woods, Constable Erskine A. Mann was commended for singlehandedly capturing two escaped prisoners from the Burwash Correctional Centre, a medium security prison farm south of Sudbury. Just after 3:00 a.m. on a cold January morning, Mann had discovered the two convicts huddled together in a boxcar in Sudbury Yard. The burly constable was more than a match for his adversaries.

In July of 1927, the company's first class Atlantic steamship, *Empress of Australia*, landed at Quebec City with His Royal Highness the Prince of

Wales on board for yet another royal visit. This time he was accompanied by his brother, His Royal Highness, Prince George, as well as by the Right Honourable Stanley Baldwin, Prime Minister of Great Britain.

Again, a special train was assembled for the exclusive use of the royal party. The district inspector from the CPR's Department of Investigation, with the aid of each local investigator on duty, was responsible for ensuring that no unauthorized persons were able to board the train. The police officers kept a running list of names and occupations for all railway officers and crew assigned to the royal train and where they would be travelling. Traffic arrangements at

and around Windsor Station for many years, earned his stripes the hard way. Many dangerous and exciting moments occurred during his dealings with the criminal underground in Scotland. While arresting one murderer, for instance, he was brutally assaulted by other members of the criminal's family. But he brought his man before the courts and had the satisfaction of seeing him convicted.

When Logan retired in 1938, Chief Panet and several other senior members of the Department were on the docks in Montreal to say farewell to the popular inspector and his wife as they boarded the Company's *Duchess of York* to return to Scotland. "Will Ye No' Come Back Again," skirled the bagpipes of CPR Constable James "Jock" Murray at the send-off.

By 1932 the Depression had become so severe that the Canadian federal government set up labour camps on the Pacific coast to clothe, shelter and feed young, unemployed single men. Working under the auspices of the Ministry of National Defence, in cooperation with the Labour Department, the men worked six and a half days a week for the paltry sum of 20 cents a day.

On April 4, 1935, 1,500 of the relief camp residents invaded the City of Vancouver by truck and train, believing that neither the provincial nor federal governments were ready to undertake any meaningful public works to create real paying jobs instead of the make work projects to which they had been assigned.

After a two month struggle, during which the unemployed men unsuccessfully tried to negotiate decent work for decent pay, a large contingency of protestors decided to confront the politicians in Ottawa. The relief camp strikers organized themselves for the journey. The "On-to-Ottawa Trek" had begun.

By June 3, hundreds had gathered in the CPR yard to board freight trains. Mindful of the potential for violence, city and provincial officials had advised all law enforcement agencies to use tact in their dealings with the unemployed workers and the thousands of citizens who had turned out to view the scene.

The railway had put together two dozen pieces of idle railway equipment alongside which about 800 Trekkers had assembled. With cooking supplies, washboards and laundry tubs safely stowed in an empty boxcar, they climbed the ladders to the roof of the freight train whooping it up and shouting out their last goodbyes.

Members of the CPR's Department of Investigation stood to one side with a small group of city police and RCMP officers who counted heads but did nothing to interfere.

The first trainload of Trekkers reached Kamloops, B.C., a day after departing Vancouver. The men climbed down from the rooftop walkways to bathe in nearby streams and eat at the local union hall. In Revelstoke, the train lingered for scarcely an hour. There some crockery was broken in a town cafeteria and two men were dismissed by the strike committee for drunkenness.

On June 6, the Trek had passed through Golden, B.C., and the next day it arrived in Calgary where it was assumed the Trek organizers would stop for two or three days to gather provisions and attract more followers. A group of sympathizers escorted the main contingent of strikers to the Calgary Exhibition Grounds where they were treated to sandwiches and coffee and offered a dry place to sleep.

Railway police sergeants and constables, normally quite accustomed to removing a transient or two from passenger trains moving through town, now stood aside in astonishment at the sheer volume of humanity on the move.

The departure for Regina followed the usual pattern. The strike leaders rode on the locomotive tender facing the men on top of the cars in back. W. S. Hall, the CPR's general superintendent for the Saskatchewan District, came up alongside and instructed the engineer to give a loud blast of the whistle before the train slowly pulled away.

In Regina, the Trekkers decided to send a committee of eight on to Ottawa to enter discussions with Prime Minister Bennett and his cabinet ministers while the remaining 2,000 or so strikers settled in to await the outcome. The railway police were instructed to take a more hands on approach to persons illegally riding on trains, and notices to that effect were posted prominently by both Canadian Pacific and Canadian National.

When the talks in Ottawa fell apart, the leaders returned to Regina. On July 1, 1935, an organized public protest got out of control and turned into a riot. Police fired their revolvers into the air. Tear gas bombs were thrown. The movement's leaders, including well-known activists Arthur Evans and George Black, were arrested from their

The strike leaders rode on the locomotive tender, facing the men on top of the boxcars.

speaking stands and detained for the duration. Dozens of protestors were injured in the mêlée and a city policeman was killed.

Finally the rioters made their way, individually or in small groups, back to the exhibition stadium where the main body of Trekkers was quartered. Many departed for their homes in the west. A long series of interminable court trials began. The movement was all but over.

In a federal election a few months later, the Conservative government of R. B. "Iron Heel" Bennett went down to defeat, largely as a result of its inability to deal fairly with the relief camp strikers and their demands for better working conditions. One of the new Liberal government's first acts was to abolish the labour camps.

Government relief or "pogey" was the principal stop gap measure for the misery of unemployment. Between 1931 and 1937, more than $800 million in relief money was distributed by the various levels of government.

The work and the difficult losses of the Department of Investigation continued throughout these years. On December 23, 1936, at Montreal's Windsor Station, Constable G. H. Howard was struck and killed by a locomotive as he searched for a parcel which had reportedly fallen from a baggage car. The engine had been switching passenger coaches. Across town a few months later on April 9, 1937, CPR Constable C. L. Bell surprised two thieves breaking into a warehouse near Outremont Yard. One of the men died in the crossfire when his accomplice opened up on Bell. The unidentified gunman was captured.

High on CPR President Beatty's agenda between the two world wars had been the reestablishment of the company's supremacy on both the North Atlantic and the Pacific.

The CPR's steamship activities were concentrated in fewer areas and were therefore easier to police. Constables were regularly assigned to the areas on and around company wharves for its inland, coastal and ocean-going fleets. These law enforcement officers worked closely with all of the various policing agencies and customs officials, both at home and abroad, to combat the trafficking of people, merchandise and especially, narcotics. Most of their time was spent watching the loading and unloading of cargoes and providing a reassuring presence. Crime was minimal, predictable and manageable—until the sticky black tar came aboard.

A half-century before, when the Canadian Pacific had inaugurated its steamship service on the Pacific, opium had not been strictly controlled. It arrived in the holds of ships from the Far East along with abundant quantities of tea, silk, sugar and rice. Some of it was used in the pharmaceutical industry and some was smoked by Asians living in North America.

In 1908, William Lyon Mackenzie King, Deputy Minister of Labour and future Prime Minister of Canada, had travelled to Vancouver to study the opium business. At the time, manufacturers in Victoria, B.C., were among the drug's biggest suppliers. Mackenzie-King found seven factories in Vancouver, Victoria and New Westminster doing an extensive business that involved both Chinese and western users. In particular, he was appalled by the casual use among women and girls that he saw in B.C.'s opium dens. As a result of his recommendations, the Canadian Parliament outlawed the importation and sale of opium that same year.

Nevertheless, use of the drug continued unabated, although on a much smaller scale and deeper underground. The use of opium was once more on the rise in the years after the First World War, partly fuelled by the prohibition of alcohol.

On July 27, 1933 the *Empress of Canada* was fined $40,500, when a large stash of opium was found hidden behind a panel in an unused cabin during a customs inspection at Honolulu. Three months later another substantial seizure was made on the same ship and a fine of more than $22,000 assessed. In each case, the ship was released with the filing of a bond, pending an appeal in Washington, D.C.

In negotiations with the U.S. authorities, the Canadian Pacific's attorney in Washington stressed how closely the ship's officers and company officials had been working with the authorities to combat narcotics smuggling. He also pointed out that the previous December a trunk containing a large quantity of narcotics had been discovered by the ship's officers on *Empress of Canada* after an unsuccessful search by U.S. Customs at Honolulu.

As a result of the CPR's lobbying efforts, the outstanding fines were reduced to much smaller token amounts.

However, despite the company's best efforts at suppressing the drug trafficking through greater vigilance, on January 5, 1934, 199 tins of opium were fished out of the harbour at Honolulu beside the dock where the *Empress of Japan* was berthed. A $40,000 fine was assessed against the ship.

President Beatty immediately authorized an exhaustive internal investigation into the hiring practices adopted by the company's steamship arm on the Pacific. Among the outcomes was a recommendation to dispense with the services of several of the Chinese crew members on the *Empress of Canada*, all of whom were employed by Yuen Wo, an agent acting on behalf of the CPR. Included on the list of suspected smugglers were the ship's number one fireman, boatswain, fitter, tallyman and electrician. Also fingered during the investigation were the number one saloon boy and his two assistants, the Chinese interpreter, the ship's doctor's cabin boy, all the Chinese writers in the chief purser's office, plus the linen room attendant and his assistant.

As for European crew members in the CPR's Pacific service, the report recommended that the chief purser, chief steward, staff captain and ship's female stenographer be dispensed with or, at least, be transferred to the Atlantic run.

In addition, it was suggested that Yuen Wo and his son, one of the fleet's Chinese interpreters, "should be instantly discharged from their employ with the CPR and barred from ever visiting *Empress of Canada*." It also suggested that "the heads of Canadian Pacific Steamships at Hong Kong and Vancouver, B.C., should be immediately notified to discontinue their friendship and intimate associations with Yuen Wo and on no consideration shall they receive gifts or presents of any kind from him, and further, that they be prohibited from attending banquets and dinners which Yuen Wo has provided for them in Hong Kong."

The thorough purge of the company's Pacific crew lists included not just those shown to be actively involved in smuggling, but also individuals found to be addicts or drug users themselves. In an accompanying initiative, Inspector Walter E. Graham of the Department of Investigation was assigned to lead a group of constables in combatting the opium traffic head on. For the foreseeable future, all four of the company's Pacific *Empresses* would set sail on each voyage with a uniformed master-at-arms and two constables aboard from Vancouver and Victoria to Honolulu, Yokohama, Kobe, Shanghai, Hong Kong, Manila and back. The ocean-going police squad conducted regular daily searches of the ships from stem to stern, looking everywhere, including the stokehold and the captain's cabin, behind wall paneling and in unoccupied accommodations.

The first general voyage report from *Empress of Canada* after the change in the CPR's approach to policing its ships included a summary of progress, both onboard and dockside:

> The Master at Arms and Constables have proven a valuable addition to the ship's staff; there is a marked improvement in the orderliness of the steerages and working Alley, especially in the Oriental ports.
>
> Fan Tan tables and Lotteries operated by the crew have been stopped, gambling among passengers not interfered with but kept under observation, they have accomplished this without the slightest friction with our Chinese passengers or crew. The closer supervision of watchmen should result in a decrease of theft and pilferage.

So thorough and successful was their operation that the price of opium in Honolulu was reported to have skyrocketed in a year's time from $85 to $250 for a five tael tin. Two years later, at the May 20 session of the Advisory Committee of the League of Nations on Narcotic Traffic, a Mr. Fuller, the delegate from the United States, read a paper outlining the various activities in the suppression and prevention of narcotics traffic. In it he praised the Canadian Pacific for spending a great deal of money to keep all of its vessels free from contact by unauthorized craft in the Far East, thereby preventing the smuggling of narcotics.

"It is the opinion of expert observers," said the delegate, "that the Canadian Pacific system could well be taken as the measuring-rod to be maintained by every steamship company."

It was the first official recognition of what the CPR and its police officers had accomplished on the Pacific, though they had been complimented on numerous occasions by U.S. officials and held up

Canadian Pacific built a reputation for being tough on smugglers, cracking down hard on the opium trade.

as an example to officers of U.S. steamship lines. The others were told that unless they could show as efficient a record as Canadian Pacific Steamships, they could expect to have the full penalties of the law imposed upon them.

For the next three years the Canadian Pacific's record was nearly spotless. Then opium was discovered in the personal baggage of a seaman aboard the *Aorangi*, a ship of the Canadian Australasian Line, jointly owned by the Canadian Pacific and the Union Steamship Company.

The Canadian Australasian Line operated between Sydney and Vancouver via Honolulu. The seaman had boarded in Sydney for his first voyage with the Canadian Pacific. At Honolulu, eight tins of opium were found by U.S. Customs in his kit bag. He was convicted and sentenced to 18 months hard labour. While testifying, the sailor admitted that his cut from the sale of the drug was to have been $800.

The company's attorney in Washington again did all he could to mitigate the $1,300 assessment against the ship. In his arguments, he cited the Canadian Pacific's admirable record in suppressing the drug trade. However, customs officials in Honolulu claimed that no apparent efforts were made by the ship's officers to keep opium off the *Aorangi*, that several hundred visitors had apparently been allowed to board the ship on sailing day to bring gifts to departing passengers, and that no formal warnings had been issued to crew members about the regulations against opium and the severe penalties for carrying it.

The Canadian Pacific argued that it was standard practice among the Matson Line and other steamship companies in Sydney to allow unrestricted access by visitors, and that the problem was a result of Australian employment practices more than anything else. The company's legal department outlined how the Canadian Pacific was compelled to hire its seamen from a specific hiring hall in Sydney, much the same as was the practice in San Francisco. If a man was certified by the hall, the ship was obligated to hire him on.

The company concluded its arguments with the suggestion that all men hired in Sydney be subjected to a thorough search of their personal effects before their ships reached Honolulu.

The 1930s were hard economic times for all steamship lines on the Pacific. It was a period of falling traffic and rising costs for the Canadian Pacific's *Empresses*. Although all four ships in the company's Pacific fleet remained in service after its initial successes at maintaining strict law enforcement on the high seas, the Department of Investigation largely withdrew its men from marine duty.

Salaries for constables and sergeants had been reduced by about 15% in 1933; four years later staff reductions at some of the company's terminals and wharf operations had also become unavoidable.

Internally, however, things were improving for the railway police as cooperation from employees was up and claim payments for lost or stolen goods was down.

"When making some remarks a couple of years ago about the theft of freight," reported CPR Inspector J. P. Burns in a presentation to a combined class of RCMP and CPR constables,

> I was able to say that we had tracked down the entire year's payment, and all of it was perpetrated by outside raiders, and none of it by our own employees—and I thought that was a very sweet advertising medium for the Company. It was not always so, and, years ago, when our annual loss and damage bill was around two million dollars, fully twenty-five per cent of the amount was paid on account of pilferages. Furthermore, it was forced on us to acknowledge that the great portion of this stealing was done by our own employees, and I'm glad that element is gone.
>
> I think it quite appropriate to remark that the continued surveillance and efforts of the Department of Investigation are essential to maintain this satisfactory situation.

Burns went on to talk about the random nature of the sporadic outbreaks of theft suffered by the CPR and its effect on customer relations.

One of these little epidemics a couple of years ago took the form of mixed merchandise cars— that is L.C.L., or less than load, freight—being broken into and thoroughly ransacked, contents of packages being pulled out and tossed about. This was being done by young fellows— later apprehended—who seemed to proceed somewhat on the basis of making "Whoopee," as very little was taken away, but they seemed to take particular delight in ripping up ladies' lingerie and throwing things around. The actual monetary loss per car did not come very high, but there was a tremendous amount of work attached to sorting out and connecting up the goods with their proper assignments to enable delivery to be made of what was undamaged.

We have never felt that it was in order to minimize in any way the bad effect of loss and damage to freight, and the claim payments made thereon. However, by comparison we have long had the best record of claim payments of any Class A railroad in America.

On July 27, 1938, the Canadian Pacific's west coast business received an unexpected blow. CPR Police Constable G. H. Lake reported wisps of smoke rising from the northeast end of Pier D, headquarters for the company's coastal fleet. Within an hour the entire 25-year-old wooden pier had been consumed by fire, along with 30 tons of cargo. Four tons of fireworks were ignited in the conflagration, which caused a great deal of excitement on the waterfront.

As the probability of war with Nazi Germany loomed large, Canada was treated to a rare and festive occasion—a visit from reigning British monarchs. For the entire westbound leg of their 1939 tour, King George VI and Queen Elizabeth were within the secure domain of the CPR's expansive network.

TOP: Despite the vigilance of the fire brigades, Vancouver's Pier D was completely consumed by the flames.

ABOVE: The police department formed special fire brigades to maintain a watch on the railway's docks and in its warehouses.

On board the company's stately *Empress of Australia*, the King and Queen walked the promenade deck, visited the bridge and attended nightly showings of movies, to which the Queen insisted all of the ship's off duty crew of several hundred men be invited.

While all the policing arrangements were being made by the Department of Investigation in cooperation with the RCMP, provincial and civic police forces, and Scotland Yard, the railway's operating department was putting together the finest railway equipment available. Since the CPR was to have the honour of running the first train outside Great Britain to carry reigning monarchs, every consideration received special attention. An eye-catching paint scheme of royal blue, silver, gold and stainless steel was applied to Hudson locomotive 2850 and 12 selected rail cars. The interiors of the coaches were completely refurbished to provide the royal couple with every possible convenience.

Two hundred of the company's finest and most experienced locomotive engineers, firemen, conductors and trainmen were readied for duty on their respective railway divisions.

Two or three hours before the royal train arrived at each scheduled stop across the country, the main line and all surrounding areas were patrolled by a railway constable and, in most cases, a sectionman who was familiar with the territory. All bridges and culverts were inspected.

Chief Panet rode the train for the entire distance along with district inspectors from the Department who acted as contacts between the RCMP and the railway.

The enormous task of policing all level crossings throughout the tour was accomplished with the cooperation of civic and provincial police, as well as the assistance of Great War veterans who volunteered by the hundreds. At points where the train stopped and Their Majesties stepped down to the platform to meet city officials or take part in

Away from the secure confines of their Empress of Britain stateroom and the luxury of their special train, the royal couple took to an open-topped automobile, escorted by a phalanx of RCMP motorcycles.

ABOVE: "What a lovely engine," the Queen was reported to have remarked to the CPR men piloting the 1939 royal train.

RIGHT: With Jim Brewster holding the reins, CPR police chief Edouard de Bellefeuille Panet rides shotgun in Banff for the visiting King George VI and Queen Elizabeth.

a state visit, the CPR police officers joined other police and militia members with carefully mapped out preparations.

Major events were organized at Montreal, North Toronto, Winnipeg, and Vancouver where the respective stations were festooned with banners, bunting, flags and shields. Additional stops were made at several CPR division points where enthusiastic receptions were prepared by local dignitaries and the private citizens who gathered along the route.

In locations where long and elaborate ceremonies were planned, such as Montreal's Windsor Station, extensive precautions were taken. Thousands of soldiers, war veterans and policemen guarded the district. One end of the station was closed off entirely to the public. Crowds were so well-behaved that there was little trouble in keeping them behind prearranged lines, and no injuries or untoward incidents were reported.

While the red-coated RCMP officers did high-profile duty at ceremonies across the country, the railway police were behind the scenes providing security and logistics support.

ABOVE: Female soldiers parade in front of portraits of the Allied leaders, maps of the various theatres of war and, most ominously, signs directing civilians to the nearest air raid shelter.

RIGHT: The new public address system, which alerted the travelling public to train arrivals and departures at Montreal's Windsor Station, could also be used for emergency broadcasts.

Inspector Machan also worked with the CPR Medical Department to hold first aid classes across the country for any employee of the railway, as well as for those working for Canadian Pacific Air Lines and Canadian Pacific Express.

In 1939, under the threat of invasion by the German army, Britain began a systematic evacuation of prisoners of war to Canada. Among the ships used to transport the prisoners was the Canadian Pacific liner *Duchess of Atholl*, requisitioned by the British Admiralty early in the war. When the ships arrived in Canada, curious citizens crowded the docks to catch a glimpse of the enemy—men of the Wehrmacht, Afrika Korps members, Luftwaffe pilots, U-boat and other German navy sailors.

Back on terra firma, the prisoners were hustled onto waiting CPR and CNR trains bound for their wartime destinations in one of the 26 internment camps set up at locations across the country. The first director of internment operations was Brigadier-General Edouard de Bellefeuille Panet, CPR's chief of police and head of the Department of Investigation. He took leave of absence from his regular duties to supervise, among other things, the complex logistics of transporting and confining prisoners of war. He is unlikely to have realized the extent to which his fellow railway workers and CPR police colleagues would help him fulfill those responsibilities.

It was the duty of all captured enemy officers to effect an escape, if possible, and there were many such attempts. Once, while a prison train was moving slowly through the yard in Smiths Falls, Ontario, two German flyers, Franz von Werra and Otto Hollman, broke a coach window and jumped to the ground. Hollman was recaptured through the vigilance of a railway employee who spotted him walking the track and immediately alerted the police. The cagier von Werra managed to make his way across the border into the still neutral United States and eventually rejoined his unit in Germany.

Three lieutenants from the Luftwaffe were outsmarted by sectionman John Fedan and section foreman S. M. Stadnyk after escaping from a train in which they were being transferred from one prison camp to another. The railway men caught the trio hiding in a toolhouse at Naughton, Ontario, not far from Sudbury. One of the POWs managed to flee into the bush, but before nightfall they were all in the hands of the law. Two Mounties and two detectives had arrived from Sudbury and successfully tracked the runaway.

The greatest escape from wartime internment in Canada occurred when 28 prisoners tunneled out of "Camp X," located at Angler, Ontario, on the CPR main line in the wilderness along the north shore of Lake Superior. So remote was the location of their imprisonment, however, that none managed to remain free for very long; most were rounded up in the immediate area. Within hours, five of the men were found sleeping in a lean-to on a nearby construction site. Four of them were shot in the ensuing mêlée and the fifth bolted into the surrounding woods, but was quickly captured. Two of the prisoners later succumbed to their wounds. The railway was the easiest and most practical route of escape. Avoiding detection was another matter.

After boarding a freight train as it slowed on a hill, two of the POWs, Horst Liebeck and Karl Heinz-Grund, forced their way into a CPR refrigerator car where they spent many chilly hours huddled in a corner before arriving in Kenora, Ontario. There they were able to secure a more comfortable ride in an empty boxcar on a westbound train. But their luck ran out when they reached Medicine Hat, Alberta, where the fugitives were apprehended by railway police and returned to Angler.

Another three escapees surrendered to CPR sectionman Mike Gopek of Peninsula, Ontario, shortly after emerging from the woods on the north side of the railway tracks. Armed with nothing more than a shovel, Gopek was able to round up the men in their weakened state, march them down to the nearby railway station and turn them over to members of the Algonquin Regiment who were passing through on a troop train.

Track watchman E. Courtemanche, armed only with a flashlight and plenty of moxie, captured one of the Angler escapees while patrolling his regular beat near Middleton, a lonely outpost not far from the internment camp. Hearing approaching footsteps at the west end of the Little Pic Bridge, the watchman switched on his light. The beam fell on the startled man, his hands stretched skyward as he pleaded, "Don't shoot." When the man quickly blurted that he was from the prison camp, Courtemanche led him a considerable distance along the railway right-of-way and had him row them both back across the river to the camp.

The sharp eyes and quick wits of nine-year-old Erik Thorsen were instrumental in rounding up two more of the runaway POWs. Provincial police constable E. W. Miller organized a citizens' posse, consisting in part of schoolboys eager to do their bit to track down the wanted men. Thorsen, son of the railway's station restaurant manager at Ignace, Ontario, joined the hunt. The two men, a pilot, and a wireless operator, had gone to the depot to enquire about trains for Winnipeg when young Thorsen identified the escaped prisoners from a police description.

Yet another escapee who made his way east for a considerable distance was apprehended under a train in Montreal's Windsor Station by CPR Constable W. E. Smith and Investigator George E. Gravel. Baggageman René Audette had spotted a pair of feet dangling under a passenger coach five minutes before the train was due to leave for New York. The POW had used a piece of clothesline and a wool scarf to secure himself to the air pipes located between the rail car's battery boxes. He was held in the Investigation Department office until he could be turned over to the RCMP.

Another unique task in which the Canadian Pacific and the Department of Investigation were involved during the early years of the war was the transfer of British government and civilian securities from England to Canada, a safe haven earmarked as the central bastion of defense if Britain were to be invaded and fall to the enemy.

In the first months of the war, more than 10,000 British children had been evacuated to Canada as "war guests," many accompanied by their school instructors or their mothers. With their most precious assets safely ensconced, Britain's leaders moved to protect the country's financial assets as well.

Late one June evening in 1940, a British warship slipped out of Scapa Flow with five staff members of the Bank of England. With them was more than a million pounds of stock script securities and a lot of gold. The documents were bound for a specially built vault, 50 feet below the Sun Life Assurance Company's building on Montreal's Dominion Square. The gold was being sent to the Canadian Mint and to Fort Knox in the United States for safekeeping.

Assisting with the packing and trucking of the United Kingdom Security Deposit, as it was officially called, were the European and head office managers of the Canadian Pacific Express Company. CPR

From the roof of Montreal's Windsor Station the most prominent buildings were the Sun Life building, below which the Crown Jewels were secreted, and St. James Cathedral.

police officers worked closely with members of Scotland Yard, the Bank of England and the RCMP to help transfer the top secret shipment to the London docks on its way to the impregnable, underground bunker in Montreal.

HMS *Emerald* transported the first batch of about $650 million worth of paper securities and gold ingots across the North Atlantic, the largest single transfer of wealth to date. A CNR train met the ship in Halifax, where the Canadian National Express and a phalanx of RCMP and provincial police quietly took charge.

Over the course of the next three months more than $5 billion in assets—including some of the British Crown Jewels—would be stashed away in Sun Life's third-level, subterranean basement vault known as the Buttress Room, where they would remain for the duration of the war.

The task required special arrangements on the ocean, special steel trains on land, and two or more specially trained guards in each railway car. Electrical and telephone connections to every car on each

Trucks lined up alongside Montreal's Windsor Station reveal the extent to which Canadian Pacific embraced door-to-door delivery service.

During the Second World War and the years immediately after, express trucks were tempting targets for thieves looking for high-value merchandise.

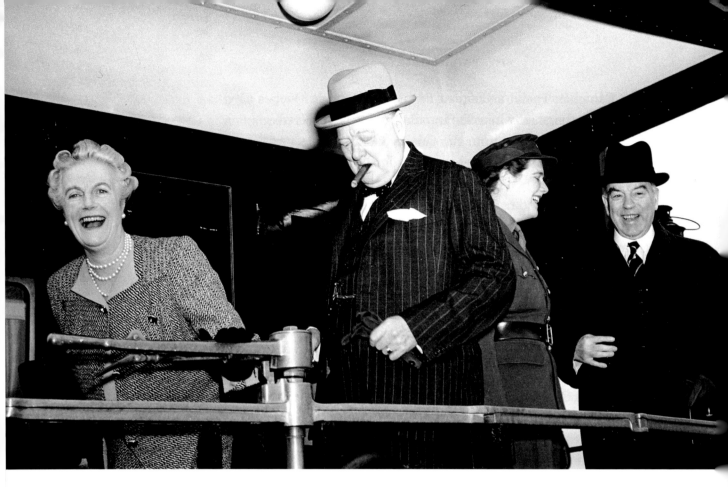

consisted of a baggage car, the dining car *Arbuthnot*, sleeping car *Summerland* and private cars *Strathcona*, *Mount Stephen* and *Mount Royal*. In 1929, Churchill had slept in the same private car, *Mount Royal*, on a much more lower key visit to Canada; he was apparently quite happy to reacquaint himself with his former first class lodgings.

"See here, Mary, this is my bedroom," he said to his daughter, in a conversation reported by the company's Staff Bulletin. It was the same room he had occupied 14 years earlier and he had not forgotten it. Churchill also greeted by name George Grant, the car steward who had attended to him on his previous visit and had again been assigned to the *Mount Royal*. The two would travel another 4,500 miles on scheduled state visits, as well as impromptu fishing trips in Canada and the United States. Few company people outside of senior management and members of the Department of Investigation would know who was on board until the tour was over, and no company dispatch would include a listing of the train's illustrious passengers.

On August 9, 1943, Canadians were informed to their surprise that Roosevelt had been a guest of the dominion the preceding week.

By that time the president had returned to Washington after a post-conference fishing vacation on Manitoulin Island.

Rest and relaxation for the two great war leaders was made possible by an impenetrable wall of secrecy. Train crews were selected after careful consideration of their service records and personal backgrounds. Maintenance-of-way men went over their routes obsessively. Roadmasters and divisional superintendents rode track motor cars ahead of the special trains. CPR police coordinated security efforts with law enforcement officers on either side of the border.

The Investigation Department posted a uniformed officer on every CPR passenger train that passed the VIP trains en route. Their assignment was to prevent passengers disembarking from any train placed in a siding to allow for the passing of the special trains. The railway police also sent out guards to secure each bridge before the trains passed across.

Throughout the conference, nothing was allowed to disturb the participants, and the lengthy strategic deliberations ultimately led to a consensus. The senior British military commanders gave their full endorsement to Operation Overlord, a plan for the invasion of Europe to take place on the beaches of Normandy less than a year later. The war's end game was about to begin.

"No more fitting and splendid a setting could have been chosen than we have here in the Plains of Abraham, in the Château Frontenac and the ramparts of the Citadel of Quebec," Churchill said in a public broadcast to all Canadians. And, indeed, proving that actions speak louder than words, the Allies staged a repeat performance at the Château over a ten-day period the following September, albeit on a much smaller scale.

By this time, threats to the security of Churchill and Roosevelt had abated to the point where the two great statesmen and commanders-in-chief could take time out from their official duties to accept honorary doctorates from McGill University.

For CPR police officers on home duty during the war, however, most days were not filled with glamorous assignments on the world stage; fraud and theft were still their primary concerns. The scarcity of some items and the social pressures caused by government programs to ration specific commodities may have been contributing factors. There were many desperate people inside and outside the war economy.

In the summer of 1943, a freight porter on Eastern Lines was arrested by a CPR constable for stealing cigarettes. During the day, he would remove a carton from a shipment while it sat in a railyard, hide it under a freight car on the car's wheel assembly, and return at night to retrieve his prize after most of the employees had quit for the day.

In view of the deliberate methods employed, all uniformed police officers on patrol in and around railway properties were asked to look underneath freight cars while they were checking seals on car doors. As a result, other items—from bolts of cloth to foodstuffs—were discovered hidden in the same fashion and the practice was greatly reduced.

On passenger trains, onboard staff members learned to protect the interests of their clientele by staying alert. Trainman Clinton Moore and Porter Arthur Johnson were manning one of CPR's daily transcontinental trains between Montreal and Vancouver just before the Christmas of 1943, when the two men became suspicious of the behaviour of a passenger walking surreptitiously through Johnson's sleeping car.

When the passenger was seen to hide something under his overcoat, the trainman and porter gave chase and apprehended their quarry in the washroom of a day coach. A search revealed a pair of air force uniform trousers stolen from the sleeping car. Another passenger reported the loss of a wallet containing money and valuable papers. It was found to have been looted by the same man before being tossed from the train at North Bay Station.

The thief, identified as Floyd Sells, turned out to be a convicted international criminal with more than 25 reported convictions against him since 1919 in the United States and Canada. He was turned over to Ontario Provincial Police officers at Chalk River and appeared in court at North Bay where he pleaded guilty to two charges of theft from rail passengers. Sells was sentenced to a year in jail.

More imaginative means were found to loot the railway's freight cars.

"In July a shipment of horses was received on the Alberta District [in] transit to Winnipeg," said an internal memo from CPR Inspector J. C. Webber to all investigators and uniformed staff in Saskatchewan. "On arrival [at] destination it was found that the tails and manes of these horses had been clipped, thus detracting from the marketable value.

"I am informed that horse's hair brings a very high rate on the market," the inspector reported. "I wish you would instruct your staff in the course of their duties to give supervision when they see stock being loaded, having the end in view of ascertaining where this trouble is occurring."

Two months later, a bulletin from the same inspector turned the attention of police officers in the field to the theft of sugar that was occurring somewhere between Raymond, Alberta, where it was refined and packaged, and points in Saskatchewan where it was sold.

The product was pilfered by thieves boring holes with a 3/4-inch auger through the floors of the boxcars in which it was being transported. The losses, which appeared to take place at some point where the cars were held for connections, had amounted to 200 pounds of sugar before the theft was discovered.

The scheme came to an end when the constables at Swift Current were instructed to routinely examine the floors of cars used to ship sugar, and local car foreman and car inspectors were alerted to keep a close watch.

More than 22,000 Canadian Pacific Railway employees had enlisted for active service in the Second World War. Of these, 658 died during the hostilities. Those that returned, many of whom suffered wounds, returned to their jobs with seniority and pension rights intact. The same applied to the couple of hundred employees who had been seconded to the Canadian and British governments for civilian war work.

The CPR had answered the call to duty and its people had met the challenge admirably. Company President and Chairman, D. C. Coleman, summed it up in a 1943 speech, just as victory appeared to be in sight: "I am convinced that no body of workers can have served the nation more loyally and effectively than the employees of the Canadian Pacific Railway."

In the first year after the war, the Canadian Pacific police made just fewer than 2,000 arrests, an average of almost five each for every member of the Department of Investigation. Their conviction rate was about 98%.

Assured that the Department of Investigation had returned to its original focus as the primary security apparatus of CPR's expansive transportation network, Panet stepped down as chief of the department in favour of A. Hector Cadieux.

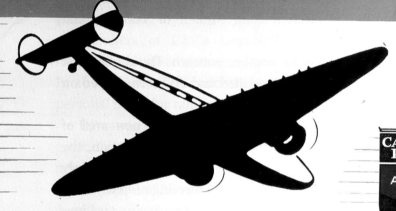

Within minutes of taking off, the plane had climbed to 3,000 feet and was just clearing the northernmost tip of Île d'Orléans when a group of passengers enjoying a down river passage on the deck of the steamship *St. Lawrence* saw a puff of white smoke coming from its fuselage.

Fearing the worst, two Canadian National sectionmen tamping ballast on a CN line in the vicinity also saw signs of distress and witnessed the aircraft's quick descent. Rushing to a nearby telegraph line to use their trackside phone, the rail workers were the first to alert the authorities to what would soon be revealed to be one of Canada's most appalling airline disasters and one of the country's most infamous crimes.

By 4:00 p.m. that afternoon, the wreckage of Flight 108 had been spotted by a search plane in a small clearing just below the crest of Cap Tourmente. The head of Canadian Pacific Air Lines, Grant McConachie, was already flying east from his headquarters in Vancouver. With the veteran bush pilot turned airline executive was the company's expert aeronautical engineer, Melville Francis. By nightfall, representatives from several government agencies were also mobilizing to investigate the disaster, among them the RCMP, the federal Department of Transport and the Quebec Provincial Police.

OPPOSITE PAGE: Early airline passengers were subjected to no greater personal or baggage security checks than if they were stepping onto a bus.

LEFT: Constables took shifts guarding the crash site and sorting out the many investigators.

Within hours a small group of police and airline officials was hiking up Cap Tourmente. With them was a lawyer named Terrence F. Flahiff, who had himself been on the first leg of Flight 108 from Montreal to Quebec City. He had been shocked and dismayed to hear the initial reports of its ultimate fate. After an arduous climb to the crash site, Flahiff was struck by a dramatic scene.

"The DC-3's back was broken," the lawyer later recalled. "From where we stood, the soft whiteness of the full moon played like a great floodlight on the aluminum fuselage. The tail assembly, driven straight into the ground and rising thirty feet in the air, looked like a silver cross."

The next day, in the lobby of the Canadian Pacific's Château Frontenac, federal, provincial and local police converged to exchange information with airline officials and members of the company's Department of Investigation. Flahiff, on hand to share a first-hand account of his earlier flight with the plane and its crew, as well as his later impressions of the crash site, was impressed with the CPR men. Jean Bélanger, inspector of the Department's Quebec Division and Jules Perreault, a senior investigator, who had been assigned to the case by chief Cadieux:

"As a former Crown prosecuting attorney, I felt that I could recognize a good detective," he said, in an award-winning story that he wrote several years later for *Reader's Digest*. "These two, I sensed immediately, ranked with the best."

Bélanger sent CPR Constable Andrew Stott out to the scene of the crash, while Perrault began to assemble passenger lists, waybill information for baggage that had been placed aboard Flight 108, and testimony from a myriad of witnesses.

On Sunday, September 11, Stott reported back to Bélanger and Cadieux that what was left of the ill-fated DC-3, as well as the remains of its crew and passengers, was being guarded night and day by the provincial police, who for the moment were not requesting any assistance from CPR's men in uniform. He also noted that several reporters, photographers and curious members of the public were converging on the site by every means possible, and disrupting an orderly and systematic probe of the wreckage despite the best efforts of the police to secure the site.

The Canadian Pacific was not unaware that if it was held responsible, substantial damage suits could certainly be filed against the company by relatives of the victims. One man already thinking along such lines was J. Albert Guay, the 31-year-old husband of one of the women who had died in the crash. Guay grieved openly and dramatically, granted interviews to the media, and was among those who tried to visit the site without proper clearance—a veritable circus of would-be looters, souvenir hunters and assorted ghouls who descended on the site in the days immediately following the disaster. His name would soon be underlined with bold strokes in the case files of the railway police.

The first task was sending home the coffins by rail.

183

Police and the protective section of the Association of American Railroads. In addition, he was a member of the Province of Quebec Police and Chiefs Association and the district of Montreal Police War Veterans' Association.

Under Bouzan's direction, CPR's Department of Investigation promoted an educational program throughout Canada to instruct children on the hazards of playing on and around railway tracks, yards and bridges.

Off the job, CPR's fourth chief of police was an Officer Brother of the Most Venerable Order of the Hospital of St. John of Jerusalem, and found time to serve as both founder and president of the Canadian Police Curling Association.

Five years to the day after taking command at Canadian Pacific, Bouzan retired on pension and moved to the west coast with his wife. He died in Vancouver, April 30, 1965.

could jeopardize the safety of railway employees and passengers. At particularly troublesome locations, it was also advantageous to have investigation officers deliver short safety lectures in schools bordering railway property. In small towns and villages, provided their offences were not too serious, young delinquents would sometimes be made to appear before a local person of authority—mayor, councilor, priest or teacher—to receive counsel and to realize the error of their ways.

Training for members of the Department of Investigation became more sophisticated and nuanced than it once was. After the war, new recruits had to be at least five feet ten inches tall and weigh a minimum of 160 pounds. Having passed a general physical, a prospect was then fitted with a uniform, sworn in and made a probationary constable for a 12 month period.

Many of the men who came to the railway were ex-servicemen, or had served with the RCMP or other law enforcement agencies. Their training was as much about familiarizing themselves with their new environment as it was about learning basic policing skills.

To accommodate the increased need for professional training, CPR's Department of Investigation opened its own police academy

in Winnipeg. Ongoing training for investigators and senior members of the Department was also conducted at the Canadian Police College in Ottawa.

Within months of the war's end, W. A. Fillingham, the Canadian Pacific's Inspector of Western Lines headquartered in Winnipeg, had standardized the training for police recruits into an intensive ten day system of instruction that began with a thorough review of how to handle a revolver in a professional manner. Continual practice on the firing range gave the probationary constable, in the words of a CPR spokesman, "the same kind of adeptness with his firearm that David had with his slingshot."

The best revolver shots with the department of investigation that year were, from left, national champion Constable E.R. Siegel, Investigator G.J. Collins, Constable O.M. Corcoran and Constable V.H. Malacrida.

The constables' manual of instruction said a railway policeman could use his gun if a person had committed a felony, but, broadly speaking, the view of the CPR and of the railway police was that there were only two cases in which he was justified in using his weapon: in defence of his life or that of someone else.

The first revolver shooting competitions for police officers were organized by the Dominion Cartridge Company and the Chief Constables Association in 1926. Each district of CPR's Department of Investigation entered a team of five men. In 1927, CPR police teams won the provincial matches in Ontario, New Brunswick, British Columbia and Saskatchewan. On four occasions in 1930, 1932, 1933 and 1934, its members scored the highest marks in Canada.

Investigator John H. B. MacDonald won numerous championships for revolver shooting in Ontario over a three-decade period. During that time, he was considered to be one of the best revolver shots in the country. Throughout his career, he helped many of the constables in Toronto with their shooting, as well as teaching archery at the University of Toronto and he set archery records at the annual Sportsman's Show that stood for decades.

Each successful student and member of the Canadian Pacific's Department of Investigation was also required to qualify in St. John Ambulance and other first aid techniques, and to take a proficiency examination every year. Over the years, numerous members of the railway police qualified as instructors and trained other police officers and civilians with excellent results.

Along with lessons in gun handling and first aid, police recruits were given a close acquaintance with the railway. In the classroom and on the property, they were shown how trains were assembled, where facilities were located, and how railway business was conducted. They learned the meaning of train symbols and signals.

Constable F.F. Pettit, a member of the Quebec District revolver team for 1932, demonstrates the proper stance for firing his service weapon.

First aid champions,
from left, P. Keogh, E.G. Wykes,
Sergeant H.W. Bailey, W. Allison
and J.A. Griffith, wore full dress
uniform for their victory portrait,
right down to the spit-and-polish.

They familiarized themselves with the various types of railway equipment and the commodities they carried, and learned to recognize when things were amiss.

Some of the recruits may have wondered why the railway companies had not devised a better method for protecting their goods than was afforded by the flimsy little seals that were applied to every door on every freight car that left the yards. They soon learned, however, that while you cannot stop a determined thief from breaking into a rail car, with the evidence offered up by a damaged car seal you can begin to pinpoint a vulnerable spot en route. If a constable checked a train in one town and found a broken seal where everything had been in order during the last inspection down the line, he would know approximately when and where a theft had taken place. He could investigate or set up a trap for the perpetrators accordingly.

Besides being a good marksman, detective, and railroader, the probationary constable also had to learn to be a competent mechanic. When railway flat cars loaded with road vehicles were delivered to terminals, as they were by the thousands during the war, it was the duty of the men from the investigation department to check the condition of every battery, plug and carburetor, not to mention more obvious features such as lights and tires. Before their training was done, each man would be checking two to three hundred railway cars a night in all kinds of conditions.

At the end of the twelve month probationary period, the prospects were ready for a proficiency test leading to a third class constable rating. Only about one out of every three potential recruits who walked through the doors of the Department of Investigation could meet the exacting requirements.

The end result from a public perspective, as outlined in a CPR publicity department brief: "Six feet of brawn, encased in blue serge and terminating in radiant black boots, a visored service cap and a pair of white gloves. That to all outward appearances is the policeman to be seen any day on the platform of any Canadian Pacific Railway station of importance, between Saint John and Vancouver."

A model of fitness and discipline, the railway policeman was also expected to be the soul of discretion and diplomacy. "Ask one of them what kind of questions he has put to him in the course of a day," the

publicity writers challenged. "He will probably smile and change the subject. Incidentally, you yourself have joined the army of inquirers. Like most people who have plenty to do, he is not given to talking about it."

The CPR policeman could handle the classically obstinate drunk with the same grace that he would shepherd a little old lady from waiting room to station platform. In the back of his head was sound knowledge of the law, the *Railway Act*, the Company's own regulations and the many things that frenzied passengers want to know in the last few minutes before their trains depart.

"In your dealings with the public, we expect you at all times to be courteous," CPR Constable Machan (later chief of the Department) was accustomed to instructing recruits. "The mere possession of a badge and the authority that goes with it means nothing, and we do not expect, nor do we want you to use that authority unless you have to. When you see something going on in the yards, whether it be an employee or an outsider, and it makes no difference, approach that person in a courteous manner. Don't jump to conclusions without

Constable W.R.B. Flett poses with local boys Mac Belanger, on the motorcycle, and Des Moore, beside the new post-war station in Cranbrook, British Columbia.

The stainless-steel streamliner, dubbed *The Canadian* by Canadian Pacific, quickly assumed its place among the country's most visible national symbols.

much more likely to be patrolling a yard or inspecting local freight sheds than he was to be walking the floor of a station concourse, or standing dutifully on the trackside platform.

The emerging rail network would require giant marshalling yards to assemble and launch the longer and longer freight trains that were soon to be criss-crossing the country. Specialty freight cars were designed to move products directly from the producer to the consumer while making their cargo less prone to theft and damage.

When the future queen of England, Princess Elizabeth and her consort, Prince Philip arrived in Canada in October 1951 for the first postwar royal visit, they would embark upon the last of the

big cross country tours organized and executed by Canada's two transcontinental railways, Canadian Pacific and Canadian National. From the point of view of the railway police, there would be no more big public events to draw much of the population of many a town down to the railway station.

Assisting with the general security arrangements while Princess Elizabeth and the Duke of Edinburgh were in the hands of the Canadian Pacific transportation network were members of CPR's Department of Investigation, under the guidance of Chief Cadieux.

Initially, the royal couple had been expected to arrive in Canada aboard the CPR's *Empress of France*. However, when the Duke suffered an illness in the days leading up to the event, the tour was postponed until he was well enough to fly over. While in Canada, not only did the royals travel hundreds of miles over the Canadian Pacific's railway lines, they also attended scheduled ceremonies at CPR stations, dined at its hotels, and were ferried back to Britain on its transatlantic liner, *Empress of Scotland*.

The uniformed staff assigned to the 1951 Royal Tour were, from left, front row: T.R. Veary, W.J. Callaghan, W.E. Graham, unidentified, H. Tetreault, G. Fairbrother; second row: H. Allison, A.W. Spence, J. Gervais, B. Dubreuil, H. MacKenzie, H.R. Giroux; back row: G. Adam, C. Ball, E. O'Hara, A. Butler, J.W. Stimson.

A state dinner at the climax of the first day, presided over by the Honourable Maurice Duplessis, premier of Quebec, was held in the CPR's Château Frontenac. The internationally known hotel rose to the occasion as it had done in 1939 when Princess Elizabeth's father and mother, King George VI and Queen Elizabeth, toured the country. During their visit Their Royal Highnesses became the central concern of the entire CPR organization, and accordingly, CPR investigators Jean Bélanger, Jules Perreault and Gaston Délorme were on site throughout the stay at the Frontenac to ensure there were no surprises or lapses in security.

In Toronto, several tracks in the passenger coach yard were prepared for the Royal Train to rest overnight. About 3,000 yards of paving and another 1,000 of white gravel were laid alongside the rails, while several 15 foot flagpoles were set in a line to accommodate the various state and royal standards. The royal couple lived on the train from their arrival on the morning of October 12 to their departure the next day.

While the exterior of the railway cars did not require a new paint job for the tour, a considerable amount of redecoration was done inside, especially in the cars that were occupied by Their Highnesses and their immediate entourage.

The Royal York, then the largest hotel in the British Empire, was the scene of a Board of Trade luncheon for the Duke of Edinburgh on October 13 at which His Highness spoke to more than 1,700 people. The highlight was the official dinner in the hotel that night, sponsored by the Province of Ontario, the Lieutenant Governor and the City of Toronto.

Much like her mother and father, Princess Elizabeth travelled part of the CPR route aboard one of the Royal Hudson locomotives assigned to the Royal Tour. Several official events were held in Winnipeg at the Royal Alexandra Hotel; luncheons and press conferences were staged in Regina's Hotel Saskatchewan and Calgary's Palliser. All venues required a high level of security.

"It was an anxious time for the investigation department," revealed an article in the Christmas 1951 issue of the CPR employee magazine, *Spanner*, "and Benedict Bouzan, assistant chief, shifted his men as required over the region as a principal aid to security. Inspector W. Fillingham, in charge of uniform personnel for lines west, led the

A CP constable stands guard, right, as Queen Elizabeth II is whisked from Toronto's Royal York Hotel to a waiting limousine.

party to their train when they came in to rest before the Government House dinner at Winnipeg. An Old Horse Guard, the Inspector had a long day on his feet supervising the security detail."

Shortly after the event, Chief Cadieux, in charge of all policing arrangements in and around the Royal Train, told members of the Montreal Lions Club what a treat it had been for many of the people who came to greet the Royals, particularly the children. Crowds were heavy at all points, he said, with people coming from as far away as 50 miles to catch a glimpse of the young, fairytale princess.

The capsized *Empress* still smolders from the fire.

In January 1953, the *Empress* suffered a devastating fire while withdrawn from service for an overhaul. The few security crewmen aboard the great liner while she was berthed at Liverpool's Gladstone Dock were unable to control the blaze. It was a total loss and the ship turned on its side from the vast amounts of water pumped into her.

The subsequent salvage operation was the largest ever undertaken in Europe. Preparatory work went on for more than 14 months before the *Empress of Canada* was righted and sold for scrap to Cantiere di Portovenere, Genoa. In the interim, there were those in intelligence circles who took to blaming the ignoble fate of the liner on the Cold War between the Soviet Union and the western powers.

"British intelligence officers here say that Ernst Friedrich Wollweber, 55, head of Communist East Germany's secret police, is probably the most expert saboteur the world has ever seen," said the *Toronto Telegram* on August 18, 1953. "They suspect him of having been involved in the destruction by fire of the 20,000-ton Canadian Pacific liner *Empress of Canada* at Liverpool last January; the two equally serious fires on board the *Queen Elizabeth* in Southampton a week later; and in the disappearance two years ago of British diplomats Guy Burgess and Donald Maclean."

Wollweber, the East German government's deputy director of sea and international shipping, was also thought by the conspiracy theorists to be responsible for explosions on board the British Navy's 23,000-ton aircraft carrier *Indomitable* in the Mediterranean. Two sailors were killed and 40 more injured.

Though the loss of the *Empress* was never conclusively linked to the Cold War and the machinations of Soviet spies, the whole issue of adequate fire protection on and around the Company's ships led the Canadian Pacific to conduct an in-depth study of the existing security measures in place at the docks in Liverpool and London.

The initial investigation of the fire on the *Empress of Canada* had begun almost immediately when Detective Chief Inspector J. G.

The salvage effort took months and ended up being somewhat of an engineering challenge, written up with enthusiasm in both the popular press and the technical journals.

Sparks of the Liverpool City Police arrived at the scene and the ship was still aflame. During the subsequent police inquiries, more than 400 people were interviewed, including nearly 300 workmen employed by shipbuilder Harland & Wolff, Ltd., and 73 Canadian Pacific employees who were engaged on board the *Empress* just before the fire broke out. There was no evidence to suggest the fire had been deliberately set; nor was the cause determined.

The outcome of the investigations blamed the rapid spread of the fire on the light timber work that literally honeycombed the vessel, as well as the general layout of the ship with all of its alleyways, stairways and ventilators feeding the fire with plenty of oxygen.

The Canadian Pacific was cited for not taking stronger safety precautions in view of the fact that the *Empress* was undergoing repairs. Factors leading to the complete loss of the ship were said to be the delay in the detection of fire along with inadequate fire prevention and firefighting equipment. If automatic sprinklers had been installed, it was thought the fire would have been held in check until the arrival of the fire brigade.

Within months, A. C. MacDonald, managing director for the Canadian Pacific Steamships, was exploring the feasibility of establishing a uni-formed police force in British ports on the same lines as the Company enjoyed in Canada. A permanent uniformed police force would require work conditions and pay equal to, if not slightly better than, those laid down by Statutory Regulation for Civil Police in Britain. This would attract and retain the right type of man.

Under the system then in place, the Department of Investigation in the U.K. employed a minimum number of permanent personnel and recruited temporary help if and when necessary. A superintendent worked out of Liverpool. The men who were hired as baggage masters and masters-at-arms, as well as firemen and patrolmen, were permanently assigned to each of the three *Empress* vessels on the North Atlantic.

In May of 1954, CPR police chief Benedict Bouzan sent Inspector W. E. Graham on an exploratory tour of the Canadian Pacific's U.K. operations with a view to making recommendations one way or the other about setting up a steamship security force there. Graham proceeded to England on the *Empress of Australia* and called at the Canadian Pacific steamship offices in Liverpool's Royal Liver Building where he interviewed the general manager, Captain A. E. Shergold and the general superintendent, Captain R. V. Burns. The two men organized further meetings with both Liverpool and London police authorities as well as with fire department officials in Liverpool. Graham also met one on one with nearly every staff member of the Canadian Pacific in both port cities.

"I directed my enquiries at the outset in an effort to learn if it would be possible to organize a regularly constituted police force to operate in Liverpool and London," Inspector Graham reported back to Chief Bouzan.

Maintaining a crisp military look, with no weapons visible, was even more important for these two CP constables assigned to dockside duty in London than it was for their counterparts across the pond.

There are only three such forces in England. The Metropolitan force is covered throughout England and Wales by uniform police regulations as laid down by the Home Office in London and which governs conditions of service, pay and allowances throughout the country. The Port of London Authority Police is a separate force, but operates largely under Home Office regulations as to pay and allowances. The third force is that of the railways, now nationalized and operating under one head, the British Transport Commission.

With regard to the Railway Police, I find that powers to form a police body was first granted in 1835 and each railway in subsequent years formed their own police forces under separate powers granted from time to time. Since nationalization, the separate acts granting authority to individual railways have all been repealed and they are now operating under one act which came into force in 1949 and while they have all been amalgamated, each force operates under the individual railway's existing rates of pay and various pension schemes. Due to the complex problems involved, I am advised it will be many years before this police body can be standardized as to rates of pay, retirement ages, and conditions of service and pension plans.

Apart from the three police forces above named, there are no other such bodies, and private companies are only allowed to form Security forces without actual police powers. In this connection, however, I find that in both Liverpool and London we enjoy such a great measure of actual protection in the Dock areas that a police force of our own would possibly conflict with the forces now operating and might more or less leave us to our own resources. On the other hand, all the police officials both in Liverpool and London welcome the idea of a Security force in uniform with which they assure me they would cooperate most heartily.

The Liverpool docks, including Gladstone Dock where the CPR's shed was located, were under the jurisdiction of the Liverpool City Police. And the Mersey Dock and Harbour Board paid the city for the police protection provided. The dock area was enclosed by a high brick wall, entrance to the docks being gained through gates manned by the police. Suspicious characters were checked when entering the dock area and all trucks and vehicles of all kinds, as well as individuals, were subject to search and inspection when leaving.

In addition to the activities of the uniformed police, plainclothes detectives from the city's Criminal Investigation Department looked into all complaints from steamship companies about theft or other unlawful acts in the same manner as if the complaint was received from a private individual.

As a case in point, Inspector Graham cited the recent activities of Chief Inspector J. Allendy of the Liverpool Police who had been conducting enquiries into the thefts of Irish linen shipments from both the Cunard Line and the Canadian Pacific. By arranging for shipments to be weighed at Belfast prior to being loaded onto the steamships and again upon being received at Gladstone Dock, Allendy proved the thefts were taking place in Belfast and was able to set a trap to catch the culprits.

In the port of London much the same conditions prevailed. The London Authority's own police force, consisting of more than 500 men, patrolled the entire dock area. All vehicles and individuals were closely checked when leaving the docks and suspected thieves were trailed to their destinations by plainclothes officers trained in detective work.

Cargo watchmen were supplied when required by the New Zealand Shipping Company.

Graham recommended a security force of 15 men be employed by the Canadian Pacific on a permanent basis. To strengthen the calibre of the watchmen, he suggested forming a pool of retired city policemen and firemen for casual employment. While these men were not ready to accept steady employment if the extra pay moved them into a higher tax bracket, they were willing to accept casual work that would augment their pensions without boosting their earnings above a certain level.

"Should it be decided to organize a Security force on the lines suggested," Graham said, "I would recommend that they be given a course of instruction in firefighting and that all concerned become conversant with the firefighting equipment on each of the ships and get to know every part of the ships so that, along with the deck officers, they will be capable of directing firemen without delay to any point at which a fire may be under way."

Significantly, he also mentioned that smoking at the Liverpool dock was strictly forbidden and that strict supervision to prevent smoking in both ports would be a most important part of the security work.

"A close watch should also be maintained in parts of ships undergoing overhaul where burning and welding operations are being carried out," Graham said, in direct reference to the devastating fire on the *Empress of Canada*.

The following August, recently promoted CP Steamships general manager, R. V. Burns, sent Inspector Graham a note of thanks to let him know his "efforts of last year have not been wasted." He enclosed a photograph of two new uniformed security officers of the Company's Liverpool Branch to illustrate, as he suggested, the "trim and businesslike" appearance of these men.

The loss of the *Empress of Canada* combined with the generally poor financial results from steamship operations in 1954 compelled the Canadian Pacific to take a hard look at every expense it was incurring. One of the heavier expenses was the monthly charge against steamships for the services provided by the Department of Investigation.

"This charge runs around $10,000 per month during the St. Lawrence season and about $7,000 per month during the winter season when we operate from West Saint John, N.B.," said ships' managing director A. C. MacDonald in a brief to Chief Bouzan. "Plus, of course, travel expenses and living allowances paid to your constables when transferred to this latter port."

Protective services were provided at the request of the steamship company. The Department of Investigation controlled the number of sergeants and constables to be assigned to steamship work, arrangement of shifts, areas of protection to be covered by each man, and how many men should be transferred from Montreal to Saint John in the winter season.

"It is these features which I would ask that you kindly examine with a view to effecting any possible economy," MacDonald said.

In reply, Bouzan sent MacDonald a detailed report of the measures that were adopted:

Our authorized staff for Steamship work at Montreal Wharf in the summer season and West Saint John in the winter season is —thirty-seven Constables and four Supervisors, but we operated at both places during the last two seasons with an average of —thirty-one Constables and four Supervisors, by working a considerable number of hours overtime.

From a thorough survey of the situation at West Saint John a few days ago, we feel that we can handle the Wharf situation, for the present at least, with twenty-seven Constables and four Supervisors by putting in approximately three hundred hours per month overtime, and I have issued instructions that this should be done pending your approval. There is a possibility that within the next month or so we may be able to reduce this number by one more Constable.

Our work at West Saint John, as you know, is spasmodic. We may be able to go along for days giving reasonable protective coverage with five or six men on a shift, when we can allow regular days off or compensating time off for overtime worked, but then we run into a period when extra men are required for protection of liquor or other valuable commodity and we have to provide for ten to fifteen men on a shift for a number of days, and we find ourselves confronted with an impossible situation, unless we work our men twelve-hour shifts and pay them four hours overtime.

The only way we can effect a reduction in living expenses paid our men is by reducing the number of men to a minimum and working overtime, and full advantage is being taken of this.

Our Supervisory staff at Montreal Wharf and West Saint John cannot be reduced economically and any rearrangement of shifts or areas of protection would seriously interfere with protective coverage.

The Angus Fire Brigade were colourful participants in the the Victory Loan drive, during the First World War.

The growth of the Canadian Pacific's hotel business also required more police presence.

The full time detachment of railway police which provided security at the Royal York Hotel was complemented by a seasonal squad of men who kept an eye on things at the Company's mountain hotels in Banff and Lake Louise. Both units reported to assistant inspectors.

At Montreal's Angus Shops, opened in 1904, the CPR maintained one of the largest, fully equipped, privately owned fire stations in Canada under the supervision of Police Inspector and Fire Chief J. Perreault. The huge complex of railway shops occupied 59 permanent buildings spread over 231 acres of land. There, more than 7,000 employees were busily engaged in building, repairing and maintaining locomotives and passenger and freight cars.

Keeping an around the clock vigilance were 12 regular and nearly 200 auxiliary firemen recruited from among the shops' employees. Throughout the shops there were about 1,000 fire extinguishers, countless sprinkler heads, ten miles of fire service water lines, 94 hydrants and 41 alarm boxes, ten of which were connected directly to the sprinkler system.

Much was accomplished in the decade after the Second World War to educate the public about fire prevention with hundreds of industrial

establishments across the country taking part. Angus Shops led the way in 1955 and 1956, winning the nation's top prize for its efforts during annual Fire Prevention Week. A long list of provincial awards also graced the walls of the Angus fire hall.

In certain sensitive areas such as its telecommunications and express businesses, the Canadian Pacific also called upon its police force to fingerprint job applicants and run checks on their backgrounds.

With the new emphasis on "special" police work details, company magazine *Spanner* reported on a railway constable stationed in McAdam, New Brunswick, whose circumstances compelled him to form a one man specialty squad of his own.

On their home grounds, two of Angus Fire Brigade's finest show off their spotlessly maintained machine for the photographer.

Nasty occurrences like this railway bridge bombing became all too common.

FAR RIGHT: Published by the Association of American Railroads, this special agent comic assured its young readers that the railway police's record of saving lives and preventing crimes "is excelled by no other protective agency."

SPECIAL AGENT

A PICTURE STORY ABOUT THE RAILROAD POLICE

"It all happened because a sick cow was in a shipment of livestock from Woodstock, N.B., to Montreal," the publicity department told CPR employees. "When the livestock shipment reached McAdam, one of the car department men engaged in drenching the hogs noticed that one of the cows in the livestock car was apparently sick. Consequently, the car was placed in the stockyard and the disabled cow removed."

That's when Constable C. C. Thomas went into action. With no veterinary surgeon available, the resourceful Thomas went to see the ailing bovine and immediately started to administer help, drawing upon knowledge gained while working on his father's farm.

"The policeman administered several different kinds of medicine, and soon the cow appeared on the road to recovery. Eleven hours after treatment was first rendered, the cow was able to get up and walk around, and the next day the shipper picked up the recovered animal and returned her to Woodstock. And that is how Constable C. C. Thomas became a 'vet' without retiring from the police force." Indeed, it was a special squad.

In 1959, the CPR changed the structure of its operating department from nine districts to four regions: Atlantic, Eastern, Prairie and Pacific. To align with the new administrative realities, the Department of Investigation abolished the position of Assistant Chief, Western Lines, as well as those of Police Inspector, Eastern Lines, and Police Inspector, Western Lines. In their place, four superintendents were appointed to take charge of each region, reporting directly to the chief in Montreal.

During this period of new challenges and changing priorities, one old problem resurfaced in the interior of British Columbia. The radical Doukhobor sect known as the Sons of Freedom had, for years, committed a series of violent acts against their own co-religionists, which sometimes spilled over into the greater community, and on occasion, commanded the attention of the railway police. The attacks came in batches and were interspersed with periods of relative quietness. But the burning of houses, schools and community centres, and the bombing of bridges and railway tracks invariably created a major problem for both the government and the CPR.

One night in December 1957, railway section foreman C. E. Mason was patrolling a stretch of track in the West Kootenays between

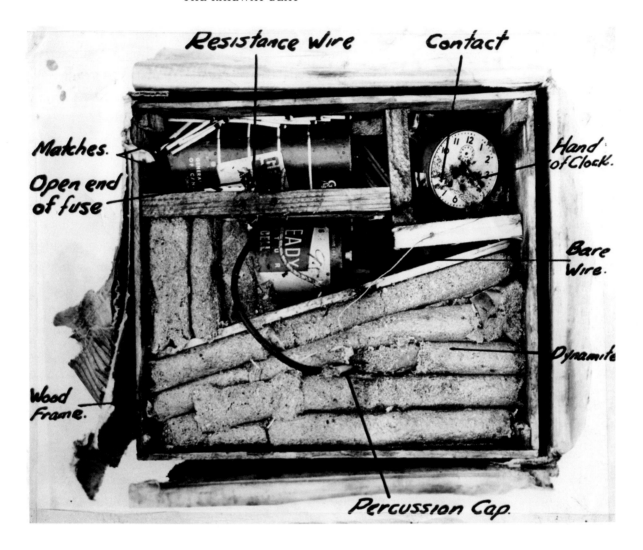

Resistance Wire   Contact   Matches.   Open end of fuse   Hand of Clock.   Bare Wire.   Dynamite   Wood Frame.   Percussion Cap.

Taghum and Beasley when he spotted a strange object up against one of the ties. When he noticed wires protruding from it, he suspected the worst and immediately wired the dispatcher at Nelson. In short order, railway divisional engineer Daniel Danyluk, investigator Herbert McGowan and two RCMP officers were rushing to the site.

They quickly determined that the foreign object was a pipe bomb similar to others planted by Sons of Freedom terrorists in the past. They had only just decided to neutralize the device by cutting one of the wires, when the whole thing began to smoke alarmingly. Dashing for cover, the men managed to get barely 20 yards away before the bomb exploded with a blast that twisted the rail, demolished a number of ties and felled three power poles. The men themselves were unharmed.

The railway police prepared a basic reference guide on bombs and their components for the edification of any unlucky officer who might encounter such things while on duty.

As a result, for the foreseeable future, passenger trains were only allowed to run through the area during daylight hours. Daily service between Penticton and Nelson was reduced to twice weekly. For several months, CPR operating men carried out track patrols ahead of all passenger trains, and several Company investigators became very familiar with the day-to-day activities of the more vocal and visible members of the various Doukhobor communities.

"An outside enemy couldn't get away with these depredations, but a fanatical group, pampered over the years as a quaint, religious sect, can terrorize Canadians and destroy their property because of lack of protection," said Consolidated Mining and Smelting's vice president and general manager, R. D. Perry, at a press conference in Trail, B.C., in March of 1962, after bomb threats at the firm's sprawling plant nearby and the complete destruction of one of the company's power towers. (Consolidated was a subsidiary of the CPR). Armed guards drawn from employee ranks had already begun to patrol the property.

"It is a tragedy that Canadians have been fed this 'sob sister' image about fanatics who have caused so much damage and unrest in the Kootenays," he said. "The RCMP have done a wonderful job with their investigations of these outbursts of violence, but the critical need now is for the protection to prevent these outrages. We do not have this."

The latest outrage by the fanatical sect, the destruction of the Kootenay Lake power line, had brought an appeal from the Canadian Pacific Railway president Norris "Buck" Crump to the federal and provincial governments. He urged them to "take whatever appropriate measures are necessary to put an end to these occurrences before other and perhaps even more serious sabotage occurs."

The Sons of Freedom were suspected of bombing the 300 foot tower and blowing a hole in Southern British Columbia's employment picture that would continue to paralyse other industries in the area for weeks to come. The act of sabotage put more than 900 men out of work in the Kimberley and Riondel areas, sites of two of Consolidated's giant mining and fertilizer operations. The lack of electric power also caused closures at local sawmills and a brewery. Service was interrupted to the homes of more than 5,000 people.

As far away as Vancouver, a firm that made special bags for shipping Kimberley produced fertilizer saw its output gutted and its profits decreased by more than $1,000 per day. Consolidated's own lead/zinc Bluebell mine and its fertilizer and pig-iron plants at Kimberley halted operations completely. Production at its huge Sullivan lead/zinc/iron mine was cut back by 60%.

"What will they blow up next?" asked Mary Comfort, a Riondel miner's wife as widespread tension gripped the area.

Over the years a large number of Doukhobors were arrested, charged and convicted of various criminal offences. The last incident attributable to the Sons of Freedom occurred in 1964. An intensive program of education for the young people in the community helped to mitigate this unique problem. Several books and many articles have been written about the Doukhobors including *Terror in the Name of God* by Simma Holt, published in 1964 with a great deal of input from the CPR's Department of Investigation. In her account, Holt credits Investigator Norval Riley of the railway police for coming to her aid when she was threatened with assault at a Doukhobor camp in Agassiz, B.C., in the wake of the death of a young Doukhobor radical who had been on a hunger strike.

Bomb threats had become an unsavoury hallmark of the fifties. During one event in the Hotel Vancouver, the CPR police area superintendent received a tip from an anonymous caller that in 15 minutes a bomb would go off in the banquet hall. With more than 2,000 people in the hall, including Canadian Governor General Georges Vanier, the superintendent ordered his men to immediately search the entire premises.

When notified of the threat, Vanier commented: "I'm staying. If I go up, we all go up."

Fortunately the deadline passed and nothing happened, but it had been a tense 15 minutes for the railway police and the hotel guests alike.

Stranger still was the threat received in May 1958 by the CPR passenger agent in Peterborough, Ontario, along with a hastily scrawled extortion letter. "Gentlemen," it began, "This is a shakedown for $25,000. We will de-rail or dynamite one of your trains unless payment is made. If you are interested, as you no doubt are, put an ad in the *Toronto Telegram* on June 6, under 'personals.' If reply is affirmative, mention the word 'thunder.' Refer to yourselves as 'baby,' to us as 'daddy.' We cannot overemphasize the fact that this is not a prank."

Members of the Department of Investigation went along with the instructions and were eventually directed to place the cash under a railway culvert in North Monaghan Township.

After nine days of keeping the drop spot under continuous observation, the tired and mosquito bitten railway police were rewarded for their perseverance. Two 16-year-olds walked right into the trap and were arrested with no further trouble. On their eventual conviction the youths were given just two years' suspended sentence despite the seriousness of the charges against them.

Annual reports from each of the railway districts during the 1950s and 1960s show that while theft was still an important issue for the Department of Investigation and bomb threats somewhat of an anomaly, the traditional concerns were quickly being overtaken by instances of trespassing, tampering with switches and placing objects on the tracks.

Members of the Department took to touring schools in railway towns across the country in an attempt to raise the level of awareness about public safety issues, supported by a variety of safety films produced for just that purpose.

One of the stories often told at these sessions was the case of the curious young man from Quebec who decided it would be a good idea to pile railway ties on the CPR main line just outside of Lanoraie yard. When a train inevitably plowed into the barrier with injury to both locomotive and crew, CPR Investigator Georges Legault was able to track down the offender after days and days of questioning people in the region.

Asked why he had done such a thing, the teenager replied that he'd recently seen the movie *The Greatest Show on Earth*, and "he wanted to find out if the CPR could put a derailed train back on the tracks as quickly as the circus people had in the film."

Clearly, more public education and work with youth groups would be required.

The Department's public safety program helped the Canadian Pacific win the National Safety Council's Public Safety Award every year from its inception in 1953 to the late 1960s. The good work helped not only to quell any misgivings the public might have had about private police forces, but also won the admiration of other police departments and law enforcement bodies across the country, and of course, the mutual cooperation and assistance was often the deciding factor in bringing criminals to justice.

Consider an instance in June 1962, when four employees of a sub-urban branch of the Bank of Montreal in Winnipeg, Manitoba, were held up by two armed gunmen, who escaped with upwards of $42,000 cash.

The next evening on the CPR's eastbound passenger train, *The Canadian*, a trainman became suspicious of two men who had boarded at Kenora, Ontario. When he pointed them out to two detectives from the Fort William City Police, the officers questioned the suspects and searched their baggage, but found no evidence they were connected with the holdup.

However, a CPR constable in Kenora discovered that a couple of parcels had been shipped that very day from the local Canadian Pacific Express office to a Montreal address in care of the same two men under scrutiny. The officer contacted CPR's assistant inspector at Sudbury and requested a warrant to examine the packages. When they were opened, they were found to contain $40,501. The information was relayed to the city police in Fort William where the suspects soon admitted their participation in the Winnipeg bank job.

Thanks to the collaborative police work, just 15 days after the heist the two holdup men appeared in court and pleaded guilty to armed robbery and automotive theft. They were each sentenced to ten years in the penitentiary on the first charge and to three years concurrent on the second charge.

By 1964, approximately 20,000 cases were being conducted annually by the Department of Investigation. An average of 1,100 to 1,200 cases was prosecuted each year with acquittals practically nonexistent due to the manner in which arrests were made and testimonies meticulously prepared.

The use of private police forces during strike actions by employees, of course, remained controversial and called for extreme diplomacy on the part of the railway police, who did not wish to risk all of the goodwill they had achieved over the years between the Railway's operating forces and themselves.

"As a general rule, in our form of industrial society, employees have the right to band together, to bargain collectively with their employer or a group of employers in regard to wages and working conditions,"

CPR president and chief operating officer, Robert A. Emerson, told the International Association of Chiefs of Police in Louisville, Kentucky, on October 28, 1964. "Moreover, our common law generally recognizes the right of a group of employees to strike to attempt to enforce their demands if the object of the strike and the means pursued to achieve it is lawful."

Fortunately, the mutual respect between the railway police and CPR employees usually precluded any physical confrontation during internal disputes. However, strikes called by third parties could and did spill over into the jurisdiction of the Department of Investigation.

In the autumn of 1963, a longshoremens' strike closed ports on the St. Lawrence River. One of the Canadian Pacific's vessels, the *Empress of Canada*, arrived in Quebec City from a transatlantic voyage with a large number of passengers. When the longshoremen refused to handle the ship's lines, the *Empress* launched a boat to take her own lines ashore. As it approached the wharf, however, violent threats and abuse by the longshoremen compelled them to abandon the attempt and, ultimately, to sail to Halifax to disembark their passengers.

"Here then," Emerson told his law enforcement audience, "was a shocking example of people, including Canadians, denied the right to land in Canada at a government owned facility by an unruly mob who trampled law and order underfoot."

The only bright spot in the whole disgraceful affair, he said, was the sense of humour displayed by the Company's police officer in charge of the small boat with the lines who, upon returning to the ship, reported to the captain that he had "attempted a landing, but found the natives unfriendly."

While Canadian Pacific took a substantial financial hit during this and other strike actions during the sixties, the Company and its police force managed to avoid some of the more nasty entanglements suffered by railroads in the United States during the same period.

"You are all familiar with the situation as it relates to the strike on the Florida East Coast Railway which commenced on January 13, 1963, and is still in effect," Emerson said. "Since the strike began—and the violence started—the Florida East Coast Railway has reported more than two hundred and fifty acts of harassment, vandalism and outright sabotage. In less than six months, twenty-two attempts to wreck trains

Vancouver "Flying Squad" members — from left, Staff Sergeant C. McCarthy and constables B. Bouzan, W. Richardson, F. Hill, F. Toop, R. Carney, A. Jasman, W. Birch, W. Richards, M. Hodge and L.R. Smith — pose with one of their three-wheeled motorcycles

with explosives were reported. At the present time, four men are free on $50,000 bail, charged with various offences in connection with these depredations. The whole story of this unfortunate affair is yet to be told."

By now Jean Edouard Bélanger was occupying the CPR police chief's chair. Bélanger was the man who had led the team of investigators probing the fatal bombing of a Canadian Pacific Air Lines flight in 1949. In the interim, the airline industry in Canada had spread its wings ever further afield. By 1959, the CPR had broken the Trans-Canada Air Lines monopoly on cross continental routes to and from Canadian locations. With the introduction in 1960 of bigger and faster DC-8 jets, Trans-Canada Air Lines cut the flying time from Vancouver to Montreal from ten to six hours. A year later, the Canadian Pacific inaugurated its own jet service, including the dramatic eight hour, nonstop route over the pole from Vancouver to London.

With the expansion of the Canadian Pacific Airlines' routes overseas, CPR investigators were dispatched by Bélanger to South Africa, Honolulu and the Orient in 1964 and 1965. The following spring, deputy police chief J. R. Johnson accompanied by J. R. Trott, superintendent of the Pacific Region, extended the exploratory visits to Mexico City; Lima, Peru; Santiago, Chile; and Buenos Aires, Argentina,

Chief Jean Edouard Bélanger

THE COMMUNICATOR

A native of Saint-Jérôme, Quebec, Jean Bélanger attended the village school in Huberdeau before moving to Montreal where he won a diploma with gold medal for composition. His communications skills would serve him well during his later career in law enforcement.

In 1923, Bélanger joined the Canadian Pacific Railway in Quebec City as a constable. He worked there and in Montreal before being named investigator in 1927 and then inspector in charge of the Quebec District in 1944. He was promoted to assistant chief of the CPR's Department of Investigation in May 1952, deputy chief on January 1, 1954, and chief on January 1, 1959.

The CPR's fifth chief of police won wide recognition in law enforcement circles for his part in the investigation of the case of the Quebec Airways plane blown up by dynamite along the north shore of the St. Lawrence River in 1949. Quebec Airways was owned by the CPR at the time and would soon be an integral part of the Canadian Pacific Air Lines. His early investigations and numerous one on one interviews indicated strong evidence of foul play which led to the arrest and execution of J. Albert Guay and two accomplices.

He also accompanied many famous people while they were travelling over the Canadian Pacific transportation network, among them the King of Siam who visited Canada in the early 1930s; U.S. President Roosevelt during the Second World War conference in Quebec City; and President Truman, who visited the Company's Seigneury Club in Montebello, Quebec.

Though the Canadian Pacific had one of the best safety records in the world during Bélanger's tenure as chief, he was doggedly

Bélanger became a media favourite during the trial and conviction of Albert Guay.

determined to get to the root causes of every accident, or nasty criminal incident, which occurred on his watch.

"No matter how difficult it looks," he said, "we have to stay at it and find out why an accident happened. There's a reason for every one. It might be the work of a careless employee; maybe a mischievous child. Perhaps even a psychopath. We just can't afford to take anything for granted."

Chief Bélanger served as the president of the Province of Quebec Police and Fire Chiefs Association, the Canadian Association of Chiefs of Police, the Airlines Security Officers' Association (New York), the International Association of Chiefs of Police, and the Canadian Highway Safety Conference (Ottawa).

He was also a member of the Canadian Railway Club and the Montreal Chamber of Commerce.

Bélanger retired on pension November 1, 1969.

developing valuable contacts with law enforcement agencies in countries served by the airline. During this period, Bélanger himself supported the outreach program as an active representative of the Canadian Pacific and its air service branch at a pair of worldwide security conferences.

Despite the increased activity to secure major airline routes and destinations around the world, however, the Canadian Pacific Airlines received another stunning blow to its safety record on Thursday, July 8, 1965.

A Canadian Pacific DC-6 lifted off that day from airline headquarters in Vancouver, bound for Whitehorse in the Yukon. While the plane was en route to Prince George, near 100 Mile House, British Columbia, forest fire guard John Hyra heard the drone of its piston engines overhead and glanced up through his truck's windshield.

"Suddenly, I heard an explosion," he later told a coroner's jury investigating the incident. "I said someone must be parachuting from the plane, because a billow of smoke came from it that looked just like a parachute opening. Then I realized what had happened. The front part of the plane seemed to continue to fly, while the tail section seemed to hesitate, then fell down away from the front part. There was a terrific blast as it hit the ground."

About 15 minutes earlier, Captain John Alfred Steele had radioed the control tower at Vancouver International Airport that he was changing course slightly to avoid turbulence ahead. The plane was flying at 15,000 feet. Then came a more frantic: "Mayday! Mayday! Mayday!" before the transmission broke off entirely.

Within minutes, British Columbia Forest Service pilot Slim Sherk was ordered to investigate from on high.

"I could see black smoke curling up into the sky," he said. "I could see it was a plane on fire. There was the smoke of magnesium burning. I have seen it burning before in plane crashes. The fuselage was smoke and raw flames. The wings were collapsing from the heat, but the plane was relatively intact except for the tail section. It appeared as though the plane dove straight into the bush. There was no trail of broken trees," the pilot recounted before delivering his most gruesome observation.

Sherk counted more than twenty bodies, until, as he said, "I couldn't find anymore."

None of the 46 passengers and six crew members survived.

A coroner's inquest concluded "an explosive substance foreign to the normal contents of the aircraft" caused the crash. Members

A CP police officer strikes a dramatic pose at the crash site of the ill-fated airliner, for a photograph that ran in the *Chicago Tribune*.

of the CPR's Department of Investigation interviewed hundreds of airline employees and others who had had access to the DC-6 in the hours preceding the crash, but were not able to draw any definite conclusions. One of the women cleaning the plane just before the fateful flight insisted a "weird-looking" man had appeared in the back part of the airliner not long before takeoff, but that trail went cold.

In the meantime, Ralph Barer, metallurgist with the Pacific Naval Laboratory, recovered a piece of copper that was foreign to the aircraft, possibly from a bomb detonator, from the body of one of the crash victims. Mrs. Rolande Rouen, a chemist with the RCMP crime laboratory told the inquest traces of black gunpowder had been found in four sections of the plane, all near the rear toilet. Traces of potassium nitrate and carbon were also found.

The official studies established beyond any doubt an explosion had taken place "in the left rear lavatory compartment of the aircraft."

When it was further revealed that the explosive had in all likelihood been placed on the floor of the compartment, slightly inboard of the toilet and sink in a fairly obvious location, the CPR investigators all but eliminated the possibility that the bomb had been planted while the plane was still on the ground.

In 1965, before mandatory security checkpoints were established in the nation's airports, it would have been relatively easy to bring weapons and explosives aboard a passenger aircraft. Passengers simply checked in, walked to a gate and boarded their flight with no more fuss than stepping onto a bus.

The investigation focused on four passengers.

A 29-year-old man on his way to accept a job in the north was found to be the owner of a considerable amount of gunpowder, the substance investigators believed was used to blow up Flight 21. Although four 11-ounce tins from his supply were unaccounted for, no plausible motive could be found for his involvement.

An unemployed man had purchased $120,000 worth of flight insurance less than an hour before departure, listing his wife, daughter, mother and niece as beneficiaries. Inquiries revealed he had reportedly been on his way to accept a job with a pulp mill in the region of Prince George, but when RCMP investigators visited all of the mills in the area, no one knew of the man or any job offer.

Another passenger was found to have had extensive experience working with explosives. Though not convicted, the man had been charged seven years earlier with a murder in Vancouver. However, the construction company for which he worked had purchased his ticket for a legitimate business trip in the north.

The final suspect was an accountant who had recently been involved in an audit of a failed financial services firm. Rumours circulated that the far reaching implications of what he had uncovered during the audit had been enough for somebody to want him silenced. Investigators later discounted the theory.

To this day, the mysterious fate of CPA Flight 21 is still an open file in CP Police case history.

CHAPTER 9
Public Safety Officers: Educating the Public

Throughout the 1960s, the salary of CPR police constables was on a par with most police salaries in Canada and in many cases higher.

The Department of Investigation had a surplus of officers arising from the reduction in rail passenger traffic on CPR lines in the 1960s and the advent of containerization that transferred goods between truck, train and ship without the need to unload or reload. One of the more difficult tasks assigned to new chief John Machan in 1969 was to reduce staff numbers in the uniformed branch by about 100 members.

In an era that predated early retirement and buyout packages, the two-year period that Machan was given to downsize the department was an aggressive one. Morale plummeted. As a result of the ensuing conflict, the constables and sergeants formed a union to negotiate working conditions and compensation on their behalf. However, it took about two years from the time the union was certified until the first collective agreement was signed, during which period wage increases were frozen. It would be nearly 20 years before the shortfall would be recovered.

Meanwhile, out on the property, the responsibilities of the railway police were evolving.

The number of bomb threats handled by the Department of Investigation increased, particularly against the Canadian Pacific Air

Lines. So, too, did the spectre of hijackings.

In the late sixties, 75 or more airplane hijackings were occurring annually. While they posed a public safety concern and a major inconvenience to passengers and airline companies alike, almost all ended without violence. In 1970, however, everything changed and aircraft hijacking suddenly became deadly serious.

On September 6, 1970, the Palestinian Liberation Organization (PLO) targeted three flights from Europe to the United States, all departing at around the same time of day. TWA Flight 741, a Boeing 707 with 142 people aboard was en route from Frankfurt to New York City when it was diverted to Dawson Field, an old military airstrip in the Jordanian desert. Swissair Flight 100, a DC-8 with 155 travelling from Zurich to New York was forced to fly to the same airstrip. Only the attempt to hijack El Al Flight 219 from Amsterdam to New York was foiled when onboard air marshals subdued one hijacker and killed another. The plane landed in London without further incident and the surviving female hijacker was arrested by British police.

Because the hijackers had been thwarted on the El Al flight, the PLO immediately targeted Pan-Am Flight 93, a Boeing 747 en route from Amsterdam to New York with 173 people aboard. This flight was diverted to Beirut, even though the airport there did not have a runway long enough to land an aircraft of that size safely.

Nevertheless, the plane landed without mishap, took on a so-called explosives expert, and continued on to Cairo. The "expert" planted explosive devices throughout the cabin and upon landing, everyone was quickly ordered off. The explosives were then detonated and the plane destroyed.

Three days later on September 9, the PLO hijacked BOAC Flight 775, a Vickers VC-10 with 117 people en route from Bombay to London. After a forced landing in Beirut to refuel, this plane, too, was taken to Dawson Field to join the TWA and Swissair planes on the tarmac. The PLO targeted this flight in an attempt to force the British to release the female hijacker arrested on the El Al flight.

On September 12, the three hijacked planes in the Jordanian desert were destroyed. All but 56 of their passengers, mostly American and Jewish men, were released. The last six of these only obtained their freedom on September 30, when the British, West German and

Swiss governments agreed to release PLO prisoners in their custody, including the female involved in the El Al hijacking.

The extensive media coverage of these events fuelled public hysteria and ushered in the first wave of stringent airline security. Hijackings and in-flight violence had become a nasty part of operating a modern air service.

Chief John Colin Machan

THE REAL ESTATE SPECIALIST

John Machan was born in Winnipeg, June 5, 1914, and moved to Montreal at an early age.

He served with the Royal Canadian Mounted Police as a secretary and constable from May 1932 until September 1937. He then joined the Quebec Provincial Police Force, December 1, 1937, but resigned a month later to take up a position as a constable with the Canadian Pacific in Montreal.

Machan was assigned to the waterfront in Montreal and West Saint John, New Brunswick, before hearing the call of duty and signing up with the Royal Canadian Navy on New Year's Day, 1941. There he served on the busy shipping lanes of the North Atlantic. By the time he was discharged on August 28, 1945, he had risen to the rank of Lieutenant-Commander. Within days, he rejoined CPR's Department of Investigation as acting investigator stationed in Montreal.

He was appointed inspector of the Quebec District, May 1, 1952, but his career took a unique turn when he accepted a job as the head of the Company's real estate department, with system wide jurisdiction. During his stewardship, all of the Canadian Pacific's land redevelopment activities were organized under wholly owned Marathon Realty Co.

Machan returned to the railway police as assistant to the chief on September 1, 1965, and advanced to assistant chief three years later. He became head of the Department on November 1, 1969, with the departure of Chief Bélanger.

Machan retired to Victoria, British Columbia, in 1979.

Machan had an odd career mix.

The 1970s brought even more political and economic upheaval.

On the back of rising unemployment, the number of transients hopping CP Rail freight trains or loitering in the vicinity of its hotels was on the rise. Members of the railway police were called upon to control situations on or near company property during labour disputes at several large firms, including the Franklin Manufacturing Company, General Motors, Firestone Tire Company and the National Farmers' Union.

The 1970 Grey Cup Football game was held in Toronto. The Montreal Alouettes were playing the Calgary Stampeders, and, predictably, the Royal York Hotel became the focal point for the festivities. Unlike the pre-game shenanigans of 1948, nobody rode a horse into the lobby of the hotel, but the staff of the Royal York did get to feed some carrots to the one equine visitor that made it to the front door, and even managed to get an imprint of its front hoof in the guest register.

The Department of Investigation, working closely with Metropolitan Toronto City Police, kept damage and disorder to a minimum by closely monitoring the situation and showing a sufficient number of uniforms in and around the Royal York. CN Police kept order across the street at Union Station.

A dramatic incident involving the police had played itself out several months before when Governor General Earl Grey's cherished mug had been stolen from a locked display case in the Ottawa Rough Riders' locker room. In response to a ransom attempt, both the police and the league completely ignored the perpetrators. In February 1970, the Toronto Police received an anonymous tip to check a phone booth at Dundas and Parliament where a key to a locker in the Royal York had been left. Metro Police sergeant Gordon Lennox recovered the Cup and promptly returned it to the Canadian Football League, which had already announced plans to order a replacement Cup if the original was not returned in time for the current season.

In 1971, CPR reorganized and a new parent company—Canadian Pacific Limited—emerged to own and manage stand-alone companies that formerly had been mere departments of the Canadian Pacific Railway Company, albeit semi-independent ones. Holders of CPR shares became shareholders of CP Limited. It was no longer possible to invest in just a railway with diverse business interests. Instead investors could buy and sell shares in a diversified operating company

whose interests included one of the largest railway companies in the world, plus an airline, a hotel chain, a shipping arm and much more.

On November 16, 1971, the Vancouver office of McKim, Benton and Bowles advertising agents for the Canadian Pacific, received a telephone call from a man claiming to be A. L. Stewart with CP's passenger department. The man asked that the following announcement be placed in both the *Vancouver Sun* and the *Province* for November 19:

Norris "Buck" Crump and Ian "Big Julie" Sinclair discuss the new branding of their ever-diversifying and expanding empire.

SPECIAL ANNOUNCEMENT

*From Saturday, November 20th to Tuesday, November 23rd,
all Pacific Coast arrivals and departures of the Canadian
will be diverted from Vancouver to New Westminster.
For further information, please call 681-2212.*

CP RAIL

Highjackings and in-flight violence became everyday concerns for those operating a modern, worldwide airline service.

The Canadian, of course, was CP Rail's premier, stainless steel transcontinental train which had been introduced to the travelling public with much fanfare in 1955.

As requests of this nature were usually received through the railway's public relations department, a representative of the agency checked with CP Rail and found the request was a hoax. The Department of Investigation soon established that a man giving the same name had telephoned the *White Rock Sun* with a similar request. The man had also contacted seven radio stations in the area with the same bogus information.

When word of the scam became common knowledge at just about every Vancouver media outlet and the fraudulent requests were ignored, the caller or callers, using both the names A. L. Stewart and R. D. Sutherland ordered a truckload of gravel to be dumped in front of the CP Rail station at New Westminster, sent several trucking firms to pick up the waiting room benches, called the utility company to turn off the electricity in the building, had five buses from Pacific Stage Lines and Trailways Bus Lines dispatched to the station—and for good measure assigned a handful of commercial photographers to take pictures at the front and back of the besieged CP Rail depot.

Many of the requests were carried out as ordered and chaos reigned for several days, though the railway police were able to get warnings out through a local photographers' association and an automotive transport bulletin which did help somewhat.

A few days later, CP received a telex from a North Vancouver CN Telecommunications office with the following message:

DIRECTOR, PUBLIC RELATIONS, CP RAIL
GRANVILLE AND CORDOVA, VANCOUVER, BC

YOU CAN TELL YOUR BOYS TO RELAX. IT'S ALL OVER WITH. ON WEDNESDAY I'M HEADING DOWN EAST FOR NEW HORIZONS TO HAVE MORE FUN IN YOUR COMPANY. DON'T THINK IT HASN'T BEEN GREAT. YOU HAD NO IDEA HOW MUCH OF A THRILL WE ALL GOT FROM IT. IT WAS TOO BAD WE DID NOT HAVE A CHANCE TO MEET GET TOGETHER BUT WHO KNOWS WHAT THE

FUTURE MAY HOLD. DON'T WORRY I'LL BE RETURNING TO THE COAST AFTER CHRISTMAS AND WE CAN GIVE IT ANOTHER GO AROUND AGAIN. I HOPE I GET SOME BETTER RESULTS. MAYBE WE COULD HAVE SOME MORE COMPANIES INVOLVED SO TELL YOUR BOYS TO BE ON THE LOOK OUT.

YOURS TRULY
RD SUTHERLAND AL STEWART

Nothing more was ever heard on the subject.

Other threats, however, were more substantive. Just after 1:00 a.m., on November 9, 1972, CP Rail Freight Extra 8761 North was rocked when an explosion occurred on the CP Rail main line near St. Martin Station, north of Montreal and right in front of the train.

Immediately following the blast, anonymous telephone messages were received by Canadian Pacific from callers claiming to represent an organization they identified as "Black September, Montreal." The ominous missives warned that the explosion at St. Martin would be followed by a second bombing at an undisclosed point in front of a passenger train unless certain demands were met. To prevent such an unwanted occurrence, CP Rail was asked to pay a quarter of a million dollars to the shadowy terrorist group.

Explicit instructions were received as to how the money was to be paid and packaged. Used $20 bills were requested, from ten different banks. Further instructions about where and when to leave the money would be received by phone. CP Rail was cautioned to remember other explosions that had recently occurred in Israel, Germany and Jordan for which Black September claimed responsibility.

A team of railway-police investigators under the leadership of Superintendent Georges Legault swung into action and following a further communiqué from the group prepared a package for the "drop." But, whether the extortionists were scared off by the exhaustive inquiries and investigations which ensued or were merely engaging in empty threats, no solid leads emerged and nobody ever showed up at the drop zone. After a considerable time CP Rail's investigating team, augmented by members of the Quebec Provincial Police and the RCMP, recovered the package and waited for further instructions. None ever came.

Theft, too, continued to dog the CP Rail and the railway police on the road as well as on the rails.

Transportation companies enhanced security measures in many of the country's major transfer centres after a rash of transport tractor and trailer hijackings. Procedures for entering and leaving shipping yards and docking areas were tightened up after thieves unleashed an epidemic of thefts at warehouses across the country, towing away containers with a myriad of consumer goods—meats, cigarettes, liquor, motorcycles, snowmobiles, car parts, carpets and even bathroom fixtures.

On November 17, 1973, thieves grabbed a 45-foot Canadian Pacific trailer full of bathtubs from a yard in Calgary. When the trailer became disconnected at a stoplight while leaving town, the driver took the tractor back to the CP Rail yard and picked up another trailer, this one full of carpets. It was later found abandoned and empty in nearby Midnapore.

New ads appeared in the *Calgary Herald* seeking railway constables over 21 years of age, at least five feet nine inches tall in good health with 20/20 uncorrected vision.

More than any issue facing the Department of Investigation, however, was the growing problem of safety at highway railway grade crossings of which there were literally thousands across the country. Unfortunately, there was—and is—no simple solution.

While the railway is required to provide visible and sometimes audible warning devices at crossings and certainly the latter on locomotives, it is the joint responsibility of municipal and provincial governments to consider topographic obstacles, traffic flows and overall visibility when laying out roads that cross the tracks. Appropriate speed limits have to be set, sufficient warnings about the existence of grade crossings given, and relevant laws enforced.

Finally, it is the responsibility of motorists to abide by the law and exercise prudence and judgement when driving over grade crossings.

Complicating these known factors are variables such as weather, temperature and whether a crossing is being used in the daylight or at night.

By law, railways are required to do their part to maintain crossings and warning devices ranging from simple crossbucks on secondary roads to complex, train activated mechanisms including such things as movable crossing gates, flashing lights, electric bells or combinations thereof. Unless specifically forbidden by municipal bylaws, railways also enforce the provisions of their Uniform Code of Operating Rules. They require a locomotive to sound its whistle for a quarter mile in advance of each crossing, and that the whistling will be prolonged or repeated until the locomotive is actually occupying the crossing.

Railway crews must undergo rigorous training and write periodic examinations, as well as submit themselves to regular medical tests to qualify and remain qualified to operate trains. There are strict regulations about the sobriety and physical condition of train personnel, as well as the adequacy of their rest periods before coming on duty. Their performance is checked frequently, both by the railway companies and government authorities.

But the moral responsibility of the railways does not end with the fulfillment of legal obligations; it also extends to educating the public and drivers in particular, to be alert at all times. That's where the Canadian Pacific has often called on its own police force to carry the ball.

The education and publicity program launched by the railway police in the 1970s included the distribution of thousands of press releases about grade crossing safety to newspapers and radio stations across the country. An audiovisual program entitled *Dead on the Level* was developed for CP constables to get in front of audiences at schools, community associations and safety conferences to promote awareness of the unequal showdowns that can occur when road vehicles meet trains at level crossings. It was a continuation of the public outreach programs practiced by the railway police for generations and the beginning of a new, more robust, multifaceted railway safety campaign that continues to this day.

Along with the diversification of the company under the corporate umbrella of Canadian Pacific Limited, new investigation techniques and changes in government regulation such as the *Bail Reform Act* and the *Human Rights Act* ensured that the old public perception of the "railway bull" or "cinder dick" was replaced by a new, highly sophisticated image of the railway policeman.

Constantly updated policing techniques, combined with new generations of computer equipment, spawned a new breed of policeman while fresh government legislation provided for greater respect of the rights of the individual. A new, two-inch-thick training manual reflected the modernization and country-wide standardization of the Department of Investigation under the brief leadership of Chief Georges Legault and, subsequently, Chief James Mickel.

Chief Georges Henri Legault

PUTTING OUT FIRES, LITERALLY AND FIGURATIVELY

Georges Legault was born October 18, 1917, in Sainte-Martine, Valleyfield, Quebec.

Legault joined the railway as a watchman in Montreal's Glen Yard in 1938. During his tenure with the railway police, he worked mostly in eastern Canada at Montreal, Quebec City, Saint John, Fort William, and Schreiber. He became a constable the same year he joined the CPR and an investigator at Montreal, in 1952. Eight years later, he was appointed assistant inspector at Fort William.

From 1943 to 1946, Legault had taken a leave of absence to go on military service, returning as a railway constable.

Legault put in 44 years of service.

His ascent through the police ranks quickened as he gained more field and administrative experience. He was appointed police inspector and fire chief at Angus Shops in 1963; inspector, Atlantic Region in 1969; staff inspector for the system in Montreal a year later; superintendent, Atlantic Region in 1971; assistant chief of investigation in 1973; deputy chief of investigation in 1977 and finally chief of investigation in 1979.

Less than a year into Legault's term as chief, a claim was filed against the Canadian Pacific by a consignee whose container shipment of fox furs from Russia arrived in Canada with many of the pelts missing. The furs had come over in a CP Ships container and CP investigators noticed its fastenings had been tampered with. With the assistance of Interpol, the Department suggested to police in Poland that the theft had probably occurred in Gdansk where the container had been transferred from a smaller ship. Five men were arrested there as a result.

Georges Legault retired to Ottawa four years later on November 1, 1982 after 44 years of service with the Canadian Pacific.

Supporting the geographic and administrative diversity of the Company's interests, members of the railway police were also sworn in as special constables for the various provinces which gave them greater jurisdiction.

Once a candidate for recruitment met the rigid physical requirements, obtained high marks on various qualifying tests and underwent a background check, he was appointed a cadet and sent to the CP Police Academy in Winnipeg for a six week training period. Along with learning about criminal and provincial law, the cadets were taught general police procedures, first aid and other related subjects.

"There's a lot more to police training at the academy than just spit and polish," said CP Inspector Walter Turchyn, one of the developers of the curriculum for trainees. "One key body of law for our police is *Canada's Criminal Code*. The men are instructed on how to use and interpret the code, as well as the *Railway Act*. That's where we get our authority. We're sworn in under the *Railway Act*."

The course also included instruction in administrative procedures such as the proper way to take notes at a reportable incident like a break-in or an accident, how to take statements and write reports, and the proper procedures for dealing with a bomb threat or derailment of dangerous goods.

If successful at the police academy, a cadet was promoted to constable and assigned to a detachment where he was paired with a training officer for a further eight weeks of advanced, on the job learning. His daily duties might entail protecting Canadian Pacific property, patrolling facilities for, or connected with, company business, or conducting cursory investigations. Uniformed members who showed investigative ability could be transferred to plainclothes duty and promoted to the rank of investigator, concerned more with serious offences such as arson, fraud and major thefts.

Approximately every four years after basic training, members of CP's Department of Investigation were sent for refresher courses at Winnipeg. They might also be selected to attend specialized courses at the Canadian Police College in Ottawa or the Ontario Provincial Police College in Aylmer, Ontario. In addition, they often were invited by city and provincial police departments where their detachments were located to join in-service training programs.

However, no amount of training could prepare you for what might occur on any given day while on special assignment.

On September 18, 1975, a guest was found to have checked in to Toronto's Royal York Hotel with a credit card stolen in the United States on which he had run up a charge of $377. Sensing that there might be trouble, the hotel's assistant credit manager, Lyanage Pryel De Silva, a 22-year old recent immigrant from Sri Lanka, asked security officer Constable Roger Saunders to accompany him to the man's room. Because he suspected a crime had, indeed, been committed Saunders requested that Metro Toronto Police Constable Gary Silliker come along as well.

The three men went to the eighth-floor room, knocked on the door and were let in by the suspect, who waved a pistol at them before their eyes had fully adjusted to the room.

Saunders was shot in the stomach. Silliker, who had turned to try to escape, was struck by a bullet in the back of his shoulder. De Silva bolted out the door and was halfway down the hall before he realized he was going in the wrong direction. It was a fatal error. Turning tail and dashing the other way, he was gunned down before he could reach the exit.

Now in full panic mode, the gunman got to the lobby and left the hotel within minutes, virtually undetected.

Meanwhile, several members of the CP Police, Metropolitan Toronto Police and Ontario Provincial Police were called to the scene to carry out a room by room search of the Royal York. With 1,600 bedrooms and public rooms to check and a well-attended convention underway, the task was both daunting and time consuming and, of course, the officers were unaware their quarry had already made good his escape.

It was soon learned, however, that a car bearing Kentucky plates and driven by a desperate looking character had recently torn out of the hotel parking lot heading west. Toronto police received a tip later in the day that the car and suspect in question had arrived in Niagara, but had managed to slip across the border into the U.S.

By now, the Royal York gunman had been tentatively identified as one Roy Allen Embry, an American citizen with an extensive criminal record for theft, fraud and other offences. A warrant was issued for his arrest on one count of murder and two counts of attempted murder.

Nearly three months later on December 10, the police in Denver, Colorado, received information that Embry was in their city and planning to take a bus to points unknown. Detectives D. DeBruno and D. Haley spotted the suspect at the Continental Bus Terminal, but did not immediately confront him in the crowded waiting area. When challenged outside the depot, however, Embry drew his revolver and opened fire on the two officers killing DeBruno instantly and gravely wounding Haley who returned fire rapidly and accurately. Embry fell to the ground and was taken to hospital with wounds to the chest, arms and face.

The Ottawa police had a file on Embry even before his escapades at the Royal York Hotel.

When he had recovered, Embry appeared in Denver City Court, pleading guilty to first degree murder and first degree assault. He was sentenced to a life term in Colorado. In addition, extradition papers were served to return him to Canada for trial should he ever be released in the U.S.

CP Police Constable Saunders made a full recovery, as did both Metro Toronto Police Constable Silliker and Denver Police Detective Haley.

Those on duty in the wilderness hotels had different challenges.

Late one evening during the summer of 1979, an ashen faced steward rushed into CP officer Rod Manson's office at the Chateau Lake Louise. "B-b-b-bear," he stuttered, pointing shakily toward the loading dock.

Manson had been assigned by the railway police to security duty at the famous Canadian Pacific mountain resort.

As the officer bolted out into the hotel yard, the agitated hotel employee hot on his heels, the two men could see that the large doors securing the garbage area had been ripped from their hinges and garbage was strewn wildly about the area.

With no perpetrator in sight, Manson instructed two hotel staff members to clean up the mess while he stood guard nearby.

It was then that the four-legged food seeker of the steward's recent acquaintance decided to return for a second helping. As the bear headed for the garbage area and the bins where the two hotel men were cut off from any escape, officer Manson drew his service revolver, a snub-nose Smith & Wesson .38 Special and fired three shots at the ground in front of the overly adventurous animal.

"I guess the noise scared him," Manson later recalled, "as the bear looked in my direction, took a few steps and then sauntered off into the darkness."

Following protocol for incidents within a National Park, the CP officer immediately called the warden's office where the speculation was that the intruder had been a grizzly bear, bigger and more dangerous than the black bears more commonly seen in the area of the Chateau.

The following night, Manson and the warden took up a position on the roof of the loading dock from where they could observe a trap they had set for the errant bear. Around the same time as it had the evening before, the grizzly once again came looking for snacks.

"When it saw the trap, it walked past, and, with one swift whack of a huge paw, slammed the trap door shut and retreated into the darkness," Manson said.

The encounter had been close enough, however, for the warden to recognize their adversary as the same problem bear that had already been relocated three times that summer.

In consultation with his superiors in Banff, the warden discovered the bear to be an elderly male, with rotten teeth and little ability to hunt for food in the wild. Given the grizzly's proclivity for encroaching on human activity without fear, the Parks Canada staff reached a decision to destroy the animal.

The very next night as Manson, the warden and an RCMP constable perched in the same spot on the roof of the loading dock, the bear came back. As the marauder moved toward the garbage area, the police shone spotlights onto the hotel yard. Manson and the RCMP officer opened fire with 12 gauge shotguns, while the warden hit the grizzly with a tranquilizer dart from a high powered rifle. The bear reared up on its hind quarters and fell to the ground dead.

"Even though it was midnight," Manson said, "a large crowd from the hotel gathered as we burnt out a winch trying to get the bear into the back of the warden's pickup. Eventually, we got it out of there, and a subsequent weighing of the bear determined that it was more than seven hundred pounds. The local media was all over the story when it broke, as there had already been a controversy brewing over hotels in the vicinity of Lake Louise allegedly being negligent with garbage disposal and, consequently, attracting bears unnecessarily. I was transferred back to Vancouver that fall, and didn't give much more thought to the incident."

But it would come back to haunt Manson soon enough.

That autumn, an article appeared in *Weekend Magazine*, highlighting a story about the recent killing of a bear at the Chateau Lake Louise.

"At the time, the superintendent of the police department for the Pacific Region, Bert McGowan, had heard nothing about this incident," Manson said, "and upon reading the magazine article, he was more than a little annoyed with me. But once the superintendent realized the hotel staff members had been in considerable danger, and that I had followed proper procedure and reported the incident immediately, my skin was spared. The following spring, I was transferred back to Lake Louise—with the promise to not shoot at any more bears."

In 1981, The Railway Association of Canada (RAC) and Transport Canada, in cooperation with the Canada Safety Council and the provincial safety councils and leagues, launched the grade crossing safety awareness program known as "Operation Lifesaver." The central message for drivers: "Trains are big and powerful. They can't stop on a dime. A 100-car freight train can weigh 10,000 tonnes or more. Travelling at 80 km/h it takes about 2,500 metres for a train to come to a full stop in an emergency. If it's a race between you and the train, you lose. Don't take a chance... it may be your last."

By then, there were more than 24,000 railway crossings in Canada. In any given year, there were about 400 crossing accidents in which about 60 people were killed.

Police investigations consistently showed that motorists were mostly responsible for these mishaps. Many ignored the horn and bell warnings from approaching locomotives. They often disregarded the automatic warning devices such as flashers and bells at the crossing. Some even had the audacity to drive around lowered barriers and very often misjudged their margin for error. In the worst case scenarios, distracted drivers would drive straight into the side of a moving train without so much as slowing down.

While reducing grade crossings fatalities was the primary objective of RAC members like the Canadian Pacific, discouraging trespassing on railway property in general was also a key strategy. Increasingly, the railway police were occupied with trying to keep all-terrain-vehicle operators, trail bikers, snowmobilers, bicyclists, and cross country skiers off railway tracks and bridges. At the same time, CP constables were rolling out the Operation Lifesaver program in public schools across the country.

TOP: Operation Lifesaver, while primarily focused on safety at level crossings, also sought to educate the public about the dangers of trespassing on railway property.

ABOVE: Railway police officers put in countless hours at schools and community centres trying to prevent accidents from occurring.

On November 1, 1982, Jim Mickel took over from Georges Legault as chief of the Department of Investigation. Mickel's most important contribution to the force was instituting formal training programs and a standard curriculum that would be taught across the country. The new chief also insisted on a strict regimen of pre-employment testing and screening for new recruits. Prior to this, hiring was pretty much left to the discretion of the local inspectors, subject of course, to the usual background checks for criminal records. A new recruit might be on the job for several months before getting any classroom instruction.

At the time, it was not uncommon to find women showing an interest in pursuing career opportunities with the police. Historically, many police forces in Canada had a few female officers on staff to deal primarily with the detention of female prisoners and some juvenile offenders. The women did not do routine police work. As early as 1912, Annie May Jackson had become Canada's first female police constable when the Edmonton Police Department hired her to work with young women immigrants to Canada who had been recruited into prostitution. Her task, as outlined by the Department, was to uphold "high morals and manners."

However, societal pressures in the mid-1970s led the RCMP to hire females and assign them to the same duties as their male counterparts. Slowly, other police agencies adopted the same practice.

Susan MacLeod, the first female constable hired by Canadian Pacific, was received with amused curiosity and unquestioned support.

While the CP's Department of Investigation traditionally had been reluctant to hire female constables because of safety concerns in the railyards, by the mid-1980s, when the railway police were recruiting for a new training class, Chief Mickel agreed that females could be hired as long as the Department's qualifying standards were met.

Sue MacLeod was one such woman, who, while studying at the University of Toronto, worked part time as a member of the Scarborough campus security team for special events.

"One of the campus police officers was a man named Jim, who had worked with the CP Police," MacLeod (now Layton) said, while reminiscing about those days. "I had planned on applying to police services right after graduation and he suggested CP Police," she said. "Jim spoke highly of the organization and told me about his former duties. I hadn't realized that the railways employed their own police personnel. It sounded interesting, so I applied."

In April 1987, MacLeod became the first female constable employed by CP's Department of Investigation. She was assigned to the Toronto Detachment.

"Introducing a new dynamic to a traditional work environment always requires an adjustment period, and my early days with CP called for some give and take on both sides," MacLeod said. "My change room was a large office-supply closet, and it took a while to convince headquarters that my uniform pants would require a different pattern than the men's trousers, but after that it was pretty smooth sailing.

"Gord Stinson was my training officer—a devoted husband and a great dad to his daughter," she said. "We often talked about how he would want his wife or daughter treated if they worked in non-traditional roles. He treated me with respect, and let me earn my confidence in my new career. His attitude toward me set the tone around the office and, I'm sure, made things easier for me than they might have been. The attitude of the rest of the railway ran from amused curiosity to unquestioned support."

Two years later, the CP's Department of Investigation was attracting additional female members. The next training class had five female applicants.

"When a police inspector from Canadian Pacific called me to ask if I would be interested in meeting to discuss a career with them, I was curious, flattered and intrigued," said Laurie Crittenden, who had initially applied for a position with the Vancouver Police Department (VPD).

"CP asked the VPD recruiting department for a list of prospective female applicants, as they too were recruiting," she said. "At the time, I felt this could lead to a fulfilling career, or at least give me some valuable experience I could take with me to a municipal police service."

As the Department of Investigation's first female member west of Winnipeg, Crittenden remembered in later years how her male counterparts adjusted to their new colleague.

"The majority of the members welcomed me without issue, particularly the younger ones who were familiar with female police officers," she said. "But some of the senior members were not excited about my presence. I learned that a spouse of one of our members did not want me working with her husband on graveyard shifts, as she had concerns."

In time, however, female officers were accepted by the department, the company and the public.

"If I had any problems with the public," MacLeod said, "it was because they weren't aware that the railways had their own police services."

Under James Mickel's leadership, the railway police also put in place a process for formally testing the potential of its members. This provided the Department with a list of candidates for promotion from the uniform branch to the investigative side.

Mickel was both liked and respected by his men.

Chief James M. Mickel

BETTER TRAINING AND EQUIPMENT

Following Chief Legault's short tenure, James Mickel was appointed head of the CP's investigation department on November 1, 1982. He, too, would have a relatively short term as chief, but, like Legault he was a respected career policeman who won people over with kindness and strength of character as much as he did through experience.

Born April 25, 1923, Mickel was raised and educated in Bathgate, Scotland. From 1942 to 1946, he served as an air mechanic with the Royal Navy, Fleet Air Arm. In April, 1946, he left the Navy to join the Edinburgh City Police. In February 1952, he came to Canada to sign up with the Canadian Pacific's railway police.

Mickel joined the Department of Investigation on March 3, 1952, as a constable. He was assigned to Vancouver, where, four years later, he was appointed investigator. In that role, he was posted to Banff Springs Hotel security duty for a period, as well as to the Edmonton area. On August 1, 1969, Mickel was promoted to sub-inspector at Ottawa, and within months was sent to Calgary. He became inspector at Vancouver in 1971 and staff inspector at headquarters in Montreal in 1973.

Liked and respected by members of the Department and CP management alike, Mickel was appointed assistant to the chief on December 1, 1973, assistant chief on July 1, 1979; deputy chief on September 1, 1981 and chief on November 1, 1982.

During Mickel's tenure, the training of recruits was centralized at Winnipeg and its length doubled. He also instituted a tough pre-employment review and appraisal program to ensure the quality of new recruits. Investigators continued to attend additional training sessions at the Canadian Police College in Ottawa.

Anticipating the growing value of new communications technologies for police officers in the field, Mickel made improvements across the board to the Force's phone, radio and computer systems, and made sure his officers were well-versed in their use.

"Our constables work alone and they must be able to call for assistance if they need help," he said, shortly after taking command of the railway police. "We feel that with better training and equipment the Force will become even more efficient."

Mickel retired in 1988.

On February 25, 1983, a shop owner in Montreal's Château Champlain reported a man causing a disturbance in her store and frightening customers. The hotel's chief security officer (CSO), Investigator Ralph Boulet of the CP's Department of Investigation, found the man in the lobby dressed as a rabbi, talking and singing to himself and appearing disoriented.

Boulet escorted the man to the security office located right behind the front desk and awaited the arrival of the Montreal Police, who had been called by the hotel's assistant chief security officer.

Under questioning the man's mood became threatening and he pulled a small revolver from his pocket which he aimed at the CSO's head. The officer who was seated behind his desk, believing he was about to be shot, threw himself to one side, drew his .32 Colt service revolver and fired twice.

One shot missed and went through the wall, where it struck the hotel's assistant manager in the back. The other struck the suspect in the right side of the neck.

"It's only a lighter," the wounded man yelled, pulling the trigger and getting a flame from the barrel.

The suspect was taken to hospital, treated for his wound and held for psychiatric observation. The assistant hotel manager had a large bruise on his back, but was otherwise unharmed by the small calibre round and the dampening effect of the hotel wall. Both the Montreal

Police and the Department of Investigation investigated the shooting and Boulet was cleared as he had no idea at the time of the incident that the gun pointing at him was a fake.

The 1980s also saw a brief renewal of bombing incidents in British Columbia. RCMP in the Kootenays investigated two explosions and the discovery of several undetonated bombs in April 1984. One blast blew a B.C. Telephone Company utility pole from its base in the early hours of the morning. Around the same time, a section of CP Rail track at Christina Lake, 22 miles east of Grand Forks, B.C., was blown up. Investigators found that dynamite and a timing mechanism had been used in that incident.

On May 1, a CP Rail track patrolman discovered a homemade bomb near the railway at Brilliant, B.C., the former headquarters of murdered Doukhobor leader, Peter "The Lordly" Verigin. Within three hours the RCMP bomb squad from Vancouver had arrived to detonate the explosive.

Extensive inquiries headed by Robin Bourne, British Columbia's assistant deputy minister of police services, were held but no charges were laid in the bombing incidents.

In Calgary, that same summer, a double killer on the run from the minimum security prison in Cowansville, Quebec was grabbed by two CP police constables. Paul Ringuette and his girlfriend, Naomi Brockman, had stepped off a Vancouver bound Via Rail train about two hours earlier and had entered the Stampede Boot & Jean store in Calgary's Palliser Square Mall. In the Western gear shop, staff saw the couple steal two pairs of jeans and a belt buckle.

When they left, a store clerk alerted mall security officials and, minutes later, the pair was arrested by the railway police. By the end of the week, Quebec Provincial Police had sent officers west to escort Ringuette back to prison. He'd been on the run since February 17, when he'd slipped an escort while visiting his mother on a "humanitarian" eight hour pass. He'd been serving a 17-year sentence for the involuntary manslaughter of a fellow prisoner at the Laval maximum security pen in Quebec. A former Hell's Angel, Ringuette had been in Laval for a previous manslaughter conviction.

A QPP spokesman lauded the efforts of the CP constables, calling Ringuette "a bad dude."

As distressing as those bombing incidents and encounters with convicted killers were, however, the CP Air detachment of the railway police was about to be enmeshed in the investigation of Canada's most infamous bombing and largest mass murder.

In the early morning of June 23, 1985, Air India Flight 182 departed Montreal's Mirabel International Airport for London's Heathrow Airport en route to Delhi and Bombay in India. Shortly after 7:00 a.m., while still about 190 kilometres offshore of County Cork in southwest Ireland, radio transmissions ceased and the plane disappeared from air traffic control radar screens.

The wreckage of the Boeing 747 Jumbo Jet and many bodies were soon discovered floating in the ocean. India's minister of civil aviation announced the possibility that the plane had been downed by a bomb. The ill-fated plane was carrying luggage from connecting CP Air Flight 60 originating in Vancouver. All 329 passengers and crew members were killed.

Less than an hour after the disappearance of Flight 182, on the other side of the world a massive explosion tore through the terminal at Tokyo's Narita Airport, killing two baggage handlers and injuring four others. The blast was traced to a suitcase that had just been removed from CP Air Flight 003, arriving from Vancouver. It was due to be transferred to Air India Flight 301.

Somebody in Vancouver was targeting Air India planes and it was beginning to look as if CP Air was being used to deliver the lethal blows.

The subsequent investigations carried on largely by a task force consisting of RCMP and Canadian Security Intelligence Service (CSIS) members, lasted nearly 20 years and at over $130 million, were the most costly in Canadian history. The main role of the CP Air detachment of the Department of Investigation was to act as liaison between the airline and the task force. Descending on the airline's audit department, the CP Police sifted through hundreds of tickets looking for the names of specific suspects. One CP officer, Inspector Cliff Hooper, accompanied RCMP officers to Tokyo to assist the Japanese Police with investigations there.

Much of the suspicion was focused on the Babbar Khalsa, a militant Sikh group whose members advocated violence to achieve their aim of an independent Sikh homeland in India's Punjab state.

Mobile investigation kits included photographic and fingerprinting equipment.

Interviews with CP Air employees centred on reservations and cancellations at the airline's Vancouver ticket offices in the days leading up to the disaster. Reservations agent Martine Donahue was questioned about an unaccompanied bag which was checked through to Narita Airport by a passenger who failed to show up for the flight; ticket clerk Gerald Duncan was grilled under hypnosis in an attempt by police to shake loose details about a suspect who had picked up tickets at Duncan's counter; and passenger clerk Jeannie Adams recalled arguing with a passenger over a request to interline a Samsonite suitcase through to Delhi, India.

Investigations of the blast in Tokyo established that a bomb had been rigged in a Sanyo stereo tuner that had been shipped by the manufacturer to a Vancouver retailer. The RCMP, assigning more than 135 officers to check every outlet where Sanyo tuners were available, discovered a recent sale to mechanic Inderjit Singh Reyat of Duncan, B.C. The searches turned up not only a receipt for a Sanyo tuner Model FMT-611K with his name and phone number on it, but also evidence of other bomb components he had purchased.

By January 1986, investigators with the Canadian Aviation Safety Board had determined conclusively that Air India Flight 182 had been downed by an explosion in the forward cargo. The report concluded that the bomb had originated in the Vancouver area and had been aboard CP Air Flight 60 prior to being placed on the Air India flight to eternity.

The task force conducted an exhaustive series of searches, wiretaps and interviews with airline employees, passengers and members of the Sikh community. Slowly a picture of the bombings emerged as a joint plot of at least two Sikh terrorist groups with extensive membership in the B.C. interior. Their lust for revenge had been precipitated by the bloody June 1984 assault by the government of India on Sikhism's most important and sacred edifice, the Golden Temple of Amritsar.

Nevertheless, the huge international scope of the investigations and the close-knit and secretive nature of the Sikh community in

Canada and abroad, led to much confusion and delays in bringing charges against any of the suspects.

Fifteen years later, on June 6, 2001, RCMP officers finally arrested Reyat on charges of murder, attempted murder and conspiracy in the Air India bombing. In February 2003, Reyat pleaded guilty to one count of manslaughter and to charges of aiding in the construction of a bomb.

Two other prominent members of the Sikh community with ties to the Babbar Khalsa—Ripubaman Singh Malik and Agaib Singh Bagri—were also brought to trial on suspicions of having orchestrated the bombings. However, on March 16, 2005, for lack of indisputable evidence, Justice Ian Josephson found the two accused "not guilty on all counts."

Within a year, an indictment was filed in the Supreme Court of British Columbia, listing 27 instances where Inderjit Singh Reyat allegedly misled the court during his testimony. While he had pleaded guilty to making the bomb, he absolutely denied any knowledge of a conspiracy.

"I find him to be an unmitigated liar under oath," said Justice Josephson at the first of Reyat's subsequent perjury trials. "Even the most sympathetic of listeners could only conclude, as do I, that his evidence was patently and pathetically fabricated in an attempt to minimize his involvement in his crime to an extreme degree, while refusing to reveal relevant information he clearly possesses."

On September 19, 2010, Reyat was convicted of perjury, and shortly thereafter, sentenced to nine years in prison.

In response to the Air India bombing and other terrorist attacks against airlines around the world, CP Air began the now universal practice of X-raying baggage before placing it on board aircraft. Interlining bags for international flights is no longer permitted. Personal luggage must be picked up by passengers after the first leg of a trip and carried through security before it is loaded onto a flight to another country.

Canadian Pacific Air Lines (as CP Air was renamed) was sold to Calgary-based Pacific Western Airlines in 1987. Many of the police officers with the airline detachment were offered security jobs with the new owners, but most were more than happy to forsake policing the skies and return to the more familiar railway beat.

Meanwhile, the Loyalist City of Saint John, New Brunswick, the Department of Investigation's most easterly post, celebrated its bicentennial in 1985. Saint John is home to the first and oldest municipal police force in the nation.

The CP Rail main line ran westward from Saint John for nearly 600 kilometres to Lac Megantic, Quebec, through the State of Maine including a stretch along the southwestern border of Canadian Forces Base Gagetown, the largest military base in North America. It was the responsibility of the Saint John detachment of the railway police to patrol all subdivisions in the Maritime Provinces, plus to keep an eye on the activities at subsidiary companies of Canadian Pacific Limited in the Atlantic Region. In addition, the detachment also served the company's rail, truck, hotel and telecommunications interests in Nova Scotia, Prince Edward Island and Newfoundland when requested to do so.

Over the years, the Department of Investigation had personnel stationed at various points in Nova Scotia including a constable at Digby, an investigator at Kentville, and other members at CP Hotels and CP Air in Halifax, and CP Express and Transport in Dartmouth. All of these positions were eventually phased out. The sale of CP Air and operational changes at CP Hotels and CP Express & Transport further reduced the number of police officers required on the east coast.

Changes in world shipping patterns reduced the number of large container vessels calling at the Port of Saint John. The last Canadian Pacific ferry, *Princess of Acadia*, which sailed from Saint John to Digby, Nova Scotia, had been conveyed to CN Marine in 1976.

CP Rail also owned 50% of Brunterm Limited's container operation at the Port of Saint John. This property was patrolled by members of the Department of Investigation. No longer were 30 extra members needed every year during the winter shipping season from November to April. Modern technology and icebreakers had ended all that. Shipping lines, including CP Ships, had begun to use St. Lawrence River ports at all times of the year, and what had once seemed like dreadful winter duty to many a railway policeman came to an end.

On September 1, 1988, CP Rail set up a separate business unit in Saint John, called Canadian Atlantic Railway (CAR). Within a decade, it too, would be severed from the CP Rail System due to changing economic and transportation patterns.

The force was then under the leadership of Chief Keith Leavitt. At the time, superintendents were based in the Eastern and Atlantic regions to coordinate police activities at a more local level. A third superintendent, located in Vancouver had responsibility for the Prairie and Pacific regions. Under Leavitt, police training at Canadian Pacific remained vigorous and stayed consistent with provincial policing standards.

Like the proverbial "cop on the beat," the railway constable was still responsible for most of the legwork. More than 150 officers were required to patrol Canadian Pacific's properties across the country. In the course of doing their duty, any number of incidents could, and did, occur. They were called upon to settle disputes, man checkpoints, control vehicle traffic, evict trespassers, inspect freight shipments, and secure buildings and premises. During quiet periods there was the inevitable paperwork to attend to. Each officer had to file "occurrence sheets" in the event of any untoward incident that required his attention.

"I've been with the Company for five years now, in Saint John, Calgary and, lately, Montreal," said CP Constable Peter De Long at the time, "and I can tell you that Montreal is where the action is. But no matter where you are stationed, the Department's concerns are the same: theft and vandalism."

In those days the favourite items to steal were VCRs and microwave ovens, and the thieves were extremely adept at inventing new ways to ply their trade. The value of goods stolen often reached tens of thousands of dollars a year, but a large percentage was recovered through good investigative techniques.

Along with thieves, transients were a source of headaches for the Department. In 1987, a couple of vagrants from California were caught hanging around a railyard in Montreal, recalled CP Constable Jean-Guy Hebert. One man had hopped freight trains all the way from South America.

"These guys are basically harmless," he said. "They just keep moving further and further north in search of work. All we can do is turn them over to the immigration people and let them handle it from there."

In 1990, CP acquired 100% of the common stock in Soo Line Corporation in the United States.

As early as 1883, several directors of the Canadian Pacific Railway had helped build the Minneapolis, St. Paul & Sault Ste Marie, the railroad that would ultimately form the basis of the CPR's wholly owned Soo Line south of the Canada–U.S. border. The value of the relationship was further enhanced when the Soo Line entered the Chicago market in 1909. Famous name trains like *The Mountaineer* and *The Soo-Dominion* would go on to carry thousands of tourists and other travelers from the Windy City and the Twin Cities of Minneapolis and St. Paul to resorts in the Canadian Rockies, and on to Vancouver and the west coast.

The cross border connections provided by the Soo Line at Emerson, Manitoba, and North Portal, Saskatchewan, extended CP's reach into the upper U.S. Midwest. The number of people in the seven U.S. states through which the Soo operates is about 36 million, several million more than the entire population of Canada. That sort of density means industry, head-to-head competition from other freight carriers, and inevitably, crime.

Milwaukee railway police looked like British bobbies with a hint of the wild west.

Early in November 1990, just after the first snowfall in Moose Jaw, Saskatchewan, CP Investigator Gordie Wharf and Constable Wayne McBride responded to a call about a suspected illegal alien.

Policing the Rails in the U. S. Midwest

Few official records have survived to corroborate near-forgotten stories about railway police shootouts with gang members on the south and west sides of Chicago, but local officers and members of the public still pay annual tribute to two Milwaukee Railroad policemen who died on April 14, 1893. The officers, Jake Frith and Henry Talcott, were shot and killed while attempting to remove transients from a passenger coach in the railyards at Dubuque, Iowa. They are the only known fatalities among the men who served the police forces of the Canadian Pacific Railway, the Soo Line and its predecessors in the United States.

When the Milwaukee Road merged with the Soo Line Corporation in 1986, most of the police officers from the former railroad accepted buyouts from their new corporate bosses—fourteen stayed on in a somewhat less formal department than they were used to. Jimmy Tubbs, who had signed up with the Soo police a decade earlier, recalled in later years the loose environment prevalent at the time:

I started with Soo Line Railroad Police in September 1976 as a special agent. I was issued a tin badge, which looked like it came out of a Cracker Jack box, and I signed a card stating that I was officially a railroad policeman. I received no training whatsoever and never went to the police academy. I bought a Colt Trooper Mark III .357 Magnum at Bell's Gun Shop in Franklin Park [a suburb of Chicago] and had to learn to shoot it myself. My duties were to inspect and protect trains, enforce [no] trespassing, make arrests and attend court. My territory was the Chicago metro area and sometimes Wisconsin. I worked with Bill Bodecker and Claude Matula on occasion, but for the most part I worked alone after the first two or three weeks.

In 1990, when the CPR acquired full ownership of the Soo Line, all of the railway police from the U.S. railroad were plainclothes officers. They are now part of a North American force, uniformed and non-uniformed, responsible for railway police operations in six Canadian provinces and fourteen U.S. states.

In the United States, members are fully commissioned police officers within the state in which they operate, empowered by that state to enforce the law. The extent, to which they may exercise their law enforcement authority, as well as the precise definition of their jurisdiction, varies from state to state.

Having learned that the individual had crossed the American border undetected at North Portal, the two police officers subsequently arrested the man under the Immigration Act and accompanied him to a cell in the Moose Jaw police station.

During questioning it became apparent that the man was missing all four fingers on his right hand, perhaps due to some industrial accident; he was not prepared to elaborate. When the man was strip searched by Moose Jaw police, he was found to have a small pouch tied around his neck. Asked what was in the pouch, he stated, "my fingers."

Obviously skeptical, Investigator Wharf had to look for himself. Removing the pouch from the man and opening it, the investigator exclaimed, "Well damn, they are his fingers." It was just one more strange incident for the railway police.

Police training at Canadian Pacific was as vigorous as ever and consistent with provincial policing standards. As CP Sergeant Jack Ridge explained to a CPR reporter, "Recruits are issued handguns and undergo strict training at the RCMP training centre in Winnipeg. They also attend an intensive course on the proper use of their nightsticks (no longer a simple club, but a sophisticated and formidable weapon), as well as courses in first aid. It used to be that you had to be six feet tall and three hundred pounds to be an effective police officer," Sergeant Ridge said, "but today the emphasis is on training and common sense."

With more and more of their working hours dedicated to public relations activities and addressing the new scourge of rampant drug use in the workplace, constables were replaced on routine patrols of Canadian Pacific headquarters at Montreal's Windsor Station by a new squad of security guards.

During the weekends and after work hours, the security guards patrolled every floor to protect records and costly equipment. On their rounds, a total of 52 punches had to be recorded on a time clock, a process which took about two hours. The footsteps required for a complete circuit was the equivalent of a two mile walk.

During regular work days, the security guards assisted people who were lost or wandering about, and ensured that all employees and visitors experienced a safe environment, protected from undue threats. They controlled the main station entrance and the two parking lots and monitored secondary entrances through a sophisticated network of 22 cameras. The guards also answered emergency phone lines in the station and initiated actions or responses where necessary.

Out on the property, CP Investigator Jack Rombs and road foreman of engines Dave Armitage put together a safety program that included the main messages of Operation Lifesaver which they shared with local schools with great success. Safety talks were held in a CP conference room in Kamloops, B.C., followed by a video and a tour of the railway offices and local yard areas. Investigator Rombs was a member of Central Interior Fraud Investigators and Okanagan District Fraud Investigators, two police organizations that shared information on known criminals.

On February 16, 1991, Rombs and fellow CP investigator Steve Gregoris set up surveillance in the CP Rail yard at North Bend, B.C., in response to numerous break-ins to trailers and container traffic. Rombs took up a vantage point above the yard and observed three youths coming out of the bush on the opposite side of the tracks from where he stood. Notifying Gregoris by radio of an imminent incident, Rombs saw the suspects proceed to break into a trailer on one of the stationary trains.

Within minutes Investigator Gregoris, CN Special Agent L. McCloskey who happened to be in the area, and Corporal M. Thompson of the RCMP detachment from Boston Bar, B.C., were directed by Rombs to the scene of the crime. The trio was successful in apprehending one of the three thieves almost immediately after a short but vigorous chase on foot up a nearby mountain. A second suspect was arrested soon after at his own residence and the third turned himself into the local RCMP station.

The offenders provided statements to police admitting responsibility for at least six unsolved thefts in Department of Investigation files, two CN Police cases, and numerous others still on the books in RCMP files in Boston Bar and North Bend. After the arrest, crimes in the area against both CP and CN all but ceased.

In 1991, the CPR purchased the Delaware & Hudson Railway for $25 million, giving its transcontinental system a connection between Montreal and the greater New York City metropolitan area. The D&H Police Service was absorbed by the Canadian Pacific Police. A superintendent of police was assigned to Clifton Park and CP detachments were retained in the newly designated D&H District at Clifton Park, Binghamton, Albany, Oneonta and Buffalo, all in New York, and in Taylor, Pennsylvania.

The expanded network created by the D&H in connection with CP Rail and the Soo Line was renamed the CP Rail System for marketing purposes.

Another step the railway police took to remain relevant under Leavitt's leadership was getting connected to the Canadian Police Information Centre (CPIC) operated by the RCMP.

"This nationwide police information system provided our members with instant access to criminal records," Leavitt said in later years. "We applied to be connected, and we were accepted. As a result we had several terminals installed across the country from which we could access CPIC, and we started to use laptop computers in our patrol cars."

The cars were also equipped with air conditioning, a rarity for police cars in those days.

Leavitt's proudest achievement, however, was getting wages for the constables and sergeants of the uniformed branch back on par with most police salaries in Canada.

"From 1972, when the union negotiated its first contract with the Department of Investigation, wage increases for constables and sergeants were in lockstep with CP's other non-operating unions," Leavitt said. "Unfortunately, during this period, wages in the public police community increased at a greater rate than the railway non-operating unions, which meant that the wages of our staff were falling behind. By 1989, our senior constables were at about $37,500 a year, while the average annual salary in the police community was about $40,000. We were, however, able to compensate our non-unionized

Policing the Delaware & Hudson

The Delaware & Hudson is the oldest continuously operated transportation company in North America and one of the first to organize an official police department.

In 1823, it started operations as a canal company. Six years later, it entered the railroad business and in 1840 it became the first transportation company to be traded on the New York Stock Exchange.

In 1907, D&H extended its railway lines into Canada to connect with Canadian Pacific at Delson, Quebec. Known as "The Bridge Line," the D&H gave the CPR access to other Class 1 railways in the U.S. northeast, as well as access to markets in and around New York City.

Following a decline in industrial traffic in the U.S. northeast and the inability of a succession of rail interests to make a go of it, CP acquired the D&H in 1991 and has since spent well over $200 million on infrastructure improvements.

As early as the summer of 1885, a Delaware & Hudson superintendent recruited a crossing gate tender from Saratoga, New York, to don a blue uniform as the railway's first police officer. In taking up his new duties, Arthur O. Lee was issued a felt helmet, a night stick and a .32 calibre revolver, and instructed to "keep order" at the D&H's busy rail passenger station in Saratoga.

By summer's end, Lee had been made a plainclothes detective in the local yard, sometimes taking on the role of yard clerk or yardmaster along with his policing duties.

L. F. Loree, the innovative superintendent who was Lee's chief sponsor went on to become general manager of the D&H and eventually achieved the presidency. Following up on his own initiative to provide security for the railroad's customers, employees and fixed assets, Loree established a full-fledged police force for the Company. On February 1, 1908, the Delaware & Hudson Police Department was launched. The department's charter listed its duties:

The D&H Police was known as an efficient force with high morale.

To protect the property of the company against carelessness, negligence, malicious mischief, depredations, and fire; to guard travelers against pick pockets, thieves and gamblers; to guard the traffic from theft and "loss or damage"; to assist in gathering facts in cases of personal injury or other claims; to preserve order upon the premises of the company and upon its trains; to aid in quelling disturbances that might arise; and to uphold and enforce the law in so far as the company's interest might be involved.

In the ensuing years, the police force expanded to take responsibility for the entire D&H property, increasing and systematically organizing the roles of its members. By December 31, 1921, there were more than 100 employees in the police ranks. The Department's structure consisted of a superintendent, inspectors, captains, lieutenants, patrolmen and watchmen. The superintendent, holding the rank of major, was in charge, with the inspectors reporting to and receiving their instructions from him and acting as his assistants.

On February 16, 1928, 42 prospective recruits for the Department were among the graduates of the Sixth New York State Police School in Troy, N.Y. Other students in that class became New York State troopers and members of the state police in West Virginia and Maryland.

Each year from the 1920s through the 1950s, the superintendent of the D&H Police would bring all of his 80 to 100 uniformed members to Albany, N.Y., for an annual military inspection. On May 18, 1932, United States Army colonel, John Franklin, presided over one such inspection.

"It doesn't take a military man to realize that this is an efficient force," Franklin told the assembled officers. "It is obviously well-equipped, neatly dressed, and made up of individuals who are intelligent and highly disciplined, all of which go to produce an efficient personnel. Your corporation is to be congratulated on having such a force, so well-equipped, and of so high a morale."

That same year, more than 900 arrests were made by D&H police officers with convictions obtained in 95% of the cases.

Right up until the late 1950s, the Delaware & Hudson Police maintained four divisional pistol teams and three divisional rifle teams with as many as eight officers per team. Travelling nationwide from 1927 to 1935, the D&H teams were known as "the best in the east," and were widely recognized as among the best small bore shooting clubs in the nation.

Today, many of the Canadian Pacific police officers assigned to the former D&H territory in the U.S. northeast have a background in municipal law enforcement and are graduates of state mandated municipal police training academies, many holding university degrees in criminal justice. Each candidate also must pass an extensive background check; each having been commissioned by the state in which he or she is employed.

The D&H's former system headquarters located in Oneonta, N.Y., is now a strategic CP Police detachment. The duties of U.S. members of the Department are similar to those of their Canadian counterparts including, to name a few, the investigation of theft from interstate shipments, suppression of trespassing (often involving illegal aliens), vandalism, and controlling the scene at railroad related accidents.

staff—investigators, inspectors and superintendents—at rates that were competitive.

"Needless to say, this caused discontent, and understandably so. In my first two years as chief, we had about fifteen or sixteen constables resign and at least twelve of them went to public police forces."

Leavitt made the case to the Canadian Pacific's senior management to address the wage discrepancy of the railway's uniformed officers vis-à-vis the public police and, in 1992 his request was approved. Over the next three years, the salaries of the uniformed branch were brought into line with public police wages.

During the early 1990s, the Canadian Association of Chiefs of Police (CACP) embarked upon a ten-year plan to produce and provide educational materials to promote lifestyles free of illegal drugs among elementary school students. With the aid of a committee of educators, health professionals, addiction research groups and various government agencies, the CACP chose a comic book as the vehicle for getting its message out.

With the good graces of Marvel Comics of New York, and the services of the firm's ever popular comic book character, Spider-Man, police constables across the country now had a winning tool with which to engage adolescents and pre-adolescents about the perils of illicit drugs. By the end of 1991, most schools in Canada had benefitted from the program with more than one and a half million anti-drug comic books being handed out to children and young people.

"Experts agree that scare tactics do not convince children to lead drug-free lives," said the promotional materials for the program. "However, they do agree that reinforcing positive lifestyles can keep a child away from drugs. For centuries, children have looked up to heroes. Today many heroes (i.e., rock stars and sports celebrities) are sending children a mixed message; that is why the CACP have chosen to use Spider-Man, an all-time favorite, to teach the children positive lifestyles."

In 1992, the railway police took inter-agency cooperation from the classroom to the street when they partnered with the Metropolitan Toronto Police Department (MTPD) to thwart a gang of thieves targeting a trailer full of Rothman's cigarettes valued at more than $2 million.

At the time, the CP's Department of Investigation had Investigator Ken Lackey assigned full time to the Company's intermodal operations in Toronto. When MTPD received a tip from an informant about an impending truck hijacking, Lackey called for assistance from four CP officers—Gerry Fish, Glen Taber, Steve Lord and Gord Stinson—working on a drug case in a nearby Ontario town.

On June 25, the MTPD put one of their officers in a tractor pulling a cigarette load from the Canadian Pacific's Obico Yard in Toronto to the Rothman facility in Brampton, Ontario. Meanwhile the five CP policemen, who had now been joined by CP Investigator Ric Ladouceur and several Toronto police officers monitored the gang's conversations on rented radios and tailed the shipment in unmarked rental cars.

The police were also watching seven gang members who were following the cigarette load in four different vehicles, including a five-ton truck.

The thieves were nervous and allowed the load to reach the

Rothman plant, but when one of the CP officers radioed the truck driver to exit the facility and drive down Highway 71, the would-be hijackers took the bait. A few miles down the road, one of the gang members hopped into the tractor at a stoplight and pulled a handgun on the driver. His accomplices closed in to assist.

Within minutes, rental cars full of policemen were flying across all four lanes of the highway.

"We screeched to a stop and rushed the suspects' vehicles," said CP Investigator Gerry Fish.

> *Our guns were drawn and we were yelling commands like, 'Out of the truck, you're under arrest,' that kind of thing— and they were really quite frightened by it all.*
>
> *Six of them gave up immediately. It turned out they had one gun between them. The MTPD officer easily took control of the situation in the tractor cab, disarming the gunman beside him in the confusion. The last gang member tried to evade capture by accelerating his vehicle directly at the MTPD sergeant who was by then standing on the road. If our guy, Glen Taber, hadn't come flying out of a side street in a rented Crown Victoria, and T-boned the bad guy just before he hit the sergeant, who knows? In my view, he saved the sergeant's life.*

That particular bad guy and all of his buddies got more than two years each.

Still, despite its solid record and ongoing success, the Department of Investigation was constantly under pressure to prove its worth to the Canadian Pacific's executive committee. That, coupled with the strain on individual officers as the force shed members, led to some resentment among the railway police—and to mixed feelings about large public showings of support for other law enforcement agencies, however friendly.

During Canada Day festivities in 1995, Canadian Pacific Limited announced it had reinforced its close relationship of more than a century with the RCMP by becoming the first national sponsor of the red coated force's Musical Ride, a world-renowned exposition of

Not everybody in the department was happy with RCMP sponsorship, given the severe budget cuts imposed on the railway police.

equestrian prowess performed by an elite corps of RCMP officers.

Ken Benson, vice president of personnel and administration for CP Limited; Hugh MacDiarmid, executive vice president of CP Rail System; Keith Leavitt, CP's chief of police; and William Mulholland, a director of both the Canadian Pacific and the Mounted Police Foundation, participated in a ceremony that took place before an evening performance of the Ride in Calgary.

"It is an understatement to say how proud and delighted we are to be joining together in what we are sure will be a long and mutually rewarding relationship with the Mounted Police Foundation and the RCMP in support of their community policing programs throughout Canada," Benson said. "The linkage between Canadian Pacific and the RCMP is not only historic, it is also wholly natural."

The cooperative nature of the relationship was shown once again

Chief R. Keith Leavitt

KEEPING IT RELEVANT

The Canadian Pacific's ninth chief of police, Keith Leavitt, was born August 22, 1936, at Saint-Basile-le-Grand, Quebec.

Leavitt entered Canadian Pacific's service on February 4, 1956, as a locomotive fireman, but within a couple of years he caught the policing bug and transferred to the Department of Investigation. As a constable and later as an investigator, he was assigned to Montreal. He also spent three winters with CP Ships at their winter port in Saint John, New Brunswick, before being named sub-inspector there on January 1, 1975. He was promoted to Inspector on February 1, 1978, at Montreal and superintendent September 1, 1982, in Toronto.

On August 1, 1985, Leavitt was appointed superintendent (System). A year and a half later, he was assistant chief of the railway police. On September 1, 1987, he was elevated to deputy chief and on May 1, 1988, he became chief.

Leavitt's priority was to keep the Department of Investigation relevant. One of the steps he took to ensure this was to continue the excellent training programs implemented by his predecessor, Jim Mickel. This training was essential, not only to improve the skills of the Department's members, but also to maintain credibility in the greater police community.

Officer safety was one of the chief's main concerns, and one that he knew had great potential for affecting morale. To ensure his officers were as secure as possible on the job, he obtained bulletproof vests for them and exchanged their outdated six-shot revolvers for the nine millimetre pistols that are now standard issue among police forces in Canada.

Leavitt retired June 1, 1996.

Leavitt emphasized training and the development of skills.

a few weeks later at the Calgary Stampede, where members of the CP Police attended the Musical Ride and were on hand to promote railway safety.

That same year, to reduce costs and put more officers on the road, the railway police—now officially known as the Canadian Pacific Police Service—chose to centralize police dispatching for eastern Ontario and Quebec at the Montreal detachment. Communications equipment, databases, telephone and voice data recording equipment were upgraded and policies put in place for dispatch constables in Montreal to handle calls.

In July 1996, the Montreal Communications Centre began fielding calls and dispatching officers to and from locations in Ontario and Quebec. Detachments in western Canada handled most of their own communications logistics, though some calls received during the night automatically would be forwarded to the Communication Centre.

The absorption of the police staff of the Soo Line and the Delaware & Hudson in 1990 and 1991 had added 31 members to the CP's Department of Investigation, but budget cuts continued to eat away at overall staff levels. A major reorganization in 1995 dropped 100 members from its roster of 340. When the Canadian Pacific reorganized its entire structure and moved its head office to Calgary in 1996, the railway police lost another 70 members.

CHAPTER 10
The Beat Goes On:
A Fresh Approach
to Policing

Much changed for CP's police department with Canadian Pacific Limited's momentous corporate decision to move headquarter operations to Calgary in 1996, the largest head office relocation in Canadian history.

The Canadian Pacific Police Service (CPPS) also relocated its management to Calgary. Chief Leavitt retired and Gerry Moody was appointed to the top post.

More budget reductions ordered by the railway's executive committee once again resulted in a significant downsizing of staff. The position of deputy chief was abolished along with those of the three regional superintendents across the country. Inspectors at each major detachment now reported to a System superintendent at headquarters.

"I didn't abolish the uniform branch, as suggested by the executive committee," Chief Moody said, "because it would have been a mistake. I was able to convince senior management that high-profile, proactive, uniformed police patrols were an effective deterrent to crime. Of course, I still had to meet the severe budget reductions imposed on me and work toward a new structure for CPPS. Department heads were given a mandate to have only five levels in their departments. For us that meant chief, superintendent, inspector, sergeant and constable.

Calgary Mayor Al Duerr welcomes CP employees and their families to Calgary during a street party in front of Gulf Canada Square.

"In 1996, we started with a thirty percent cut to our staff; over the next few months more than seventy additional positions were abolished. It was devastating."

With the reorganization of both the company and the police force, and the inevitable search for additional cost savings, Moody elected to outsource the dispatch function of the Communication Centre. He was, however, adamant about maintaining a high standard of service.

CP Inspector Brian Taupier put together a comprehensive package of standards and qualifications. After a screening process which ensured the most competent candidates were selected, a professional training program was implemented by Sergeant-Detective David Larivière.

On a typical day, an employee of the Communication Centre might deal with calls related to theft of company property, signal malfunctions, unauthorized train riders or noise complaints.

"The types of calls we received were often fairly routine, but every call was a challenge; it was never boring," said new recruit Bob Parent.

For example, one call might be about a homeless man and his dog hopping a train or seeking food and shelter, while another call might be about an escaped convict hopping another train in an attempt to exit the United States and enter

Canada. Rarely were two calls alike.

I think the most common issue was trespassing—people who, intentionally or not, were walking along the tracks or right of way. This was always a safety concern and, on occasion, became an incident where the trespasser was struck and injured or killed by a train. In the latter case, we had to notify everyone from the local police department, fire and ambulance service to CP's public affairs and general claims people.

Regardless of the time of day or night, we also had to notify the chief of the CPPS. For the most part, there were two communicators on duty, so when one of us received a call like this, the other person on duty would pretty much have to handle all of the other calls for the next 30 or 40 minutes.

Over time, the communicators became comfortable in their new environment and were able to take on additional duties. Databases were upgraded and local street maps were added to enable them to handle more calls from the rest of Canada.

In most North American cities crime statistics had leveled off and, in many cases, had begun to wane. The hard economic realities of the 1990s compelled law enforcement agencies to do considerably more with less, but better communications, sophisticated technologies and a commitment to getting police officers back on the beat paid dividends.

Chief Moody emphasized the same kind of interaction between the police department and its parent company that characterized the recent CP reorganization: less red tape and fewer administrative hoops through which to jump. Though the number of officers on the police force had been trimmed from about 400 in 1971 to 235, and more cuts were expected, the railway police's focus on crime prevention brought them closer to their constituents—employees, shippers, management and the public.

"We're taking a very close look at our overall strategy," said Moody at the time. "As a professional organization, we are committed to meeting the police and security requirements of the railway, while recognizing the current realities and strategies of the company."

In 1995, CP Police had investigated more than 4,000 criminal offences, among them 328 break and enters, 69 switch tamperings,

Moody relocated the force from Montreal to Calgary, with Canadian Pacific's head office move.

Chief William Gerald Moody

DAYS OF DIFFICULT DOWNSIZING

Gerry Moody was born in Guelph, Ontario, on September 11, 1950, and raised in the village of Glen Williams, Ontario.

He graduated from Georgetown High School and took courses at Sheridan College.

Moody's uncle, and namesake, started his policing career with the Ontario Provincial Police (OPP), before serving as chief of police in a number of small towns in Ontario. He was a role model for Gerry, who soon resolved that police work was what he wanted to do as well.

Moody was a correctional officer at Mountain Prison in Aggassiz, B.C., when he resigned to sign up with Canadian Pacific as a constable in the Department of Investigation located in Toronto. Moving up through railway police ranks, he served as acting sergeant and investigator for Toronto Terminals, inspector in charge of personnel, and by April 1, 1988, regional inspector at Winnipeg.

A staff inspector in Montreal by 1990, he was promoted to superintendent, Atlantic Region, in 1994, and chief, effective June 1, 1996.

Chief Moody was a graduate of the Canadian Police College. He took much of his training in criminal investigation with the RCMP and the Ontario Provincial Police, graduating from the OPP program at Brampton College.

Moody's early career was highlighted by his involvement with staff training, not only leading the charge internally for high levels of professionalism, but often being called upon to give lectures to local groups and associations, as well as at the police academy.

In 1995, Moody was awarded the Alberta Centennial Medal for outstanding service to the people and Province of Alberta. That same year, he also received a certificate of commendation from director of the FBI, Robert S. Mueller, for his contributions to the U.S. National Joint Terrorist Task Force.

As head of the railway police, Moody was in charge of the department's move from Montreal to Calgary in 1996. There he devised a security plan for the company's new headquarters in Gulf Canada Square.

Faced with repeated calls from Canadian Pacific's executive committee for significant budget reductions, Moody benefitted from courses he attended at the Richard Ivey Business School, making formal presentations on various business models for his department to students and staff. He was the first chief to put together a formal business plan for the railway police, complete with key performance indicators.

A member of the Alberta Chiefs of Police, the Canadian Association of Chiefs of Police and the International Association of Chiefs of Police, Moody also served a term as president of the Railway Police Section of the International Association of Railway Police (IARP). The far-reaching mission of the latter organization was "to identify and resolve issues related to the protection of railway passengers, employees, property, equipment and freight in transit, and to strive to eliminate criminal activity throughout rail transportation systems worldwide."

In a bid to improve the productivity and efficiency of his members in the face of the significant downsizing that had been imposed on the police force, Moody was able to second a police officer for a year from the Ontario Police Services Board (OPSB) to audit existing policies and conduct a full environmental scan of the Department. In exchange, an officer from the CPPS spent a year with the OPSB closely observing and auditing several other forces' operations and procedures.

The bold initiative led to the CPPS being the first major freight railway in North America to be recognized by the Commission on Accreditation for Law Enforcement Agencies (CALEA) in 2002. This achievement gained kudos for Moody within Canadian Pacific and throughout the law enforcement community.

He is the recipient of both the 20 year Canadian Governor General's Police Exemplary Medal and its 30 year Bar.

Chief Moody retired March 1, 2008.

With officers in the United States and Canada, the work of the railway police crosses the international border nearly seamlessly.

276 incidents of signal vandalism, 208 track obstructions, 199 cases of vandalism, 148 instances of theft, 27 arson cases and, most alarmingly, 115 incidents where trains were shot at or stoned.

CP's railway police dealt with a wide range of criminal activity, but the greatest problems it faced were theft of goods in transit, theft of company property, fraud, and mischief. Theft, fraud and other criminal offences accounted for about $5.5 million in losses, a whopping figure by any standard, but one that was mitigated considerably by the more than $2 million of goods recovered through the diligence of the railway police.

The railway runs through many cities' most crime-ridden areas and much of the right of way is unfenced and difficult to patrol. Nevertheless, year-end results continued to show criminal activity remaining fairly consistent—up in some areas, down in others.

While Chief Moody was concerned about the deep cuts the railway police had to accept, he was optimistic that new, marked patrol cars equipped with computer terminals and a newly invigorated commitment

Rarely are these vehicles so clean as in this promotional shot.

to educating employees and the public about safety and crime prevention, would keep unwelcome statistics on a downward trend.

"There's a very positive benefit to just being seen out there on the property," he said. "I've had a lot of good feedback from employees and the police community about the new marked cars that are patrolling in Calgary, Toronto and Montreal. The traditional blue and white colour scheme identifies us as a mainstream police force, while the outline of a steam locomotive painted on the sides of the cars emphasizes our main area of responsibility at a glance."

To continuously improve its police and security services, CP Police also introduced a new toll free telephone number across Canada and the U.S. With the police contact number widely distributed and painted on crossbucks and signal huts across the system, any railway employee, government agency representative or member of the public with an immediate need to contact the railway police could now do so without delay.

The World Police and Fire Games were first organized in 1985 by members of the Southern California Police Athletic Association. Since that time, the event has been staged every two years in locales such as San Jose, San Diego, Vancouver, Memphis, Colorado Springs and Melbourne, Australia. Calgary was awarded the Games in 1997.

Canadian Pacific and the CP Police were front and centre throughout the international event in Canada, hosting the first ever Youth Games Day. More than 4,300 children and their parents came down to participate at Calgary's Olympic Oval—a legacy venue from the 1986 Winter Games. The railway safety display, model train layout and marked police vehicle were big hits with the young police and firefighter wannabes.

The railway's internal newspaper, *CP Rail News*, detailed the efforts of both the company's operating department and its police in keeping the trains running.

"An important part of our activities is to make the public, especially children, aware of the dangers in and around railway yards and tracks," said Chief Moody. "Our sponsorship of Youth Games Day gave us a special opportunity to reach out to young people in the community with this important safety message."

By the winter of 1997, however, the warm and fuzzy images of good corporate citizenship in the west were replaced in the east by very real pictures of a railway struggling to overcome the greatest operational crisis in its history. After two and a half days, unrelenting freezing rain imposed a mini ice age on the St. Lawrence & Hudson Railway (StL&H), the CPR's eastern North American operating subsidiary at the time. Utility poles and power lines were strewn across the right of way, tracks and switches were encased in ice and virtually all two-way radios, automatic signals, level crossing barriers and warning lights were out of commission.

At the height of the chaos, an unusual convoy of six CP Police patrol cars set off from Toronto on a relief mission.

"As they drove through the darkness, the landscape began to change," reported an article in Canadian Pacific Railway News. "East of Belleville, Ontario, ice-coated trees had shattered and split as though hit by artillery fire. Utility poles had toppled like

OVERLOAD: Communications facilities gave out under strain of days of accumulated ice.   Photo by Bill Hildebrand

StL&H and CPR forces in East overcome greatest operational crisis in railway's history

ROBERT STEWART
CORRESPONDENT

MONTREAL – Picture a railway with fallen trees, utility poles and live power lines strewn across the right-of-way, the track and switches completely coated in ice, no two-way radios or automatic signals, no barriers or warning lights at level crossings.

That was what CPR's eastern North American subsidiary, St. Lawrence & Hudson Railway, looked like on Jan. 7

this year, after two and a half days of unrelenting freezing rain imposed a mini ice age on some 2,400 km (1,500 miles) of its track.

The desolation stretched east to Montreal, west to Belleville and Smiths Falls, Ont., and south well into New York State. The accumulation of ice was awesome. Some switches were encased in eight inches of the stuff, and it was almost as hard as cement.

Montreal-area employees were aware of exactly how serious the

situation was. On that grim Wednesday, most of them were without electric lighting in their own homes – which usually meant they were without heat, cooking, refrigerated food and hot water as well.

When weary StL&H department heads gathered that evening at a meeting chaired by Chief Operating Officer Paul Gilmore, they came to an unhappy decision: They would shut down all operations, then immediately

(See "War rooms" on page 2)

It's Colourful, But is it Art?

Underground urban art has been a highly visible aspect of alternative culture since the 1960s when graffiti "artists" began to spray paint their names, or "tags," on various structures in major cities across North America and around the world.

Soon the taggers moved from simply scrawling their names on buildings and other stationary structures to executing "pieces," short for masterpieces, in their stead. These more complex forms of graffiti employed multiple colours, more elaborate lettering styles and a plethora of designs, fills and backgrounds.

At the same time, as their work was becoming more sophisticated, the renegade artists were seeking out mobile canvases on the sides of subway coaches and railway cars to take advantage of the more extensive exposure offered by those ubiquitous travelling billboards. Passenger equipment, in particular, is sought out by the painters as the supreme opportunity to get in the faces of city commuters and splash their work across the urban landscape.

Preserved examples of historic locomotives get no more respect from 'taggers' than the freight equipment that is targeted for the colourful abuse on a daily basis.

The railways, of course, looked at the graffiti artists as trespassers and vandals. Spray paint is both difficult and expensive to remove from the sides of railway equipment, although a number of cleaning companies have cultivated just such an expertise in recent years. Though faced with felony convictions for damage of $1,000 or more to freight cars, many hardcore graffiti practitioners embraced their covert lifestyle with enthusiasm.

By the late 1970s, it was not unusual to read about the exploits of graffiti artists, well-known or otherwise, in mainstream newspapers and magazine articles.

One such group of five, known as the Downtown Crew, left several colourful calling cards in New York, Boston, Detroit and Toronto, during the early 1990s. When the self-styled artists—Santi, Soak, Terse, Erock and Sike—began to leave their mark on commuter coaches sitting at Canadian Pacific's Glen Yard in western Montreal, their days were numbered.

Inspector Robert LaRoche and Investigator Johnny Donovan led the CP Police investigative team, aided by investigators Laurent Croteau, Francis Desquilbet, Denis Legacé and Yvon Beauchamp. In a late night operation, the team, which also included constables François Dubuc, Jean Sevigny and Sergeant Jack Ridge, nabbed Santi and Terse midway through the execution of a detailed piece.

"At their homes, we found all the evidence we needed to find the other three guys and to make a solid case against them all," said Investigator Donovan at the time. Among the items unearthed by the police were photos and journals documenting all of the work of the graffiti vandals, including dates and locations.

"I've heard some people say they actually like this stuff," Donovan said, "but I don't think they'd want it on their property. If it's art, let them do it on canvas. Once they trespass and mess with someone else's property, they've crossed the line into mischief."

Unfortunately, though, most graffiti occurs when nobody is around and the culprits remain at large to inflict their "art" on yet another victim. While the railway police keep their vigilance, it is impossible to watch every car, every minute of the day.

In the fall of 2007, the CPR received a very visible reminder of just how vulnerable the railway really is.

On a November night, Security Guard Paul Boudreau was assigned to keep an eye on several railway cars assigned to Fred Green, the railway's chief executive officer, while they sat on a siding in Montreal's Lucien-L'Allier station between business meetings and onboard receptions. During the 12 hour shift, from 7:00 p.m. Saturday until 7:00 a.m. Sunday, Boudreau watched the cars from a table and chair set up against the front window inside the station. He was required to walk up and down the track periodically and to call into the Police Communication Centre every hour on the hour.

Though the security guard reported regularly all night long, he got quite a surprise when he did a walk around the next morning at the end of his shift. There, on the opposite side of the track from where he had sat undisturbed was a large pair of multicoloured pieces festooning the once pristine side of dining car *Craigellachie*.

Yes, indeed, graffiti is an ongoing and never-ending battle for the railway police.

rows of dominos. Downed power lines mingled with the broken branches that littered the ground."

The police officers were heading to Montreal to support their 25 Quebec colleagues who had already been toiling for days to cope with the escalating crisis caused by the great ice storm. They arrived at Windsor Station at 2:00 a.m. and headed for the conference room which was now serving as an emergency command post.

"The crisp, uniformed appearance of the man at the centre belied the fact that he had slept but a few hours in the week since the storm started," said *CPR News*.

> He was the officer in charge of Canadian Pacific Police Service's Quebec District, Inspector Robert LaRoche. All 35 police officers on LaRoche's special ice storm squad would see service above and beyond the call of duty. And the call of duty would be plenty demanding. They

stood in the cold beside inoperable level crossing gates to stop traffic when trains came by. They rerouted traffic while work crews de-iced bridges and overpasses. They cordoned off Windsor Station as large chunks of ice crashed to the streets from its roofs and turrets. They answered reports of wires, trees and branches across StL&H tracks, and helped to get them safely removed.

But it's the things the police did for their fellow employees for which they will be remembered. They drove over treacherous roads to isolated houses to check on the safety of employees whose telephone service had failed. They made good use of their heavy duty cruisers to evacuate children, elderly people, and even pets of employees and pensioners in terrible driving conditions. They scoured hardware stores to buy hundreds of litres of fuel for employees in areas without power. Two constables found a place to rent a sump pump for an employee whose basement was flooding, then found a worker to get it running. Errands of mercy were all in a day's work—and all too often a 16 hour day's work.

When the decision was made to suspend regular work shifts in favour of an emergency schedule, Inspector LaRoche, whose own home was without power for eight days, told his men to look after the safety and security of their own families first. They quickly made alternative arrangements for their kin, and then prepared to be away from home indefinitely.

In the end, LaRoche was relieved to say that his Force had come through the dangerous episode without having to report a single serious injury. He had the highest praise for everybody in the emergency squad: "They worked day and night, through very uncomfortable times, but I never heard a complaint," he said. "And they were willing to do almost anything."

In 1998, the CPR was enlisted by the Calgary Police Service to help launch Alberta's first comprehensive crime prevention program for people with disabilities.

"People with disabilities are among the most vulnerable to crime," said Rob Ritchie, CPR president and chief executive officer. "When the Calgary Police Service approached Canadian Pacific Railway to become its corporate partner in this program, we did not hesitate. Our hope is that this program will help improve the quality of life for people with disabilities and foster greater understanding of their special needs."

A donation of $10,000 from the CPR was used to produce crime-prevention guides in print, braille, and audio formats for people with disabilities.

"The Calgary Police Service worked closely with groups representing people with disabilities to develop this crime-prevention guide, which is the first of its kind in Alberta," said Calgary Police Chief Christine Silverberg. "This initiative is reflective of my commitment to reach out to all diverse communities in Calgary to ensure their needs are met."

Inside the Canadian Pacific Police Service, however, resources were once again squeezed when the department was asked to cut another 15% from its budget. Another 23 police positions were lost.

"That's when I decided a complete re-engineering of the department was necessary," Chief Moody said. "I put together a team from human resources, industrial relations, rail operations and legal services to examine options. In the end, I decided the only way to save the department was to create a one-tier, uniformed police service to focus on proactive crime prevention."

The new structure demanded police officers who were generalists, capable of doing both uniform and plainclothes investigative duties. The ranks of detective and detective-sergeant were abolished. Officers holding those ranks were demoted to constable; their wages were frozen.

"I had the support of CP management and industrial relations, but I still had to negotiate this plan with the Canadian Pacific Police Association," Moody said. "It was a difficult time and a dangerous change. We had to change our focus to community-oriented policing and problem solving. I worked to improve training and redefined our business plan accordingly."

In 1999, the CPPS Crime Prevention Unit was rechristened the Community Service Unit (CSU) and a problem solving model was developed to identify and tackle the root causes of criminal activity. All CPPS members across the system were required to participate in

Voice communications are supplemented by computer connections with law enforcement agencies throughout North America.

CSU programs, whether trespass prevention, crossing safety or driver education. Customer oriented policing and problem solving required the railway's clients to help identify areas of concern and share the responsibility of implementing solutions.

"Our reduction in staff, and our new community-focused approach meant we had to police smarter," Moody said. "We organized a system of intelligence gathering and analysis, and we established a strong and trusting relationship with other intelligence agencies in both Canada and the U.S.

"It sure paid off after the events of September 11, 2001, when the world changed. The fact that we were linked into the intel community allowed us to obtain information quickly, react when necessary, and keep senior management at CP informed about our activities.

"Every member of the unit—headed up by Scott MacAskill—was a trained criminal-intelligence analyst who could correlate data and conduct studies to uncover pertinent information and crime trends. They worked with other agencies to investigate organized crime, recover stolen property, intercept contraband and illicit drugs, and monitor potential terrorist organizations and activities."

Individual members within the CP Police Service were also looking at ways to meet the needs of the many communities within their constituency. "Our workforce [at the railway] is much more diverse than it was twenty years ago," said CP Police superintendent Gerry Fish in a 2001 interview about violence in the workplace.

> *Age gaps can create different perspectives. People have different values now and want different things from the workplace. We can no longer assume, as we sometimes did in the past, that a railway job is a job for life.*
>
> *What we experience on the policing side is both external and internal violence. Internally, threats, intimidation or even assaults. Externally, people throwing rocks or projectiles at trains, mischief and vandalism to track, and equipment that can endanger our employees, and cases of domestic violence spilling over into the workplace. A policy focused on root causes and prevention gives us a process to deal with both internal and external problems.*
>
> *We're emphasizing conflict resolution. One of the biggest causes of stress today is the rapid pace of change. People have bad days at home and take it out in the workplace. Different things stress different people. And stress has side effects that affect people on the job. We're trying to help people with that.*

Many of the rapid changes occurring in the workplace at Canadian Pacific were driven by the momentous decision of its board of directors to break up the parent company into five independent, stand-alone companies: Canadian Pacific Railway, PanCanadian Petroleum, CP Ships, Fording Coal, and Fairmont Hotels & Resorts. The move was expected to unlock value by allowing the individual companies to have full control of their assets.

"CPR shares are back on the New York and Toronto stock exchanges," said Paul Bell, CPR vice president of investor relations, at a stock launch tribute in Calgary's Canadian Pacific Railway Pavilion

Chief Ivan McClelland

POLICING IN A POST 9/11 ENVIRONMENT

Ivan Robert McClelland was born July 20, 1960, in Berkshire, U.K. Five years later, his family moved to Northern Ireland where he received his schooling, culminating with his studies in geophysics and mapping.

In 1979, McClelland joined the Royal Ulster Constabulary (RUC). In the late 1960s, the terrorist campaign in Northern Ireland had marked the beginning of what was referred to as "The Troubles." Extra policing was required throughout the province, and civil law enforcement worked very closely with the British Army and intelligence services to quell local disturbances and deal with instances of terrorism. McClelland worked with this high caliber, effective police service, tackling such problems as serious crime, racketeering and a general breakdown in public order, while deeply enmeshed with countering ongoing political terrorist campaigns perpetuated by Irish nationalist and British loyalist terrorist organizations.

After 11 years with the RUC, McClelland transferred to the Metropolitan Police in London—a territorial force responsible for the Greater London area, excluding the square mile in the centre of the city that is the responsibility of the City of London Police. There he was stationed at the historic Bow Street Police Station attached to the Bow Street *Magistrates' Court*. He was one of a group of officers known as "the Bow Street runners."

The Metropolitan Police Service, then as now, had significant national responsibilities such as protecting the British Royal Family and senior members of Her Majesty's Government, safeguarding Parliament and Buckingham Palace, and leading counterterrorism activities in the United Kingdom.

McClelland transferred to Heathrow Airport in 1994 where he joined the counterterrorist team providing security to the airport.

McClelland was part of a counterterrorism team at London's Heathrow Airport.

During this time, he responded to several major incidents including mortar attacks by the Irish Republican Army (IRA), bombing attempts by the Palestinian Liberation Organization (PLO), and the hijacking of a Boeing 727.

In 2001, McClelland came to Canada where he worked as an Edmonton bylaw enforcement officer for five weeks before accepting a job with the Canadian Department of National Defense as an investigator with the military ombudsman.

Along with the earthshaking destruction of 9/11, there was an explosion in the world of corporate security. McClelland went to work for EPCOR Utilities, an Edmonton-based company that builds, owns and operates electrical transmission and distribution networks, water and wastewater treatment facilities and infrastructure in Canada. There, he worked as a manager and later director of corporate security, IT protection, and emergency and contingency planning.

In 2008, McClelland was hired by the CPR as chief of the Canadian Pacific Police Service.

on October 3, 2001. "While not everyone could be here today, we want you to know that every employee, every pensioner, everyone who is or was part of the CPR and our incredible story is an important part of today's ceremony."

From now on the Canadian Pacific Police Service would have but one main area of focus—the railway and its employees, suppliers, customers and, of course, the public. As the railway struggled to match the financial results of its North American competitors, the pressure to reduce costs was unrelenting.

"In late 2001, I made more changes and implemented more budget reductions," Chief Moody said. "I eliminated a large number of inspector positions across Canada, and I promoted sergeants to supervisory positions in the detachments.

"Needless to say, I wasn't a very popular chief."

The severe reductions in staff dating back to the railway's move from Montreal to Calgary drastically reduced the ability of the CP

Police Service to keep up its former pace of crime prevention. Arrests fell precipitously.

But the years immediately after 9/11 were not without their successes. In 2001 and 2002, the CPPS worked closely with Canadian National and the Railway Association of Canada (RAC) to develop "Canadian Railway Incident Investigation" guidelines for police departments and coroners in Canada. Chief Moody himself, along with members of the CN Police and the CPPS' own Community Service Unit, gave presentations across the country selling the Canadian Association of Police on the process.

Most Canadian police officers, including those with the RCMP, now carry these guidelines in their briefcases while on patrol.

With a more focused mandate and fewer staff members, Moody embarked on a program to bring the CP Police up to a level of administrative efficiency that would be second to none. On July 27, 2002, the CPR became the first major freight railway in North America to be accredited by the Commission on Accreditation for Law Enforcement Agencies (CALEA). To achieve the official designation, the railway police had to comply with more than 300 standards covering every aspect of law enforcement.

However, the drastic reduction of manpower in recent years, combined with too many single-man detachments and too much paperwork at the local level, resulted in fewer arrests and more criticism from management. Despite the kudos the police force received from CP management and others for earning its CALEA designation, many CPPS members looked upon this period of severe downsizing and retrenchment as "The Dark Years."

When Chief Moody retired in 2008, the Canadian Pacific Police Service was looking for somebody who could do more with less. In recent years, tighter resources had compelled senior railway police officers to adopt a strategy that was, for the most part, reactive, leaving many of the Company's assets exposed to an increased level of risk. In addition, the terrorist attacks of September 11, 2001, in the United States had changed the North American concept of security and opened people's eyes to the immense public threat posed by disenfranchised religious and political splinter groups. In the face of these shadowy and difficult to confront forces, it was not surprising that Canadian

Pacific's search for a new chief of police culminated with the selection of a candidate with the ability to both assess risk effectively and assign appropriate resources to mitigate it. Ivan McClelland was that man.

McClelland conducted a risk analysis of the CPR network and met with senior executives to assess their operational need for a dedicated police force. Armed with a business degree, he was able to present a realistic course for the future of the CPPS in language that management could understand.

Above all, the chief emphasized that the railway police force was all about public safety. "Our goal is to stop bad people from doing bad things," he said, "and good people from doing stupid things." Securing the property and catching bad guys would go a long way toward supporting the railway's need for fluidity in its operations. A safe and secure railway is an efficient one.

Along with the hiring of a new chief of police, Canadian Pacific's senior officers reaffirmed their belief that targeted and appropriate policing would enhance public safety, support service reliability and preserve shareholder value by managing and reducing risk exposure.

Bicycles are effective vehicles for patrolling rail yards and other expansive company properties.

A railway police officer, armed with the latest radar gun, puts the brakes on speeding through company property.

During Railway Safety Week 2009 which ran from April 27 to May 3 in Canada, the Canadian Pacific Police Service took its public safety message directly to the street. CP police officers from Montreal to Vancouver conducted more than 100 safety and enforcement blitzes in communities across the country. They reminded motorists, cyclists and pedestrians about the importance of staying safe around railway property, at level crossings, in particular.

"This week our focus is to build on the education efforts of programs such as Operation Lifesaver by deploying officers to enforce the laws that relate specifically to railway safety," said CPPS Chief McClelland at the time. "We are taking a more proactive approach and confronting the problem head-on, shifting our focus from education to enforcement activities. Our aim is to reinforce the need for safety and to deter people from taking unnecessary risks."

With a new emphasis on getting constables back out on the

property, the railway police raised their public profile. The Police Communication Centre, now renamed the Police Control Centre (PCC), was moved to a more centralized location in Winnipeg where the labour market was good and fewer staff turnovers would be experienced. Railway employees and members of the public alike were actively encouraged to call the CP Police at the first sign of any illegal or suspicious behaviour. By 2010, the number of calls fielded annually by the PCC had grown to more than 56,000, and the Department had conducted upwards of 20,000 investigations each year.

In many busy areas in both the United States and Canada, the CP Police ramped up the effort to invite municipal, provincial and state police officers to ride through their districts in the cab of a railway locomotive in what has come to be called the Officer Aboard Program. Through this level crossing safety initiative, law enforcement officers of all stripes experience the harrowing reality faced by train crews on a daily basis as motorists endanger their own lives and those aboard trains by ignoring safety precautions. Police use the lessons learned from the program to educate the public on railway safety, work with the railways to install better warning devices, improve sight lines at crossings and enforce the law with more authority.

Literally hundreds of tickets are issued each month by railway police officers to speeders or vehicle operators who approach grade crossings while using hand-held communications devices. It's a telling statistic, posing considerable frustration for the officers trying to protect lives that nearly 50% of collisions at crossings occur where there are active warning devices in operation. Even more alarmingly, many vehicle/train collisions occur when a car or a truck runs smack into the side of a train already occupying a crossing.

One incident in the spring of 2010, however, caused much handwringing at railway headquarters, while demonstrating to all concerned that the CPPS was charged with investigating all crime no matter where it occurred or who were the offenders.

In the aftermath of a derailment near Golden, B.C., in which three locomotives and 26 cars had left the track, it was alleged that the "situational awareness" of the crew members had been compromised by marijuana and cell phone use.

During the course of a four-month investigation, Superintendent

Unless the offense is a serious one, the railway police — concerned more with accident prevention than punishment — typically issue a warning to motorists.

Gerry Fish and Constable Larry Parsons served two search warrants on Canadian Pacific to turn over all records related to the internal investigation of the collision and another two search warrants on national telecommunications giant, Telus, to retrieve cell phone and texting records.

The report of the Transportation Safety Board of Canada (TSB) "determined that the locomotive engineer had been exposed to marijuana sometime prior to the accident." The TSB also found the crew members had used their cell phones multiple times just before the crash.

Significantly, the investigation demonstrated that, operationally, the CPPS was truly independent of Canadian Pacific, answering only to the Crown. The derailment led to formal charges of dangerous operation of railway equipment against both the engineer and conductor.

A CP spokesman confirmed the engineer and conductor involved in the incident had been dismissed from the company. Ed Greenberg stressed the railway's safety record as well as compliance with the TSB investigation into the incident. He also emphasized that as a result of their internal investigation into the crash, the CPR had introduced new, stricter rules for the use of personal electronic devices.

"This was considered a significant accident, caused by crew error, and it served as a clear reminder why the safety of our employees and the safety of the communities in which we operate must be an ongoing commitment," Greenberg said. He went on to explain how the railway conducts drug screenings when it hires employees, as well as after accidents. However, he said that Canadian law prevents the company from conducting regular or random drug testing on employees, including those who operate trains.

"This is something we do not take lightly," Greenberg said at the time. "It was serious. Safety is a priority with the company. We are the safest railway in North America and we have been for the past five consecutive years [2005-2009] and eleven of the past thirteen. But it was a stark reminder."

On December 8, 2011, the dismissed engineer entered a guilty plea and was sentenced by Provincial Court Judge Sheard who imposed a $500 fine. During sentencing, the engineer apologized to the Court and expressed the wish that his prosecution might help his former coworkers avoid such incidents in the future. The Crown advised that the public interest had been served in the case, and directed a stay of proceedings on the conductor, officially closing the matter.

Fortunately, while the case had still been in the courts, better news was in the offing for the Department.

Canadian Pacific Railway was chosen to be the official rail freight carrier of the 2010 Olympic Winter Games in Vancouver. The CP Police deployed 40 men and women around the clock in an attempt to minimize any disruptions to its operations, while enhancing security and safety on railway property in and around West Coast Express commuter facilities in the greater Vancouver area. The Department's close working relationship with the RCMP's Integrated Security Unit and Joint Intelligence Group leading up to and during the Games was indicative of its enhanced, targeted and cooperative modus operandi.

Today, trespassing remains the number one problem. In response to Chief McClellend's maxim that "every crime begins with trespassing," and believing that prevention is preferable to prosecution, the CP Police have posted thousands of no trespassing signs on railway property everywhere that the CPR operates.

Trespassers often are found to have arrest warrants against them. Sometimes the railway police catch suspects with tools for breaking into freight cars; sometimes they find drugs. In recent years, many of the transients travel with their dogs. Riders caught trying to sneak from Canada into the U.S., through the railway tunnel from Windsor, Ontario, to Detroit or at other locations, are turned over to the U.S. Border Patrol. The depredations of copper wire thieves, as much as graffiti artists, are endemic.

The CPPS created new detachments in Minot, North Dakota, and Bettendorf, Iowa, to strengthen its presence in the United States, supplementing the detachments already established in St. Paul, Minnesota; Taylor, Pennsylvania; Bensenville, Illinois; Binghamton, Albany and Oneonta, N.Y.; Milwaukee, Wisconsin, and Detroit, Michigan.

The CP Police take pride in being one of the truly international police agencies in the world, with law enforcement operations in both Canada and the United States. "Having offices close to the border strengthens our relationship with U.S. Customs and Border Patrol," said Chief McClelland at the opening of the Minot detachment. "This allows us to develop closer working relationships, which should translate into fewer delays in cross-border traffic."

Putting more boots on the ground in Iowa was a logical response to the CPR's purchase of the Dakota, Minnesota & Eastern Railroad (DM&E), the Iowa, Chicago & Eastern Railroad (IC&E) and Cedar American Rail Holdings (CARH), approved by the U.S. Surface Transportation Board in September 2008.

"With the acquisition of the DM&E and IC&E, our territory grew significantly in Iowa," said CP Special Agent James Vaughan. "Bettendorf was the obvious choice for a new detachment because it puts us in the middle of a high-risk area, giving us the opportunity to respond quicker to problems that arise."

The two-man Bettendorf detachment was the first to be deployed on DM&E territory.

"CP is also the first rail police organization to go through the Iowa State Commission," said Chief McClelland, "which means that our Iowa-based CPPS members all have a card saying they are Iowa State police officers."

Before the new detachment, the CP Police investigations in the U.S. were conducted from Chicago, making it difficult to monitor and deal with incidents in Iowa and Missouri. Another detachment, opened in Mason

City, Iowa, was created to patrol and secure the railway's properties in the northern part of the state, as well as in southern Minnesota.

But it was across the border in its Ontario District that the CPPS had serious problems with theft.

Canadian Pacific's priority, double stack container traffic, moves on what are known as the railway's 100 series trains. During May and June of 2011, 88 containers, all of which originated in either Montreal or Toronto, reached their destinations in various western Canadian cities with seals broken and freight missing.

Preliminary investigations by the CPPS determined all the break-ins were occurring in the vicinity of Cartier, Ontario. Numerous damaged seals had been found along the CPR main line, about a mile south of the town, an area only accessible by boat, all-terrain vehicle or foot.

On July 5, Acting Sergeant Ron Morrison and constables Ron Kirst, Steve Pagliuso and Keith Donnelly set out through the heavily wooded area near where the tail end of trains are stopped while crew changes are made in Cartier. The CPPS officers, all in uniform, were soon quietly approaching a rough camp they discovered in close proximity to the tracks from where they could hear male voices. Old boxes and garbage strewn around the area indicated the men had been there for some time.

The officers got very close to the camp before the alarm was raised.

"Run!" yelled one of the five men in the clearing. Three of the suspects were apprehended immediately as they attempted to flee the area. The other two dove into the nearby lake, fully clothed, and made good their escape by swimming for the opposite bank.

In the camp, the officers found stolen merchandise from a number of trains including air powered finishing nailers, ice cream makers, tents, portable gazebos, wheelbarrows, camp chairs, basketballs, boxes of matches, a deck box and a gas powered lawn mower. Numerous empty boxes that had once contained other items were also discovered in the bush. A set of bolt cutters lay on the ground.

Because of the isolated location of the thieves' camp, the railway police made arrangements for a CPR hi-rail track vehicle to go to the site and assist with transporting both suspects and merchandise from the bush.

The three captured suspects were arrested and charged with possession of property obtained by crime and possession of break-in instruments. The two escapees were never identified.

But that wasn't the end of the problems with Canadian Pacific's 100 series trains.

Within a couple of months, eastbound containers were also being broken into while in the vicinity of Cartier. Sometimes the thefts took place at night and other times they occurred during the day. It didn't seem to matter if trains were stopped for quick crew changes or if they were held over in Cartier for several hours, all were targeted.

Once again a group of CP officers—this time Inspector William Law, with constables Ron Kirst, Steve Pagliuso, Ron Morrison, Paul Fish and Kristian Iversen—travelled to the site to set up surveillance.

For nearly six days, the railway police spent long hours in the bush without incident or lead. On October 6, however, they saw two men climbing onto the tail end of a 100 series train and breaking open containers. It was the break they needed—or almost.

As the officers moved in to make the arrest, the suspects spotted them approaching. Abandoning all caution, the pair climbed over the couplers between two cars on the slow moving train and escaped into the bush.

Just when it looked like the police might return home empty-handed, one of the officers discovered a vehicle which they suspected might belong to the thieves hidden in the woods not far away. By an incredible stroke of luck, they also found the birth certificate of one of the suspects on the ground beside the car.

As darkness closed in, the CP policemen contacted the Ontario Provincial Police (OPP) to request the services of a tracking dog and handler. Within 40 minutes, three members of the OPP Emergency Response Team were trackside and their dog had picked up the scent. It was only a short time before the suspects were tracked to their hiding place in a nearby swamp and arrested.

As it turned out, one of the thieves had just been released from a nine month prison term for a variety of offences. The other may have been the one to suggest robbing trains as his father had apparently been implicated in a series of similar crimes dating back more than ten years.

In any case, the two arrested men were charged with seven counts of break and enter with intent, one count of possession of break-in instruments, and four counts of breach of probation.

The thefts ceased.

Given the deep cutbacks of recent years, and the accompanying reduction in manpower, the police department had some good news to celebrate in 2011. In July, ten new recruits were added to the CPPS ranks; the first officers hired by Canadian Pacific since 2005. Seven of the new constables attended an 18 week training program at the Saskatchewan Police College and another six weeks of intensive on the job training with CPR. In 2012, another 15 members were recruited.

"All we had were generalists before we started actively recruiting," Chief McClelland said. "These new recruits give us the resources we need to specialize and diversify our functions. Previously we were very reactive about putting police in areas where there is high crime; we can now deploy police to areas where we determine there is a risk."

What the future holds for the railway police is consistency of training, an administration that is aligned with the needs of the entire police service as well as those of the individual detachments, centralized budget control, overall accountability for proper internal governance, and unerring responsibility to the Crown and to the public which it serves.

"We will add staff members to inefficient and risky one-man detachments, and establish a small nucleus of detectives who are highly trained in both intelligence and investigative work," Chief McClelland said. "Our focus on public safety and infrastructure security will help Canadian Pacific keep the trains running."

Image Sources

FRONTIER JUSTICE

p. 2 Map of Canada in 1873 - NA 4395-1(Glenbow Museum)
Before the Mounted Police came west, the proposed trans-continental railway ran through a sparsely populated, wild frontier.

p. 4 Sam Steele (portrait) - 15695 (CPR Archives)
Dashing and brave, Sam Steele set the tone for every movie and dime-store novel Mountie to come.

p. 6 NWMP on horses - 15212 (CPR Archives)
Shot during the mid-1920s near Amulet, Saskatchewan, the motion picture "Policing the Plains" romanticized the role of the Mounties in building the transcontinental railway.

p. 7 Ties unloaded at end of track - NA 1315-4 (Glenbow Museum)
The haphazard unloading of railway ties belies the speed with which the main line was spiked down across the prairies.

p. 9 NWMP standing at end of track – NS 15209 (CPR Archives)
The 1920s motion picture, "Policing the Plains," building on the Mounties' already formidable mythology, put one of their red-coated constables literally at the end of track.

p. 10-11 Letter from Van Horne to Col. Irvine - 17248 A&B (CPR Archives)
The 'railway general' sends his thanks to the NWMP's commander in the West for maintaining "perfect order" along his rail line.

p. 14 Piapot - NA 532-1(Glenbow Museum)
Piapot smiles for the studio photographer in better days.

p. 16 NWMP, Indians, railway officers on Medicine Hat station platform - NA 529-1(Glenbow Museum)
On the station platform at Medicine Hat, Alberta, a NWMP sergeant is caught between a group of bundled natives and a delegation of natty railway officials.

p. 18   Two Indians and NWMP on station platform - NA 660-2 (Glenbow Museum)
Stylish Hudson Bay coats and red serge jackets add a splash of colour to dusty prairie station platforms.

p. 20   First station at Calgary - NA 659-18 (Glenbow Museum)
Standing at the east end of Calgary's first, temporary, railway station, from left, are land agents R.G. Marsh and W.T. Ramsay; *Calgary Herald* employee T.B. Braden; watchmaker G.E. Jacques; and Constable Fay.

p. 24-25   NWMP detachment at Farwell - NA 294-1(Glenbow Museum) /5370 (CPR Archives)
Sam Steele, seated, commanded the rugged NWMP detachment at Farwell (later Revelstoke), in British Columbia.

p. 27   Police cabin at Donald - NA-782-3 (Glenbow Museum)
Early NWMP frontier posts, like this one at Donald, British Columbia, were hastily erected, but functional 'wild west' structures.

p. 28   Construction camp at Beavermouth - NA 782-5 (Glenbow Museum)
Hotels, bars and brothels were among the first buildings to rise from the woods in construction camps like this one at Beavermouth, in British Columbia.

SPECIAL SERVICE

p. 32   Watchman and dog - (Canadian Pacific Police Service)
A double-barreled shotgun and a dog with a good nose were the tools of the trade for this 'watchman' in the rail yard.

p. 35   Constables and railway coach - (Canadian Pacific Police Service)
With little training and virtually no centralized control, most of the men reported to whoever the highest ranking railway official was in the area where they were hired.

p. 37   Dominion Express truck c1901 - 84-58-11 (CPR Archives)
With Canadian Pacific's purchase of the well-established Dominion Express Company, the railway added another link to its rapidly expanding intermodal chain.

p. 38   Wanted bulletin/poster - A293 and A294 (CPR Archives)
Following the lead of the pioneer Pinkerton's Detective Agency, CPR's Special Service Department kept detailed files on criminals.

p. 41   Dalhousie Square Station (artwork) - A106 (CPR Archives)
Half of Montreal's police force was needed to supplement the railway's own ad-hoc security arrangements when the first transcontinental train steamed West from Dalhousie Square Station.

p. 41   Windsor Station 1901 - A20224 (CPR Archives)
Windsor Station is festooned with decorations for the visit of the Duke and Duchess of Cornwall and York, in 1901, the first of many royal tours for which the railway police would provide security.

p. 42   Pinkerton's Private Eye logo - (www. Pinkerton.com)
Pinkerton's unsleeping eye oversaw a spying and security apparatus with a greater reach than the US federal government.

p. 44   Chinese with government inspector - 16429 (CPR Archvives)
Chinese workers, many just youngsters, were closely watched while carried in bond to various work sites in the United States and Cuba.

p. 44   Chinese seated at table - 16435 (CPR Archives)
Located in the recesses below Windsor Station, the guarded quarters for Chinese workers and families in transit were spartan.

p. 49   Antonio Cordasco - PA122612 (Royal Commissions Collection, LAC)
Even as Antonio Cordasco was being crowned 'King of the Workers,' the labour boss was losing his grip on his cushy monopoly.

p. 51   Italian workers in the Rockies - PA038620 (Frontier College Collection, LAC)
Seasonal railway workers, most of whom are Italian, hunker down in a Rocky Mountains cabin before shipping home.

p. 52   Royal Train 1901 - NS1934 (CPR Archives)
Luxury and security went hand-in-hand in what were said to be the finest set of railway cars ever constructed.

p. 55   Yosemite - (Canadian Pacific Police Service)
Tied up at the CPR docks, the paddle-wheeler Yosemite served as a floating hotel for the railway's strikebreaking forces during a labour dust-up in Vancouver.

HANDS UP

p. 61   Mail car - NA 1315-35 (Glenbow Museum)
Even the most mild-mannered railway clerk kept at least one firearm close at hand while sorting Her Majesty's mail en route.

p. 63   Dominion Express logo - (Canadian Pacific Police Service)

p. 66   Dominion Express poster - A6426 (CPR Archives) A poster for the Dominion Express promises timely delivery of holiday gifts across North America.

p. 64   Bill Miner portrait - NA 837-1(Glenbow Museum)
'The Gentleman Bandit' became a local folk hero.

p. 68   Bill Miner wanted poster -1786 (Vancouver Public Library)
The 'Grey Fox' used all his wiles to escape a life sentence in the New Westminster Penitentiary.

p. 69   Imperial Limited brochure cover - x2267 (CPR Archives)
In the early years of the 20th century, the transcontinental *Imperial Limited* was CPR's most luxurious public offering.

p. 72   Lewis Colquhoun portrait - NA 837-2 (Glenbow Museum)
Lewis "Scotty" Colquhoun died of tuberculosis while in prison.

p. 72   Shorty Dunn portrait - NA 837-3 (Glenbow Museum)
             Shorty Dunn was also known as "Little Billy."

p. 78   Victor McLaglen in Windsor Station - 20114 (CPR Archives)
             Following a short stint as a railway constable, Victor
             McLaglen went on to stardom in Hollywood.

p. 80   Constable and staff at McAdam Jct. - A272 (CPR Archives)
             A railway police officer takes place of pride, front and
             centre with railway officers and other workers at McAdam
             Junction, New Brunswick.

THE IMPERIAL POLICE

p. 85   Policeman on platform at Smiths Falls - (Canadian Pacific
             Police Service)
             A CP constable stands guard over the mail and express car,
             while the train boards passengers at Smiths Falls, Ontario.

p. 86   Announcement of department - A18655 (CPR Archives)
             Shaughnessy's notice was the birth certificate of a fully
             professional police force.

p. 87   Departmental photo (small) (Canadian Pacific Police Service)
             The crisp lines and military trim of their new uniforms lent
             the recruits an air of competence and efficiency, qualities
             they would soon demonstrate in the field.

p. 88   Rufus Chamberlin portrait - 3818 (CPR Archives)
             Rufus Chamberlin was the only man considered for the
             top job.

p. 92   *Empress of Asia* - 21448 (CPR Archives)
             Empress of Asia was luxuriously appointed throughout,
             with plenty of imaginative places to stash illicit things.

p. 95   *Empress of Ireland* - 20631(CPR Archives)
             In just fourteen minutes, the pride of the CPR's steamship
             fleet vanished beneath the waves.

p. 95   Constable on *Empress of Ireland* - A36121 (CPR Archives)
             A CP constable sits with divers among the gear to be used
             in a salvage attempt on the sunken *Empress of Ireland*.

p. 96-97   Troop train - NA 2548-2 (Glenbow Museum)
The railways and the railway police were intimately involved with the movement of troops to the European theatre.

p. 99   Guard on bridge, WWI- A1557 (CPR Archives) Every bridge and tunnel on the system was guarded against sabotage by ex-military men and other volunteers unable to enlist for overseas duty.

p. 101   Silk train and detective -15641(Vancouver Public Library) Patrolling the Vancouver yards, a CPR inspector does a quick check around the engine before a silk train and its high-value cargo depart for markets on the East Coast.

p. 102-103 Gold train - A20298 (CPR Archives)
Gold bullion from Imperial Russia moves in a special train from warships at a Vancouver dock to safekeeping in Ottawa and London, England.

FRIENDS IN HIGH PLACES

p. 108   Winnipeg riots, June 10, 1919 - NA 1775-4 (Glenbow Museum)
The overheated mobs marched shoulder to shoulder through the city streets in the days leading up to 'Bloody Saturday.'

p. 109   Royal Alexandra Hotel - 9817 (CPR Archives)
The Royal Alexandra Hotel, a prominent Winnipeg social centre, became a convenient meeting point for impromptu labour negotiations.

p. 112   Prince of Wales in Vancouver - A3841(CPR Archives)
A CP constable at the entrance to Vancouver Station keeps onlookers at a respectful distance, while the Prince chats with members of his ceremonial guard.

p. 114   Prince of Wales shaking hands - (Canadian Pacific Police Service)
The Prince insisted on meeting each of the men assigned to the security detail for his first royal tour of Canada.

p. 115   Tom Basoff - NA 1146-1(Glenbow Museum)
Basoff left a trail of blood disappearing into the woods as
he staggered away from the murder scene.

p. 115   Ausby Auloff - NA 1146-2 (Glenbow Museum)
Even wanted posters had a hard time pinning down train
robber Ausby Auloff's real name, a problem no doubt
exacerbated by the man's many aliases.

p. 116   Bellevue Cafe - NA 1146-3 (Glenbow Museum)
The murder at the Bellevue Cafe was reenacted in great
detail by police investigators.

p. 118   Funeral of constable Usher shot by Basoff - NA 2814-11
(Glenbow Museum)
RCMP Constable Ernest Ussher, shot down in cold blood,
was laid to rest with full honours on August 11, 1920.

p. 120   Wembley pavilion - (Canadian Pacific Police Service)
The Canadian Pacific pavilion stood proudly, side-by-side
with the Canadian government building on 'Empire Way.'

p. 121   Wembley poster - A6013 (CPR Archives)
Twenty-seven million people visited the greatest trade
show the world had ever seen.

p. 122   Wembley constables - (Canadian Pacific Police Service)
The four railway constables sent to Wembley were chosen
for their spotless records, as well as their bachelor status.

p. 127   Wanted poster - (Canadian Pacific Police Service)
There were many suspects, but no one was ever charged
with murdering the Doukhobor leader.

129   Peter Verigin funeral train -179 (Thomas Gushal, Vancouver
Public Library)
Crowds of supporters turned out to pay tribute to their
fallen leader, as Verigin's funeral train arrived in his
hometown of Brilliant, B.C.

COMPETITION & CHAOS

p. 133   Royal York poster - A6356 (CPR Archives)
The magnificent new hotel was the full-time stomping ground for a small squad of house detectives.

p. 134   1920s hotel fire, Lake Louise- NA 937-9 (Glenbow Museum)
A series of devastating hotel fires struck Lake Louise, above, Banff Springs, and Quebec's Chateau Frontenac.

p. 135   Edouard Panet portrait – (Canadian Pacific Police Service)
Panet served as aide-de-camp for two Canadian governors-general.

p. 137   Windsor Station police- NS 11812 (CPR Archives)
CPR founding president, George Stephen, stands guard on his pedestal in Montreal's Windsor Station, while a couple of railway police officers watch over things at ground level.

p. 139   PM Baldwin, Prince of Wales, Prince George on E. of Australia - NS17898 (CPR Archives) On board the *Empress of Australia* are, from left, Captain R. G. "Jock" Latta, Prime Minister and Mrs. Stanley Baldwin, the Prince of Wales, Prince George, and Staff Captain R.N. Stuart, V.C.

p. 141   Hobo riding on roof - NC-54-3604 (Glenbow Museum)
During the Great Depression, many unemployed or itinerant workers hopped into empty boxcars to travel down the line or, as in the case of this young man, climbed up top for a more scenic view.

p. 146-147 On-to-Ottawa Trek - NA-4532-2 (Glenbow Museum)
The strike leaders rode on the locomotive tender, facing the men on top of the boxcars.

p. 152   Empresses of the Pacific poster - A6024 (CPR Archives)
Canadian Pacific built a reputation for being tough on smugglers, cracking down hard on the opium trade.

p. 156   Fire at Pier D - 1938-1305 (CPR Archives)
Despite the vigilance of the fire brigades, Vancouver's Pier D was completely consumed by the flames.

p. 156   Fire brigades badge - (Canadian Pacific Police Service)
              The police department formed special fire brigades
              to maintain a watch on the railway's docks and in its
              warehouses.

p. 157   Royal Tour at Quebec - A7252 (CPR Archives) Away from
              the secure confines of their *Empress of Britain* stateroom
              and the luxury of their special train, the royal couple took
              to an open-topped automobile, escorted by a phalanx of
              RCMP motorcycles.

p. 158   Royal Tour Chief of Police with Royals - NA 4325-11
              (Glenbow Museum) With Jim Brewster holding the reins,
              CPR police chief Edouard de Bellefeuille Panet rides
              shotgun in Banff for the visiting King George VI and Queen
              Elizabeth.

p. 158   Royal Tour Queen in locomotive - A7308 (CPR Archives)
              "What a lovely engine," the Queen was reported to have
              remarked to the CPR men piloting the 1939 royal train.

p. 159   Royal Tour 1939 with PM- A7237 (CPR Archives)
              While the red-coated RCMP officers did high-profile duty
              at ceremonies across the country, the railway police were
              behind the scenes providing security and logistics support.

p. 160   Royal Tour Calgary Constable white gloves - NA 5258-13
              (Glenbow Museum) collection
              A white-gloved railway constable gives a cameraman
              a warning glance, as the royal train prepares to depart
              Calgary Station and the Palliser Hotel, at left.

HOME GUARD

p. 162   World War II poster - A6714 English (CPR Archives)
              Canadian Pacific was proud of the employees who left
              the company's many services to join the armed forces,
              maintaining a running total of recruits on a series of posters
              in English and French throughout the Second World War.

p. 164   Concourse/sign for bomb shelters - D195 (CPR Archives)
Female soldiers parade in front of portraits of the Allied leaders, maps of the various theatres of war and, most ominously, signs directing civilians to the nearest air raid shelter.

p. 164   Windsor Station public address - NS3396 (CPR Archives)
The new public address system, which alerted the travelling public to train arrivals and departures at Montreal's Windsor Station, could also be used for emergency broadcasts.

p. 168   Sun Life building 1940s - 22720 (CPR Archives)
From the roof of Montreal's Windsor Station the most prominent buildings were the Sun Life building, below which the Crown Jewels were secreted, and St. James Cathedral.

p. 169   Express trucks lined up at Windsor Station - 20106 (CPR Archives)
Trucks lined up alongside Montreal's Windsor Station reveal the extent to which Canadian Pacific embraced door-to-door delivery service.

p. 169   CP Express truck 1940s-84-58-6 (CPR Archives)
During the Second World War and the years immediately after, express trucks were tempting targets for thieves looking for high-value merchandise.

p. 172   Churchill family - War116 (CPR Archives)
Winston Churchill, along with wife Clementine and daughter Mary, was entertained by Canadian prime minister Mackenzie King on CPR's railway car Mount Stephen.

p. 176   Auxance Hector Cadieux portrait (Canadian Pacific Police Service)
Cadieux was widely known throughout Canada among his fellow officers.

p. 179   CPAL bombed plane CF-CUA (www.murderpedia.org/male.G/g/guay-joseph-photos.htm)
Canadian Pacific Air Lines Flight 108 flew to its doom that fateful autumn day.

p. 180   Airlines poster - A6255 (CPR Archives)
              Early airline passengers were subjected to no greater
              personal or baggage security checks than if they were
              stepping onto a bus.

p. 181   CP Air bombing, 1949, crash site (Canadian Pacific Police
              Service)
              Constables took shifts guarding the crash site and sorting
              out the many investigators.

p. 185   CP Air bombing, 1949, loading coffins - (Canadian Pacific
              Police Service)
              The first task was sending home the coffins by rail.

p. 187   Albert Guay and police - web (www.mysteriesofcanada.com)
              "At least I die famous," airplane bomber and murderer
              Albert Guay was reputed to have said before his execution.

p. 189   Ben Bouzan portrait – (Canadian Pacific Police service)
              Bouzan learned the ropes suppressing the opium trade.

p. 191   Shooting champions- (Canadian Pacific Police Service)
              The best revolver shots with the department of investigation
              that year were, from left, national champion Constable E.R.
              Siegel, Investigator G.J. Collins, Constable O.M. Corcoran
              and Constable V.H. Malacrida.

p.192   Constable Pettit with pistol- A36123 (CPR Archives)
              Constable F.F. Pettit, a member of the Quebec District
              revolver team for 1932, demonstrates the proper stance for
              firing his service weapon.

p. 193   First aid champions - 15863 (CPR Archives)
              First aid champions, from left, P.Keogh, E.G. Wykes,
              Sergeant H.W. Bailey, W. Allison and J.A. Griffith, wore
              full dress uniform for their victory portrait, right down to
              the spit-and-polish.

p. 195   Policeman on platform at Cranbrook - 0220 - (Cranbrook Archives)
          Constable W.R.B. Flett poses with local boys Mac Belanger, on the motorcycle, and Des Moore, beside the new post-war station in Cranbrook, British Columbia.

SPECIALTY SQUADS

p. 198   Brochure for *The Canadian* - A15428 (CPR Archives)
          The stainless-steel streamliner, dubbed *The Canadian* by Canadian Pacific, quickly assumed its place among the country's most visible national symbols.

p. 199   Police assigned to Royal Tour in Quebec 1951 - (Canadian Pacific Police Service)
          The uniformed staff assigned to the 1951 Royal Tour were, from left, front row: T.R. Veary, W.J. Callaghan, W.E. Graham, unidentified, H. Tetreault, G. Fairbrother; second row: H. Allison, A.W. Spence, J. Gervais, B. Dubreuil, H. MacKenzie, H.R. Giroux; back row: G. Adam, C. Ball, E. O'Hara, A. Butler, J.W. Stimson.

p. 201   Royal Tour at Royal York 1951 - R278 (CPR Archives)
          A CP constable stands guard, right, as Queen Elizabeth II is whisked from Toronto's Royal York Hotel to a waiting limousine.

p. 203   Great Lakes brochure cover - A18309 (CPR Archives)
          Providing steamship security was a pleasant assignment, unless you were patrolling alone at night among the extensive docks, warehouses and grain elevators in Thunder Bay, Ontario.

p. 204   *Empress of Canada* on fire - (Canadian Pacific Police Service)
          The capsized Empress still smolders from the fire.

p. 205   *Empress of Canada* in Quebec - (Canadian Pacific Police Service)
          The Empress of Canada was the first CP steamship to return to the St. Lawrence route since V-J Day.

p. 206   Empress of Canada salvage - (Canadian Pacific Police Service)
The salvage effort took months and ended up being somewhat of an engineering challenge, written up with enthusiasm in both the popular press and the technical journals.

p. 207   UK police - (Canadian Pacific Police Service)
Maintaining a crisp military look, with no weapons visible, was even more important for these two CP constables assigned to dockside duty in London than it was for their counterparts across the pond.

p. 212   Angus Fire Brigade - 5172 (CPR Archives)
The Angus Fire Brigade were colourful participants in the Victory Loan drive, during the First World War.

p. 213   Angus fire truck- A233 (CPR Archives)
On their home grounds, two of Angus Fire Brigade's finest show off their spotlessly maintained machine for the photographer.

p. 214   Bombed bridge - (Canadian Pacific Police Service)
Nasty occurrences like this railway bridge bombing became all too common.

p. 215   Comic book cover - (Canadian Pacific Police Service)
Published by the Association of American Railroads, this special agent comic assured its young readers that the railway police's record of saving lives and preventing crimes "is excelled by no other protective agency."

p. 217   Bomb - (Canadian Pacific Police Service)
The railway police prepared a basic reference guide on bombs and their components for the edification of any unlucky officer who might encounter such things while on duty.

p. 223   Vancouver Flying Squad - (Canadian Pacific Police Service)
Vancouver "Flying Squad" members—from left, Staff Sergeant C. McCarthy and constables B. Bouzan, W. Richardson, F. Hill, F. Toop, R. Carney, A. Jasman, W. Birch, W. Richards, M. Hodge and L.R. Smith—pose with one of their three-wheeled motorcycles.

p. 224 Jean Belanger portrait- NS8204 (CPR Archives) Belanger became a media favorite during the trial and conviction of Albert Guay.

p. 226 CP Air bombing 1965 - *Chicago Tribune*
A CP police officer strikes a dramatic pose at the crash site of the ill-fated airliner, for a photograph that ran in the *Chicago Tribune*.

PUBLIC SAFETY OFFICERS

p. 231 John Machan portrait - (Canadian Pacific Police Service)
Machan had an odd career mix.

p. 233 CP Limited/Sinclair and Crump - E674 (CPR Archives)
Norris "Buck" Crump and Ian "Big Julie" Sinclair discuss the new branding of their ever-diversifying and expanding empire.

p. 234 Airlines 1960s - Marc H. Choko collection
Highjackings and in-flight violence became everyday concerns for those operating a modern, worldwide airline service.

p. 239 Georges Legault portrait - (Canadian Pacific Police Service)
Legault put in 44 years of service.

p. 242 Embry/Royal York - (Canadian Pacific Police Service)
The Ottawa police had a file on Embry even before his escapades at the Royal York Hotel.

p. 245 Operation Lifesaver, officer/kids on bridge - E7458-5 (CPR Archives)
Operation Lifesaver, while primarily focused on safety at level crossings, also sought to educate the public about the dangers of trespassing on railway property.

p. 245 Operation Lifesaver, officer in classroom - E6981(CPR Archives)
Railway police officers put in countless hours at schools and community centres trying to prevent accidents from occurring.

p. 246   Female officers/Sue MacLeod - (Canadian Pacific Police Service)
Susan MacLeod, the first female constable hired by Canadian Pacific, was received with amused curiosity and unquestioned support.

p. 248   Jim Mickel portrait - (Canadian Pacific Police Service)
Mickel was both liked and respected by his men.

p. 252   Fingerprinting cars - E7164-59 & E7164-80 (CPR Archives)
Mobile investigation kits included photographic and fingerprinting equipment.

p. 256   Milwaukee police - (Canadian Pacific Police Service)
Milwaukee railway police looked like British bobbies with a hint of the wild west.

p. 261   D&H badge - (Canadian Pacific Police Service)
The D&H Police was known as an efficient force with high morale.

p. 266   RCMP musical ride - E7715-47 (CPR Archives)
Not everybody in the department was happy with RCMP sponsorship, given the severe budget cuts imposed on the railway police.

p. 267   Leavitt portrait - (Canadian Pacific Police Service)
Leavitt emphasized training and the development of skills.

THE BEAT GOES ON

p. 270   Move to Calgary - Photo by Rick Robinson
Calgary Mayor Al Duerr welcomes CP employees and their families to Calgary during a street party in front of Gulf Canada Square.

p. 272   Gerry Moody portrait - (Canadian Pacific Police Service)
Moody relocated the force from Montreal to Calgary, with Canadian Pacific's head office move.

p. 274   Cops briefing - (Canadian Pacific Police Service)
With officers in the United States and Canada, the work of the railway police crosses the international border seamlessly.

p. 275   New vehicle with locomotive - (Canadian Pacific Police Service)
Rarely are these vehicles so clean as in this promotional shot.

p. 276   Ice storm - (Canadian Pacific Police Service)
The railway's internal newspaper, *CP Rail News*, detailed the efforts of both the company's operating department and its police in keeping the trains running.

p. 277   Graffiti on railway car - Photo by Andy Cassidy
Preserved examples of historic locomotives get no more respect from 'taggers' than the freight equipment that is targeted for the colourful abuse on a daily basis.

p. 282   New vehicle interior - (Canadian Pacific Police Service)
Voice communications are supplemented by computer connections with law enforcement agencies throughout North America.

p. 284   Ivan McClelland - (Canadian Pacific Police Service)
McClelland was part of a counter-terrorism team at London's Heathrow Airport.

p. 287   Bicycle police - (Canadian Pacific Police Service)
Bicycles are effective vehicles for patrolling rail yards and other expansive company properties.

p. 288   Cop with radar - (Canadian Pacific Police Service)
A railway police officer, armed with the latest radar gun, puts the brakes on speeding through company property.

p. 290   Cop writing ticket - (Canadian Pacific Police Service)
Unless the offense is a serious one, the railway police—concerned more with accident prevention than punishment—typically issue a warning to motorists.

p. 293   Double-stack train - Photo by Jim Brown
Slow-moving container trains on uphill grades can be tempting targets for acts of vandalism and theft.